A Rhapsody of Love
and
Spirituality

A Rhapsody of Love and Spirituality

David Fekete

Algora Publishing
New York

Library of Congress Cataloging-in-Publication Data

Fekete, David J.
  A rhapsody of love and spirituality / by David J. Fekete.
      p. cm.
Includes bibliographical references.
  ISBN 0-87586-245-4 (alk. paper) — ISBN 0-87586-244-6 (pbk. : alk.
paper) — ISBN 0-87586-195-4 (ebook)
  1. Love. 2. Spirituality. I. Title.

  BD436.F39 2003
  128'.46'09—dc22

                        2003018466

Cover: Pierre Auguste Cot, *The Storm*; thought to illustrate a scene from
Daphnis and Chloe

Printed in the United States

TABLE OF CONTENTS

ACKNOWLEDGMENTS

This book grew out of a rich spiritual environment. It developed from love and friendship, the tutelage of mentors, the lively culture of the university, and above all from a consuming personal passion for the issues this book raises. Considering when it was that I first thought of writing a book like this, the final product was a long time in the making. You could say that it grew out of my many years in graduate school at Harvard and The University of Virginia, followed by more years of study, teaching, experience, and reflection. Many influences went into the creation of this book. Several people, however, were especially influential. Professor Ralph Potter started me on my scholarly interest in love and spirituality with a course he taught at Harvard, entitled "Conflicting Interpretations of Love." In that class I was introduced to many of the texts that are considered in this book. For that solid beginning I am deeply grateful. I continued to research these issues in other classes at Harvard. I thank the general faculty of Harvard University not only for giving me the latitude to study the themes of this book, but for guiding me in my quest. Professor Larry Benson and Professor James Miller in particular provided me with valuable guidance in the field of literature.

I was given further direction and encouragement from Professor Stanley Hauerwas, who was a visiting professor at The University of Virginia while I was enrolled in Ph.D. studies there. Professor Hauerwas's professional interest in friendship, happiness, and virtue lent support to my own project. He also got me thinking in the methodologies of virtue ethics. And he brought me, too, into contact with important texts in the philosophy of love. I am deeply indebted to him for inspiring me and supporting me in the study of erotic love and spirituality.

I would like to thank my friends, Arnold Thompson and Philip Hogan, and my mother, Joyce Fekete, for reading this book as I wrote it. They provided me with valuable feedback, and their much appreciated encouragement kept me writing.

This book is the culmination of a long pilgrimage. I hope that it brings the reader as much satisfaction as it brought me as a searcher and a writer.

PREFACE

Consider the curious irony of a celibate priest conducting a marriage ceremony between man and wife.

Where did such an irony come from?

What does it say about sexuality and love?

Consider Martin Luther's typically strong language, commenting on 1 Corinthians 7, "Those who cannot contain are commanded to marry."

Can it be that the Puritans, who have a popular reputation for prudery, were in fact champions for Romance?

Can marriage today yet be haunted by an ancient Greek expression of oppression whereby women are to be held subservient to men (Ephesians 5)?

History shows that love and spirituality have been in tension for ages. Perhaps today's sexual anarchy is a reaction to conflicts in our past. Or do our culture's sexual tensions merely represent humanity's ongoing engagement with sexuality and spirituality? In either case, it may be valuable to examine the origins of some of our fragmented culture's traditions on love and spirituality. It may be beneficial to lay bare hidden suppositions that are no longer useful and to reexamine buried or forgotten ideals. Along the way, we may be able to find traditions that we will want to recover or adopt, or simply to say, "Yes, that's the way I always thought it should be!"

For these reasons, I have written this book, entitled *A Rhapsody of Love and Spirituality*. I consider a vast kaleidoscope of humanity's relation to love: Platonic "Eros," Christian mysticism, friendship, religious ritual, and sexual love as

3

people experience it. In order to control these topics, I refer them to two categories: Transcendental Platonic "Eros" (love), and Romantic, personal love. I define these two categories in the first chapter. Then, I select definitive historical texts that relate to one or the other category. I draw on poetry, literature, theology, the Bible, philosophy, and music lyrics.

The book speaks to all lovers — be they scholars or interested readers of less rigorous appetite. By considering definitive texts from various perspectives, this work surveys humanity's reaction to love and spirituality. The reader may find her or himself resonating with one or another text or tradition. In a time of such great social alienation, the reader may find kinship with a voice from the past, still alive in the present.

CHAPTER I. TWO VAST ANTAGONISTS: LONGUS AND PLATO

Introduction

Today we live in an age of great amorous plurality — or even anarchy. This may well have come about partly by a failure to resolve the kinds of tensions that we will look at in this book. We have no comprehensive cultural tradition about love. In the times of Longus or Plato, the two authors to be discussed in this chapter, a deeply-held cultural understanding about love informed their society. Today, we have highly conflicted traditions of love. Sensing that something doesn't mesh when it comes to love, many have turned away from primary texts and traditions of love that our culture has generated, and instead of following traditions, they follow the whims of personal desire. Some consider a departure from tradition liberating. Others consider living according to personal desire to be unstable and capricious, even unholy.

In this chapter, and throughout this book, I will introduce a particularly strong conflict between two traditions of love, illustrated by the works of Longus and Plato. Our society still preserves the two conflicting traditions, but today the incompatibility of these two authors is blurred by respect that has arisen for both traditions and the attempts that have been made to harmonize the two. By spelling out the contrast between Plato and Longus, we will be able to understand the origins of some of today's confusions: we will understand where we have come from, and so, where we are now.

Musing On Phaedrus
Did we ride in heaven together —
Following our God in the circle of stars,
Two pairs of winged steeds drawing our souls
To gaze on the beauty of eternity as if ours.

Here, fallen to dirt, when we look in each others' eyes,
Is it the faint, dimmed memory of our former company
And the semblance of eternity in those skies —
Is this the unnamed thing we two recognize —
The unnamed, but for each other, would not be shared with any.

— David J. Fekete

When two lovers look into each others' eyes, they remember heaven, where they used to live, and their souls begin to grow wings. So goes Plato's poetic description of love in his book Phaedrus[1]. His description of love is passionate: the lover shivers and experiences holy dread; he grows hot and falls into a sweat; he struggles helplessly as against a flood; in a frenzy, he cannot sleep at night and is restless all day when his beloved is not present. Nothing equals the sweetness the lover feels in his beloved's company. Mother, brother, friends are all forgotten in the lover's passion for his beloved; his property means nothing to him; he scorns civilized behavior if only he can live near his beloved. If he didn't fear being called a madman, the lover would offer sacrifices to his beloved as to a god.

Clearly, Plato has experienced the intensity of love. Yet, in the long run, this strange lover delivers the strongest blow against love that Western civilization has known. Plato comes close to saying that one is better off not loving at all. But as a pious Greek, Plato knows that Love is a god. And despite Plato's philosophical vocation, he doesn't completely abandon reverence for the god of love; but by the time he gets done saving Love from his own philosophy, little is left that looks like love. Ultimately, to get back to heaven, the lover must leave behind his personal beloved. The soul must purify itself from all passion. And poetry, since it "waters" the passions and "makes them grow," must be replaced by dispassionate philosophy.

---

1. Plato, *Phaedrus and the Seventh and Eighth Letters* (New York: Penguin Books, 1973).

Our culture still reels under the effects of Plato's onslaught. In the centuries that followed, Plato's philosophy became the model for the entire Mediterranean world's view of the universe and a person's place in the universe. Christianity's early educated Fathers wrote in such a philosophical climate. And through these educated Fathers, Christianity imported Plato and passed him on to Europe. And even in more recent times, Poets who are all too familiar with Plato's philosophy write with their backs up against a wall. Some important writers who felt compelled to write defenses of poetry are Plato's own pupil Aristotle, Sir Philip Sidney, William Wordsworth, and Percy Bysshe Shelley.

But love will have its way. In Longus' *Daphnis and Chloe*, an ancient Romance has been preserved from the second or third century C.E. that still speaks to lovers, today. It represents a tradition of Romance that was highly popular in the ancient world. Unfortunately, through time, we have lost all the texts of the genre excepting this one gem.

Longus narrates the innocent life of a young couple that grows up in the Greek pastureland. Their love develops naturally, since it is uncomplicated by urban distractions. This rustic couple spends their days together tending their herds of goats and sheep. Right at the time of puberty, they become aware of one another in a troubling and at times painful way. The story moves on to tell how they come to know the god of love (whose Greek name is "Eros") and the emotions they have been experiencing. They become emblems of Eros, protected and nurtured by the god himself.

Thus the battle lines of this book are drawn by Plato and Longus. Neither writer wrote with the other in mind. Rather, each author represents a way of loving that generates a vast tradition of literature. For Plato, love involves merging with an infinite, immortal Idea of The Good or The Beautiful that transcends every finite mortal — so you must give up every finite, mortal thing for the Ideal. For Longus, on the other hand, love finds its home in a particular, finite person. Love finds its fulfillment in that special someone; and this personal love is intended by God. It is just as spiritual as is Plato's love. Thus both writers claim to be worshipping the god of love, but their way of doing so is at odds with the other's. These two ways of seeing love have been influencing our culture for millennia, and in the pages that follow we will enjoy and compare important texts that have been generated by various writers since the time of Plato and Longus.

My two introductory authors merely represent traditions of love. I do not claim that the literature that grew up after them was written with them in mind; rather, I choose them as examples of two powerful traditions of love in our society. Once Plato was incorporated into Christianity, his ideas took on a life of their own; and the Romance writers of the Middle Ages did not draw on Longus, despite the appeal of his approach. So, in Plato and Longus, we have examples of two vast and incompatible traditions that have permeated Western culture.

Daphnis and Chloe

No reader of Longus can come away unmoved by the innocence and simplicity of this tale. The story is an idyllic Romance set in the pastoral landscape of ancient Greece. When approaching a fairytale of this sort, one leaves behind the expectations of realistic modern novels. The author knows that he is painting with ideal brushstrokes. His work is "an offering to Love and the Nymphs and Pan." But though *Daphnis and Chloe* is an idyllic pastoral romance, nevertheless it has realistic points to make about the nature of love. Its author hopes his book will heal broken humanity. His book is,

> . . . something to heal the sick and comfort the afflicted, to refresh the memory of those who have been in love and educate those who have not. For no one has ever escaped Love altogether, and no one ever will, so long as beauty exists and eyes can see.[2]

Longus hopes to reawaken feelings of love by writing a simple story. I have seen apparently jaded and cynical readers come away thoroughly charmed by his magic. Longus' work seems to have touched a Renaissance author, who adds telling adjectives to the title of a translation of the book,

> Daphnis and Chloe: Excellently describing the weight of affection, the simplicitie of love, the purport of honest meaning, the resolution of men, and disposition of Fate.[3]

The work was highly popular and it influenced art and music in the 19th century. Corot's pastoral paintings can be seen as reflections of the setting of

---

2. Longus, *Daphnis and Chloe* (New York: Penguin Books, 1989), p. 17-18.
3. Longus, *Daphnis and Chloe*, p. 11.

Daphnis and Chloe. Both Ravel and Offenbach wrote musical adaptations of the work. Some consider it a "European bestseller."

Love is nurtured by love stories. And even as Longus nurtures love in us, so the Greek myth of "Eros" (the Greek word for the love god) gives meaning and purpose to the love of Daphnis and Chloe. In a way, Daphnis and Chloe is a kind of quest; the couple searches for a cultural interpretation for the raw emotion that they are feeling for one another. Longus holds up his ideal couple as a symbol for the working of "Eros." The couple is adopted and protected by the god of love. We first glimpse this in a mystical dream given to both of the couple's adopted parents:

> They dreamt that the Nymphs . . . were handing Daphnis and Chloe over to a very autocratic and very beautiful small boy who had wings growing out of his shoulders and carried tiny arrows and a tiny bow. This boy hit both of them with a single arrow. . . .[4]

In this dream, the reader may recognize the trappings of the Roman god, Cupid. Cupid is yet another Roman copy of a Greek original. The Romans borrowed all of Cupid's attributes from the Greek god "Eros"; as in the dream, "Eros" is a youth with wings and a bow and arrows. Whoever is shot with the golden arrows of "Eros" will fall in love. In the dream, Daphnis and Chloe are both shot with the same arrow, meaning that they will fall in love with each other.

The dream given to the parents of Daphnis and Chloe symbolizes an important theme that underscores the entire tale. In the culture of Longus, love has a divine origin. Love comes from God. It is more than a mere instinct or biological drive. It is a sacred experience nurtured with reverence. And throughout the story, Daphnis and Chloe show their reverent attitude by presenting offerings to the Nature gods that they know.

The interaction between Daphnis and Chloe and their gods adds charm and color to the tale. The gods of this pastoral romance are not the awesome sky gods of Olympus, such as Zeus, Apollo, or Athena. In this story, Daphnis and Chloe present offerings to the Earth-bound demi-gods of Nature. There are the Nymphs: beautiful young ladies who are given charge of mountains, valleys, rivers, and trees. Also aiding the couple is the woodland god, Pan. (Pan has a human torso, but the legs and horns of a goat. He is the primary god of goatherds.

---

4. Longus, p. 22.

Associated with music and dance, Pan is often depicted playing the flute and dancing in the woods with the Nymphs.) These "supporting" gods are all ruled by the power of the primary deity, "Eros."

The dream shows that Daphnis and Chloe will be singled out by the god of love, their love being his emblem. But until they knew their culture's story about the origin of love, the myth of Eros, the couple did not know what to do with their feelings for one another. They did not even know what they were feeling. "They wanted something, but they did not know what they wanted."[5]

Although the love of Daphnis and Chloe is given a mythological base, their love develops in accord with human nature as we experience it. Daphnis and Chloe were friends for a long time before they fell in love. They were constant companions in the hills of Lesbos since their childhood. Daphnis tended his herd of goats and Chloe tended her flock of sheep. Longus tells us that,

> They did everything together, for they grazed their flocks side by side; and often it would be Daphnis who rounded up the sheep that had strayed, and Chloe who drove down the more adventurous goats from the high rocks. In fact, it sometimes happened that one of them would look after both the flocks, because the other was busy playing with some toy.[6]

In their idyllic setting, they had an opportunity to grow familiar with one another over a long period of time before they became sexually aware. Thus, they had a firm foundation in friendship before the stirrings of adolescence.

Then, when Daphnis was fifteen and Chloe thirteen, they began to feel something strange for one another. Again, the arousal of their sexual feelings was completely natural. Modern readers might be interested to know that the girl first feels love. Perhaps this fact is natural in adolescent development. Chloe first felt the stirrings of desire when she watched Daphnis bathing. The cause for Chloe's feelings is attributed to the god of love — "While they were playing like this, Love ["Eros"] made something serious flare up."[7] Longus describes Chloe's observation of Daphnis in highly sensual terms:

> [H]e stood in front of the spring and started washing his hair and his whole body. His hair was black and thick, and his body was slightly sunburnt — it looked as though it was darkened by the shadow of his hair. It

---

5. *Ibid.*, p. 34.
6. *Ibid.*, pp. 23-24.
7. *Ibid.*, p. 24.

seemed to Chloe, as she watched him, that Daphnis was beautiful; and as he had never seemed beautiful to her before, she thought that this beauty must be the result of washing. Moreover, when she washed his back, she found that the flesh was soft and yielding; . . . she had set her heart on seeing Daphnis washing again.[8]

Daphnis was now continually in Chloe's thoughts. While she was watching her flock, "most of the time she was looking at Daphnis." Then he played on his Pan-flute, and "While he was piping he again seemed to her beautiful, and this time she thought that the beauty was caused by the music." She persuades Daphnis to wash again and she watches him again; and again, "She went away full of admiration, and this admiration was the beginning of love."[9]

Chloe does not know what is wrong with her because, as Longus tells us, she "had never heard the word 'love' used by anyone else." As her pangs continued, she "tried to find a name for love." In a poignant internal monologue, Longus describes Chloe's distress:

> There's something wrong with me these days, but I don't know what it is. I'm in pain, and yet I've not been injured. I feel sad, and yet none of my sheep have got lost. I'm burning hot, and yet here I am sitting in the shade.

She compares her feelings to nature, which is all she knows, but can't understand this new experience.

> How often I've been scratched by brambles and not cried! How often I've been stung by bees and not screamed! But this thing that's pricked my heart hurts more than anything like that. Daphnis is beautiful, but so are the flowers. His pipe does sound beautiful, but so do the nightingales — and I don't worry about them.

She longs for a more intimate relationship with Daphnis. "If only I were his pipe, so that he'd breathe into me! If only I were a goat, so that I could have him looking after me!" She even begins to despair for her life:

> Oh, Nymphs, I'm dying — and even you will do nothing to save the girl who was nursed in your cave. Who will put garlands on you when I'm gone? Who will look after my chattering locust? I had a lot of trouble catch-

---

8. *Ibid.*, p. 26.
9. *Ibid.*, p. 27.

ing her, so that she could talk me to sleep in front of the cave — and now I can't sleep because of Daphnis.[10]

Longus brings alive a young girl's feelings of love in touching detail.

> [S]he was always talking about Daphnis. She took no interest in food, she could not sleep at night, she paid no attention to her flock. One moment she would be laughing, the next she would be crying. Now she would be lying down, now she would be jumping up again. Her face would grow pale, and then grow fiery red.[11]

Chloe becomes the sexual aggressor in her own inexperienced, rustic way. At one point in the narrative, Daphnis and another youth act as contestants in a beauty contest that Chloe is to judge. The prize is to be a kiss from Chloe. Of course, the outcome is a foregone conclusion, but each contestant makes his speech as to why he should be chosen. Naturally, Chloe jumps forward and kisses Daphnis. The kiss awakens Daphnis' sexuality. Now Longus paints a graphic picture of the experience of love in Daphnis.

> He suddenly looked almost indignant and shivered several times and tried to control his pounding heart; he wanted to look at Chloe, but when he did so he blushed all over. Then for the first time he saw with wonder that her hair was as golden as fire, that her eyes were as big as the eyes of an ox, and that her complexion was really even whiter than the milk of the goats. It was as if he had just got eyes for the first time, and had been blind all his life before.[12]

The interior monologue that Longus gives Daphnis again relies on nature motifs. And now in Daphnis, Longus arouses in his readers the early promptings of love.

> Whatever is Chloe's kiss doing to me? Her lips are softer than roses and her mouth is sweeter than honey, but her kiss hurts more than the sting of a bee. . . . My breath's coming in gasps, my heart's jumping up and down, my soul's melting away — but all the same I want to kiss her again. . . . Had Chloe drunk poison just before she kissed me? If so, how did she manage not to be killed? Hear how the nightingales are singing — and my pipe is

---

10. *Ibid.*, pp. 27-28.
11. *Ibid.*, p. 27.
12. *Ibid.*,p. 30.

silent. Look how the kids are frisking about — and I'm sitting still. Look how the flowers are blooming — and I'm not making any garlands. Yes, the violets and the hyacinths are in flower, but Daphnis is withering away.[13]

Like Chloe, Daphnis searches for a name for his new experience — "I don't even know what to call it."

Daphnis and Chloe's search for the name for their feelings brings up an important point about the Mediterranean world-view. In their world, the name for the emotion called "love" is the same as the name of the god of love. In this case, the word is "Eros." Learning the word for their emotion is the same as learning the myth of the god.

Love is a dialogue between raw emotion and culture. Our cultural stories tell us what love is, and how love is to be expressed. The early feelings that Daphnis and Chloe felt for one another were naive. Being raised in nature, away from civilization, they were at a loss for how to love. They had no cultural grounding for their emotions. They had no way to participate in their culture's options for loving. They needed to know the name of their god. They needed a story about "Eros."

An elderly cow-herd named Philetas provides the story they need. Philetas tells Daphnis and Chloe about a time when he found a young, naked boy playing in his garden. Unaware of the boy's identity, Philetas tries to catch him for fear that he will ruin his garden. He discovers, though, that he is actually in the presence of a god. The boy announces that despite his youthful appearance he is older than "time and the universe itself." Philetas also discovers that he has been cared for by this youthful-looking god throughout his long life. But Eros informs Philetas that he is now looking after Daphnis and Chloe. Philetas informs the young couple that they are "dedicated to Love, and Love is looking after you."[14]

After being informed that they are dedicated to Love, Philetas tells Daphnis and Chloe about the nature of the god.

> [H]e can do greater things than Zeus himself. He has power over the elements, he has power over the stars, he has power over his fellow gods . . . The flowers are all Love's handiwork. . . . He is the reason why rivers run and winds blow.[15]

---

13. *Ibid.*, p. 31.
14. *Ibid.*, p. 47.
15. *Ibid.*, p. 48.

Philetas suggests an idea articulated by an ancient Greek philosopher named Empedokles. For Empedokles, the universe was created by Love. Love brings together all the elements of matter. The world of Daphnis and Chloe and of Empedokles is quite different from our own. For us, or for some of us, the universe is governed by cold Newtonian forces. We inhabit Einstein's vast and impersonal time-space continuum. But for Empedokles, the same feeling that brings humans together in love also brings together the elements of the created universe. Empedokles' universe is alive and filled with love; so in learning about their feelings for one another, Daphnis and Chloe also learn that they live in a universe ruled by Love — "He is the reason why the rivers run and winds blow."

Philetas also tells the couple the only way to find relief for their feelings: "The only remedies are kissing and embracing and lying down together with naked bodies."[16] The story enters its "quest" phase, following this revelation. Daphnis and Chloe try to discover the meaning behind Philetas' tale about the god of love, and the remedies for their feelings.

As the couple seeks to understand the meaning of love, their love for one another develops and deepens. Their love develops freely because they live in a state of nature, far from the complexities of man-made structures. At the end of the tale, both Daphnis and Chloe come into an inheritance and have the opportunity to live in a state of luxury in the city. However, they turn down the chance of living amongst the man-made structures, even a luxurious life, there. They prefer to stay with their herds in the natural world they grew up in, with the Nymphs, Pan, and "Eros." In later tales, such as Tristan and Isolde, and even in The Scarlet Letter, the lovers in each tale are only able to express their love in a state of nature, as in this much earlier tale of Daphnis and Chloe.

The couple soon finds that the world can intrude on their love and threaten it. They discover what Martha Nussbaum calls The Fragility of Goodness.[17] They discover that their love can be thwarted in many ways, and that the good experience of love is exceedingly fragile.

Since this is an idyllic tale, their problems are solved by the gods. But the calamities that they undergo suggest that for others who are not personally selected for protection by a god, love may not survive the trials and whims of worldly fortune. Lovers are vulnerable to forces outside their control. (It may be

---

16. *Ibid.*
17. Martha Nussbaum, *The Fragility of Goodness* (Cambridge: UP of Cambridge,1987).

that Plato's own transcendental love was generated by a realization that personal love is all too fragile for this world.)

Being a Romance, Daphnis and Chloe contains the obligatory adventure scene. Chloe, and some of her herd, are kidnapped by pirates from a neighboring village. Daphnis witnesses the kidnapping but is impotent to prevent it. His only recourse is prayer to the Nymphs. The Nymphs ask Pan to intervene and the god comes to Chloe's rescue. He causes vines to grow on the antlers of the kidnapped flock. The pirates hear eerie music coming from a cliff ashore. Dolphins pound the sides of the ship's hull with their tails. Then the god himself appears to the ship's captain, scolding him for taking Chloe and the cattle. Pan threatens to sink the ship if Chloe and the cattle are not returned. Afraid of these omens, the captain returns Chloe and the cattle to their homeland.

The gods intervene again when Daphnis wants to ask Chloe's parents for her hand in marriage. Being a poor goatherd, Daphnis has nothing to offer as a dowry. He again prays to the Nymphs and finds an answer in a dream. A purse containing 3,000 drachmas has washed ashore and a Nymph guides Daphnis to its location.

Geography becomes a problem for the couple during the dreary winter months. The roads are blocked by snowfall and all the people are shut up in their homes. Since the home of Daphnis is distant from Chloe's, the two are no longer able to meet. Distance increases their longing for one another. Winter is endured with "sleepless nights and miserable days." The couple looks forward to the return of spring, "as to a resurrection from death."

Several suitors seek the favors of the young man and woman, pursuing their desire by any means possible. One of Chloe's suitors ruins a garden, intending to blame Daphnis's goats for the destruction and thereby alienate Chloe's parents from Daphnis. A prostitute seeks Daphnis' favor. A dissolute homosexual named Gnathon from the nearby city also pursues Daphnis. This threat is more serious than others because Gnathon is of a higher social standing than Daphnis. In fact, he asks the master of Daphnis' land to hand Daphnis over to him as a slave. But in each of these threats from rival suitors, the love between Daphnis and Chloe prevails.

The episodes above are all evidence that the natural course of love can be threatened by outside forces, whether kidnapping, financial trouble, distance, or envy from others who covet one's partner. The love of Daphnis and Chloe might have failed without special aid from the gods. The tale suggests to modern readers how hard it is to maintain love. With all the stresses of our present culture — job mobility, financial strains, disruptions due to time commitments and the lack of leisure, and our fragmentary traditions of romance and religion — it is a wonder that any couples find a way to stay together, today. In addition to its testimonial to the beauty of innocent love, Daphnis and Chloe reminds the reader just how precarious the institution of love can be.

The tale Daphnis and Chloe brings up several issues relating to love. First, love comes from a god; it is not of human origin. The love for god is bound up in a couple's love for each other. In fact, reverence for the god of love is shown by the very act of remaining faithful to one's lover. Second, love finds its fulfillment in another person. Love is a union of two partners who want nothing more than to live together and share their love for each other. Finally, love between two persons conspires with the love that has created the universe. The universe is made from love, and this same love brings together loving couples. For Daphnis and Chloe, the god of love gave meaning to the love they had for each other, and the love they had for each other gave meaning to their lives.

Plato and Transcendent Love

Plato's philosophy of love is difficult to describe. It is a rich tapestry of mythology, art criticism, psychology, anatomy, and, of course, philosophical argument. When we begin to talk about one aspect of his thought, all the other aspects arise. Talking about Plato's philosophy is like Hercules fighting the Hydra. As soon as one head is cut off, two others grow back in its spot.

Perhaps we should begin in the comfortable setting of a dinner party devoted to a discussion of love. This is the opening scene of Plato's *Symposium*.[18] Famous playwrights and notable gentlemen are gathered together for dinner at the home of Agathon. As the evening proceeds, each member of the dinner party gives a speech about love. One interesting speech comes from the famous comic writer Aristophanes. He suggests that humans were originally round in shape. We had four legs and four arms, and rolled when we wanted to move. Then arrogance overtook us and we attacked the gods. To weaken us, the gods cut us in two. Our search for love is an attempt to find our other half and become whole.

---

18. Plato, *Symposium* Alexander Nehamas and Paul Woodruff, tr. (Indianapolis and Cambridge: Hackett Publishing Co., 1989).

As amusing as Aristophanes' and the other stories are, Socrates — Plato's mouthpiece for almost all his philosophical works — gives a speech which is held up as the true account of love. But Socrates' speech is actually a speech within a speech. In a rare literary move, Socrates puts his truths in the mouth of another philosopher. And still more remarkable, for the time period in which the dialogue was written, the philosopher that Socrates quotes is a woman, Diotima: Plato's great work on love is presented by a woman philosopher. More shocking still, Diotima even doubts whether Socrates, usually a rather arrogant "know it all," can grasp the truth she is about to teach — "the final and highest mystery." Her doubts are clearly expressed — "I don't know if you are capable of it." And as a final coup de grace, she bestows a patronizing encouragement on Socrates: ". . . you must try to follow, if you can."[19]

In a speech filled with metaphors of giving birth, she explains the pathway that the philosopher should follow throughout his or her lifetime in order to attain true love. Love is considered a pursuit of the Beautiful. And love follows a kind of ladder — Plato's famous "Ladder of Love" — up toward ultimate Beauty. The way up the ladder is an affair of pure reason. Plato keeps this emphasis on reason in all his works.

The ladder begins in the philosopher's youth. As a youth, one devotes oneself to beautiful bodies. Initially, he or she chooses one beautiful body. "First, if the leader leads aright, he should love one body. . . . " But even in this early stage, reason enters the course of love. The lover "begets" beautiful ideas in his beloved. "First, if the leader leads aright, he should love one body and beget beautiful ideas there; . . ."[20] At the very beginning of love, it would appear that the "intercourse" between lover and beloved is philosophical, Platonic dialogue.

Very soon, the lover moves beyond a single beloved to a recognition of many bodies:

> . . . then he should realize that the beauty of any one body is brother to the beauty of any other and if he is to pursue beauty of form he'd be very· foolish not to think that the beauty of all bodies is one and the same.

Diotima almost ridicules love for one single beloved. "When he grasps this, he must become a lover of all beautiful bodies, and he must think that this wild gaping after just one body is a small thing and despise it."[21]

---

19. Plato, *Symposium*, p. 57.
20. *Ibid.*

The lover steps up another rung on the ladder by moving from a love of bodies to a noble interest in souls. A love of souls can be directed even at those who are not yet of a sexual age.

> [H]e must think that the beauty of people's souls is more valuable than the beauty of their bodies, so that if someone is decent in his soul, even though he is scarcely blooming in his body, our lover must be content to love and care for him. . . .[22]

Again, Diotima uses the image of giving birth. And again, it is ideas that concern Plato's lover — "our lover must be content to love and care for him and to seek to give birth to such ideas as will make young men better."[23] This doctrine follows Plato's general philosophy that society is the soul writ large. The same components that make up a good soul make a well-ordered state (cf. *The Republic*).

Since we are now interested in making young men better citizens, the next logical step on the ladder of love is to see the beauty of laws. Now, bodies don't matter. "[T]he beauty of bodies is a thing of no importance." Laws are ideas, and from legal matters the lover becomes a lover of ideas. Knowledge is now his pursuit, and we are becoming "lovers of wisdom," "philosophers." (In Greek, *philos* means "friendly love," and *sophia* means "wisdom" — hence *philosophia* — a lover or friend of wisdom.) "The lover is turned to the great sea of beauty, and gazing upon this, he gives birth to many gloriously beautiful ideas and theories, in unstinting love of wisdom (*philosophia*)."[24]

The philosopher then "sees" a beatific vision. I put the word "see" in quotes because the "vision" is not sensual. It is grasped by reason, not the eye. It is beyond every color or anything that is created, mortal, or finite. It is Beauty itself:

> But how would it be . . . if someone got to see the Beautiful itself, absolute, pure, unmixed, not polluted by human flesh or colors or any other great nonsense of mortality . . . Beauty itself in its one form.[25]

---

21. *Ibid.*, pp. 57-58.
22. *Ibid.*, p. 58.
23. *Ibid.*
24. *Ibid.*
25. *Ibid.*, p.59.

The philosopher here has ascended to the final rung of the ladder of love. And viewing this one, transcendent Beauty, he has reached the goal of love.

Here we have arrived at a difficult point in Plato's philosophy. We are considering the doctrine of "Ideal Forms." We now need to pause and reflect on this doctrine in order to understand Plato's philosophy of love, and the way our soul is meant to function in it.

Consider three beautiful things, things of this world. Consider the Parthenon in Greece; Marilyn Monroe; and Monet's painting, "The Water Lilies." They are three different things, indeed: a building, a person, and a two-dimensional combination of colors. Yet, we say that they share one thing in common: they are beautiful. There are many beautiful things.

There is another aspect to the beautiful things that we see on this Earth. The temple will crumble. Persons age and lose their good looks. Paintings fade. The beautiful things we experience are subject to change. They come into the world; and they go out of the world. They are not eternal.

Plato's concept of Ideal Forms addresses these two points: multiplicity and change. While in our world a beautiful thing comes into being and goes out of being; for Plato, Beauty Itself always Is. Beauty Itself belongs to another world altogether. Beauty belongs to the world of Being, where things don't change. While we are here on Earth, we see a multitude of beautiful things; but Beauty Itself is singular. There is only one Beauty Itself. The many beautiful things that we see down here all share the one concept, Beauty Itself. There must be something Beautiful that they all "participate" in since, we call them all beautiful; and that Idea of Beauty existed before they came into being in order for us to recognize them as beautiful.

Thus, there is something that all beautiful things possess: Beauty Itself. We can reason our way to such a concept, but the idea of Beauty Itself transcends every beautiful thing. It is the measuring rod against which every beautiful thing is measured. We can comprehend with our mind that there must be a concept, "Beauty Itself," but we cannot see it with our senses. Our senses give us only beautiful things that have come into existence and will go out of existence. These things are beautiful by partaking of Ideal Beauty in a finite, sensual way.

But the Ideal Form of Beauty is eternal. Beauty Itself is not subject to change — it must always be beautiful. And all of it is beautiful:

> First, it always is and neither comes to be nor passes away, neither waxes nor wanes. Second, it is not beautiful this way and ugly that way,

nor beautiful at one time and ugly at another, nor beautiful in relation to one thing and ugly in relation to another; nor is it beautiful here and ugly there, as it would be if it were beautiful for some people and ugly for others.[26]

There are other "Ideal Forms," such as Justice Itself, and The Good Itself, but we need not concern ourselves with these in the present discussion.

The entire universe depends upon these Ideal Forms. (This is expounded in Plato's book *Timaeus*.[27]) When the world we inhabit was created, the creator god created this world by imitating them. It is sometimes said that he stamped into matter an image of the Ideal Forms; but matter is an imperfect material and the copy isn't exact. Thus, for Plato, there are two vast worlds: the realm of Ideal Forms, and the created universe that imperfectly copies them. Things come into being and go out of being and are always in flux in this world. But things are eternal and unchanging in the world of Ideal Forms.[28]

We all possess human souls that relate to both worlds. To the extent that our soul clings to changing material things, we become like this world and are repeatedly reborn into it. But if our souls cling to the eternal Forms, we become like them and are lifted from this world up into eternity.

In Plato's mythology, we don't start our life here on Earth; we begin in heaven. The soul is compared to a winged charioteer driving a chariot pulled by two different horses. One is noble and responds to his charioteer, and the other is disobedient and wild:

> The horse that is harnessed on the senior side is upright and clean-limbed; he holds his neck high and has a somewhat hooked nose; his color is white, with black eyes; his thirst for honor is tempered by restraint and modesty; he is a friend to genuine renown and needs no whip, but is driven simply by the word of command. The other horse is crooked, lumbering, ill made; stiff necked, short throated, snub-nosed; his coat is black and his

---

26. *Ibid.*, p. 58.

27. Plato, *Timaeus and Critias* (New York and London: Penguin Books, 1977).

28. Reflection on a Christianized version of Plato's Ideal Forms troubles the poet Wallace Stevens:
    Is there no change of death in paradise?
    Does ripe fruit never fall? Or do the boughs
    Hang always heavy in that perfect sky,
    Unchanging, yet so like our perishing Earth,
    With rivers like our own that seek for seas
    They never find, the same receding shores
    That never touch with inarticulate pang?
    ("Sunday Morning," in *The Palm at the End of the Mind* (New York: Vintage Books, 1972), p. 7.

eyes are bloodshot grey; wantonness and boastfulness are his companions, and he is hairy-eared and deaf, hardly controllable even with a whip and goad.[29]

At first we follow a god around the circle of stars, far above the Earth. On high feast-days, we ascend up through the middle of the sky and stand outside the arch of stars. There, we ride around on the back of the arch of stars. It is here that we "see" the eternal Ideal Forms, that is, we grasp them by our intellect. The realm of Ideal Forms is a place of knowledge, reason, and intellect.

> The region of which I speak is the abode of the reality with which true knowledge is concerned, a reality without colour or shape, intangible but utterly real, apprehensible only by intellect . . . sustained as it is by pure intelligence and knowledge.[30]

There the soul is made happy by "the contemplation of truth."

But since our soul has two horses at its command, one obedient and the other unruly, the going is not easy. Some of us can't control our team, and others of us get caught up in a kind of traffic jam. Then, the unruly horse can pull us down to Earth — the realm of coming into being and going out of being. Life on Earth is always the result of a "fall," for Plato. (The Christian Fathers had difficulty with this aspect of Platonism, since Genesis says that all creation is good).

Now that we are down here on Earth, when we see a beautiful form (such as a beautiful body), we are sub-consciously reminded of the Ideal Beauty we "saw" in heaven. Our bodies grow warm and our souls begin to grow the wings back that were broken when we fell. But if we ever want to get back to heaven, we must nurture the rational quality in our souls. The Ideal Forms are grasped only by reason and intellect.

But an encounter with beautiful bodies also arouses passion and a desire. "[H]e feels a desire to see, to touch, to kiss him, and to share his bed."[31] The physical expression of love is treated with loathing by Plato; he considers it beastly:

---

29. Plato, *Phaedrus*, p. 62.
30. *Ibid.*, p. 52.
31. *Ibid.*, p. 64.

Now the man . . . who has been corrupted does not quickly make the transition from beauty on Earth to absolute beauty; so when he sees its namesake here he feels no reverence for it, but surrenders himself to sensuality and is eager like a four-footed beast to mate and beget children, or in his addiction to wantonness feels no fear or shame in pursuing a pleasure which is unnatural.[32]

But those who remember the Ideal Forms restrain their passions and contemplate Beauty Itself. Restraining passion is graphically described by Plato in a metaphor. The charioteer violently restrains the unruly horse:

When the driver beholds it [the beautiful body], the sight awakens in him the memory of absolute beauty. . . . At the thought he falls back in his fear and awe, and in so doing inevitably tugs the reins so violently that he brings both horses down on their haunches; . . . he falls back like a racing charioteer at the barrier, and with a still more violent backward pull jerks the bit from between the teeth of the lustful horse, drenches his abusive tongue and jaws with blood, and forcing his legs and haunches against the ground reduces him to torment. Finally, after several repetitions of this treatment, the wicked horse abandons his lustful ways; meekly now he executes the wishes of his driver, and when he catches sight of the loved one is ready to die of fear.[33]

Thus the philosopher has won his victory over passion. Dispassionate reason becomes master and the philosopher ascends to heaven upon his happy demise.

So, if the higher elements in their minds prevail, and guide them into a way of life which is strictly devoted to the pursuit of wisdom, they will pass their time on Earth in happiness and harmony; by subduing the part of the soul that contained the seeds of vice and setting free that in which virtue had its birth they will become masters of themselves and their souls will be at peace. Finally, when this life is ended, their wings will carry them aloft.[34]

This discussion of Platonic love outlines his ethics. Reason should dominate and moderate "desire and its mixture of pain and pleasure, and fear and

---

32. *Ibid.*, p. 57.
33. *Ibid.*, pp. 62, 63.
34. *Ibid.*, p. 65.

anger; . . . mastery of these would lead to a good life, subjection to them to a wicked life."[35] In the *Timaeus*, Plato lists the passions to be avoided:

> . . . pleasure, the chief incitement to wrong, pain, which frightens us from good, confidence and fear, two foolish counsellors, obstinate passion and credulous hope . . . irrational sensation and desire. . . .[36]

In fact, in Plato's psychology the source of these desires is in the loins — as far away from the mind and its reason as is possible. The creator god did this so that these passions would do as little damage to our reasoning faculties as possible.

Thus for Plato, the beauty of the beloved is meant to call the soul to contemplation of Ideal Beauty, and to lift the soul up into the realm of Ideal Forms. Plato wants no union of lovers as we saw in *Daphnis and Chloe*. I call Plato's love "Transcendental Love," because it causes the lover to transcend every created thing. It calls upon the lover to subdue passion and live in dispassionate contemplation. The Ideal Forms are eternal; if the soul wants immortality, it must contemplate the eternal Ideal Forms.

Either Or

We have looked at two authors and their approaches to love. Both authors come from the Greek tradition. Both authors see love as a divine blessing. They both do homage to the same Greek god "Eros." But there, the similarities end.

Longus sees a loving interpersonal relationship as a divine gift. For this reason, we can call the love expressed by Longus "Interpersonal Love." It's what most people today mean when they think of a loving relationship.

Plato sees the soul merging intellectually with a concept that is beyond every finite thing. It merges with The Beautiful. The Beautiful is otherworldly. It is infinite and eternal. It transcends everything we experience with our senses on this Earth. For this reason, we can call Plato's expression of love "Transcendental Love."

A little reflection will show that these two traditions are incompatible. A person cannot embody both traditions and remain one person. If one chooses to

---

35. Plato, *Timaeus*, p. 58.
36. *Ibid.*, p. 97.

love another person, he or she has stopped short on Plato's ladder. In order to ascend further, one must move past the early attraction to a beloved body in order to merge with Beauty Itself.

For Longus, love finds fulfillment in the single beloved that an individual has chosen. The god of love wants it to be this way. When this happens, the god of love has shot both persons with his arrows and they are thus meant for one another.

By contrast, for Plato the god of love feels shame at the passion expressed in the love shared between two bodies. To follow god's commands, the Transcendental Lover must subdue the unruly horse and bend his passion to reason's rule. Only in the clear, impassive light of reason can the Ideal Form of Ideal Beauty be comprehended. Everything mortal and finite will drag the charioteer down from heaven. Only by merging with the eternal Ideal Form can the soul become eternal and find its place in heaven.

Thus the two traditions we have looked at in Longus and Plato are irreconcilable. It is important at this point to see the absolute incompatibility between these two traditions. Later writers would attempt to blur the distinctions between these two traditions, and, furthermore, Western culture has come to hold respect for both traditions. The great modern philosopher Alfred North Whitehead has said that "all philosophy is a footnote to Plato." But countless popular novels and self-help books extol the virtues of Interpersonal Love. Although our culture respects both traditions, the same person cannot be a lover in both the Platonic sense and the sense of Longus.

The tension between these two traditions can be seen in the writings of Plato's student Aristotle, in writings of the early Christian Fathers, in the Chivalric Romance writings of Thomas Malory, in Martin Luther's theology, in the poetry of Spenser, even in the late Romantic writings of Percy Bysshe Shelley, and in the teachings of the Christian Church to this very day.[37]

We need to keep straight in our minds the distinction between love as it is expressed in Longus and in Plato, if we want insight into Western culture and our world. Time, and deliberate attempts to harmonize these two contrasting traditions, have weakened the dissociative effect that these two incompatible approaches would have in a single person. We cannot totally merge with a transcendental Form and yet keep a particular personal lover. To do so would

---

37. This conflict is also highly marked in the Eastern religious tradition, notably in the god Shiva, but that is a subject that lies outside the scope of this narrative.

drag us down from the infinite to the finite. But to give up a personal lover for an abstract philosophical Idea means to deny ourselves a rich and fulfilling, God-given emotional life. To love another person means to reject Plato. And to embrace the eternal Idea of Beauty is to reject Longus. To live with a coherent world view, we must see clearly and choose. To keep one means to reject the other.

In the pages that follow, I will attempt to cut through the accretions of time and sophistry, to lay bare these two traditions where they appear in powerful texts of Western Culture. In watching the textual evolution of these two traditions, we will come to understand some of the complexity of our current culture when it comes to loving. We will understand where we have come from, and so, where we are now.

CHAPTER II. THE LOVER'S COACH AND THE APPLE FALLEN FROM PLATO'S TREE: OVID AND ARISTOTLE

OVID: THE LOVER'S COACH

I put Ovid into the category of Interpersonal Love, but he is dramatically different from Longus. Longus was pastoral; Ovid is urban. Daphnis and Chloe were devout to their pastoral gods; Ovid is irreverent. Daphnis and Chloe's love developed naturally; Ovid's form of love is guided by art. But their subject matter is the same: both want to see love expressed between two loving partners.

Ovid wants to bend Cupid to his will — "Love, to be sure, is wild and often inclined to resent me;/Still, he is only a boy, tender and easily swayed/ . . . So Love will yield to me, though he wounds my heart with his arrows."[38] Ovid thinks that love arises through human art: "Art is a thing one must learn, for the sailing, or rowing of vessels,/Also for driving a car: love must be guided by art." Ovid sets himself up as a "master of Arts" in the area of love: "Thanks be to Venus, I too deserve the title of master,/Master of Arts, I might say, versed in the precepts of love."

Ovid is irreverent about Cupid — he is irreverent about all the gods. "Gods are convenient to have, so let's concede their existence."[39] Indeed, Ovid's approach to loving might be considered irreverent, even scandalous; at least, Caesar Augustus thought so. Augustus blamed Ovid for some unknown scandal

---

38. Ovid, *The Art of Love*, trans. Rolfe Humphries (Bloomington, Indiana: Indiana UP, 1957), p. 105.
39. Ovid, *The Art of Love*, p. 124.

and banished him to the crude, barbaric outlands of the Black Sea. One could hardly devise a more devious torment for this highly cultured and urbane gentleman. Ovid spent the rest of his known life writing tiresome poems bewailing his fate: the lack of culture, the foreign language (he loved the Latin he used so artfully!), the frequent raids from barbaric tribes. In these tedious poems he constantly begs Caesar to allow him back into Rome. Caesar wasn't moved by any of this, and so Ovid remained in the Black Sea territories till his death.

But he left us the first known "how-to" manual on love. Although written in the first century C. E., Ovid's book is remarkably current. Some things don't change.

Ovid also adds a sequel to his book on love. He appends a book on remedies for love, should none of his ploys in the arts of love work. Some of his remedies are dreadful, but so are the consequences of unrequited love.

Reading Ovid in the twenty-first century is a delicate matter. Readers are polarized; some love the time-honored truisms Ovid puts forth about love, while others find him politically incorrect and offensive.

I think Ovid is best approached as a comic. He himself admits his comic style — "If my muse is accused of being a little funny,/I would plead guilty and win; throw the case out of court!"[40] Ovid's perspective shows us that much of love is funny, and fun. Ovid asks his readers to dive deeply into the logic, or should I say the illogic, of emotion. For Ovid, the way our emotions operate is comedic. Our emotions are sometimes best coached in ways that might not make rational sense. The way we respond to things — the way a kind word will make us break down into a fit of tears, while an insult may fire us up with resolve for conquest; the way a flower we picked for free warms the heart, while an expensive present may leave the recipient unmoved; the things at which we grow indignant or react to happily — all suggest that from the perspective of our emotional life we are humorous animals.

To work on emotions is to dispense with reason, and delve into persuasion. To move another person to love, we may need to persuade and titillate, to arouse the other's will — not his or her reason. And the same holds true for us. We won't look at the other person objectively and study with cool calculation the virtues and vices, and thus come to a lasting philosophical appraisal of his or her character. We may be passionately drawn to someone and minimize all his

---

40. *Ibid.*, p. 193.

shortcomings in the throes of love — only to hate and denounce the same person, should our love be unrequited. Ovid gives us the freedom to hate what doesn't bring emotional satisfaction and to love what grants emotional satisfaction — something that would give an ethicist nightmares, but ought to make a psychologist pay attention.

All the strange illogic of emotional life is bound up in the defining style of Ovid's poem — play. Emotional language includes a liberal portion of play. Why not approach a "how-to" manual in that spirit? Ovid is playful, if anything.

Some serious readers argue that there is nothing funny about emotional manipulation, which they then accuse Ovid of employing. But humor is often on the boundary-line between offence and hilarity. Some of the best comedians cause offence to some, while making others laugh. From a logical point of view, grown men slapping each other in the face for a half an hour is cruel; but the Three Stooges continue to make people laugh. I find Ovid's play delightful, and hope to present him in that spirit. At times, I feel I need to cite at length in order to allow Ovid's playful style to speak for itself. Ovid conscripts the limits of his manual to three areas:

> First, my raw recruit, my inexperienced soldier,
> Take some trouble to find the girl whom you really can love.
> Next, when you see what you like your problem will be how to win
> her.
> Finally, strive to make sure mutual love will endure.
> That's as far as I go, the territory I cover,
> Those are the limits I set: take them or leave them alone (p. 106).

In other words, Ovid will teach us how to find our mates, how to win them over, and how to keep them. This citation reveals an aspect of Ovid that is easily overlooked. He tells his raw recruit to "Take some trouble to find the girl whom you really can love." Although much of Ovid is playful and affected, his first teaching is to find someone for *real* love. It would be well to remember that line, as we continue through Ovid's manual.

Thus, Ovid begins his teaching with the quest to find someone. We must go out and search — "She is not going to come to you floating down from the heavens/For the right kind of girl you must keep using your eyes" (p. 106). Ovid uses several metaphors in his instruction manual. Hunting and conquest turn up often:

Hunters know where to spread their nets for the stag in the covert,
Hunters know where the boar gnashes his teeth in the glade.
Fowlers know brier and bush, and fishermen study the waters
Baiting the hook for the cast just where the fish may be found.
So you too, in your hunt for material worthy of loving,
First will have to find out where the game usually goes. (p. 106)

Ovid is a great coach. He continually keeps up your spirits as he encourages you on your quest. You won't have to travel far to find someone:

I will not tell you to sail searching far over the oceans,
I will not tell you to plod any long wearisome road.
. . . Rome has all you will need, so many beautiful lovelies
You will be bound to say, "Here is the grace of the world!"
(pp. 106-107)

I'm not sure how to translate Ovid's geography. Is he telling people everywhere that there is ample game nearby, or is he talking specifically to Romans? Do I need to move to New York, a modern-day Rome? Or is there sufficient game here in my home town? In any event, his list of locations to search are Roman, so let us follow him on his rounds and translate that into our own culture, individually.

His first piece of advice seems apt: "Take your time, walk slow" (p. 107). In your wanderings around ancient Rome, notice the monuments to the royal family, or the open-air shrines to the gods. Here, people mingle. Keep your eyes open. One can find love in the most unlikely places. "Even the courts of the law, the bustle and noise of the forum,/(This may be hard to believe) listen to whispers of love" (p. 107). Even the skillful lawyer can be caught by his romantic betters — his arts of legal pleading of no use to him:

Hard by the marble shrine of Venus, the Appian fountain,
Where the water springs high in its rush to the air,
There, and more than once, your counsellor meets with his betters,
All his forensic arts proving of little avail;
Others he might defend; himself he cannot; words fail him,
Making objections in vain; Cupid says, Overruled!
Venus, whose temple is near, laughs at the mortified creature,
Lawyer a moment ago, in need of a counsellor now (p. 107).

Then there is the theater:

> Here you may find one to love, or possibly only have fun with,
> Someone to take for a night, someone to have and to hold.
> Just as a column of ants keeps going and coming forever,
> Bearing their burdens of grain, just as the flight of the bees
> Over the meadows and over the fields of the thyme and the clover,
> So do the women come, thronging the festival games,
> Elegant, smart, and so many my sense of judgement is troubled.
> Hither they come, to see; hither they come, to be seen (p. 108).

Horse races make an excellent "contact-sport" for amorous spectators:

> Furthermore, don't overlook the meetings when horses are running; . .
>
> Sit as close as you like; no one will stop you at all.
> . . . Whether she likes it or not, contact is part of the game.

Then you need to be noticed — "Put your bet down, fast, on whatever she plays." Let your interests be known. Cheer for the goddess of love when they bring in the statues of the Roman gods: "Then, when the gods come along in procession, ivory, golden,/Outcheer every young man, shouting for Venus, the queen" (p. 109). Once the races have begun, the real game begins — the game of love:

> Often it happens that dust may fall on the blouse of the lady.
> If such dust should fall, carefully brush it away.
> Even if there's no dust, brush off whatever there isn't.
> Any excuse will do: why do you think you have hands?
> If her cloak hangs low, and the ground is getting it dirty,
> Gather it up with care, lift it a little, so!
> Maybe, by way of reward, and not without her indulgence,
> You'll be able to see ankle or possibly knee.
> Then look around and glare at the fellow who's sitting behind you,
> Don't let him crowd his knees into her delicate spine.
> Girls, as everyone knows, adore these little attentions: . . . (p. 109).

Public parades are another good ground for happy hunting. When Caesar brings home prisoners from far-off lands, the Roman crowds loved to gather and watch the victory parade. There will be girls here, too. When the one you have your eye on asks who the various foreigners are, tell her. This gives a man the air of authority — always an attractive quality:

> Answer her questions, each one, and don't always wait till she asks
>   you;
> Things that you don't know tell her as if you were sure.
> Why, that's Euphrates, of course, with the reeds hanging over his
>   forehead;
> The one with the dark-blue hair? That would be Tigris, his twin.
> Those are Armenians there; the one just passing is Persia . . .
> (p. 111).

Ovid also advises his students to visit the unlikely gladiatorial contests, and, more likely, parties to find game for their hunting.

What is a modern reader to do? We don't have gladiatorial contests or open-air temples to the gods to wander through. "Where do you go to meet people?" is a question we often hear. Ovid simply means to encourage us to get out where the people are. Don't sit at home waiting for the phone to ring. Go where the girls are, says Ovid. They aren't going to come floating down from heaven to you. Spread your nets. Go to a park! Join a volunteer group! Answer phones for PBS! Take a dance class! Find a support group! If you don't have any problems, invent them! Hunt your game. A good woman can be found, right here in your own city.

Having told his readers where to find a lover, Ovid turns his attention to securing her favor. As a good coach, Ovid encourages the lover to be optimistic. Think positive! Ovid assures his pupil that victory is certain:

> First: be a confident soul, and spread your nets with assurance.
> Women can always be caught; that's the first rule of the game.
> Sooner would birds in the spring be silent, or locusts in August,
> Sooner would hounds run away when the fierce rabbits pursue,
> Than would a woman, well-wooed, refuse to succumb to a lover;
> (p. 113).

Banish all fear — "Venus favors the bold!" (p. 124). Resorting to a martial metaphor, Ovid repeats his injunction to be bold — "Love is a kind of war, and no assignment for cowards" (p. 137).

Ovid tells us that both men and women are equally interested in finding a lover. But the rules of the game are that the man must be the pursuer:

> It's a convention, no more, that men play the part of pursuer.
> Women don't run after us; mousetraps don't run after mice.
> In the soft meadows the heifer lows for the bull to come to her,

Stallions respond, but the mare gives the first whinnying call
(p. 113).

Any man of my age knows that we are the pursuers. We all know the courage that must be mustered up to seize our stomachs, swallow hard, and walk across the dance floor or barroom, all alone, to ask our lady for a dance. We all know, too, the shame and humiliation we endure to walk back across that same dance floor or barroom all alone, having been spurned. But Ovid coaches us to keep at it. Although men must be the pursuer, feminine desire is on our side. They are as eager to be caught as men are to catch them. "Keener in their desire, fiercer, more wanton than ours./So, you need have little doubt when it comes to winning them over;/Out of the many there are, hardly a one will refuse" (p. 115).

In beginning to woo the desired woman, Ovid advises one to make friends with her maid. The maid can be a great asset to the lover's cause:

> While her maid is at work, combing her hair in the morning,
> Let her keep urging her on, let her add oars to the sail,
> ... Then let her talk about you, and add some words of persuasion,
> Let her swear that she knows you must be dying of love (p. 116).

If one is to succeed, it is important that you are favored by those close to your intended woman. Your going will be rough, if her girlfriends don't like you. We know only too well that women talk! If her girlfriends don't like you, you don't stand a chance. On the other hand, a good word from a girlfriend will favor the lover.

Ovid advises one to begin by learning oratory, as if one were pleading a case before the lawcourts:

> Young men of Rome, I advise you to learn the arts of the pleader,
> Not so much for the sake of some poor wretch at the bar,
> But because women are moved, as much as the people or Senate,
> Possibly more than a judge, conquered by eloquent words,
> (p. 119)

Ovid suggests that you make your early pleading through letters, letters using a "natural, easy, familiar style." Keep trying, no matter what the response:

> If she refuses to read, or sends back a letter unopened,
> Hope that some day she will read, don't be discouraged. Some day!

> Time brings the most obdurate ox to submit to the yoke and the
>   ploughshare,
> Time brings the fiercest steed under the bridle and rein.
> . . . What is harder than rock, or more gentle than water?
> Yet the water in time hollows the rigidest stone.

Ovid continually encourages his student to keep up his hope, even if she won't respond at first:

> What if she reads, and won't answer? Do not attempt any pressure.
> Only supply her with more flattering missives to read.
> What she is willing to read, some day she'll be willing to answer —
> Every thing in its time, every thing by degrees. . . .
> So go on with your work; some day the day will be won (pp. 119, 120).

Here we encounter a modern problem. How aggressively can a man pursue a woman before he becomes a stalker? Ovid suggests that we need to persist. Time will bring her to our side. He even suggests something that our society loudly opposes. "No" might mean "yes," to Ovid; but today we are taught in no uncertain terms that "'NO' MEANS 'NO'!" But sometimes, a woman is slow to come around, or slow to show her assent, and time will pay off. Women don't want to appear easy. In fact, Ovid advises women to be non-committal at first. For Ovid, a man must sometimes sleep on a woman's doorstep overnight if she won't let him in. (That, I suppose, would be stalking, in today's terms.) Sending repeated letters may be annoying, but what about repeated phone calls? This matter is one that our culture has yet to fully resolve.

Ovid gives advice on our appearance, too. Men should not be too well-dressed, but we should be neat and clean. We need to pay some attention to our appearance, but we don't want to look like fops or dandies:

> Men should not care too much for good looks; neglect is becoming. . . .
> Let your person be clean, your body tanned by the sunshine,
> Let your toga fit well, never a spot on its white,
> Don't let your sandals be scuffed, nor your feet flap around in them
>   loosely,
> See that your teeth are clean, brush them at least twice a day,
> Don't let your hair grow long, and when you visit a barber,
> Patronize only the best, don't let him mangle your beard,
> Keep your nails cut short, and don't ever let them be dirty,
> Keep the little hairs out of your nose and your ears,
> Let your breath be sweet, and your body free from rank odors,

Don't overdo it; a man isn't a fairy or tart (p. 121).

In fact, Ovid warns women against men who are too concerned with their own appearance. These dandies are up to no good.

> Keep away from men who show off their elegant natures,
> Boast of their looks, and arrange every fine hair in place.
> What they are telling you, they have told to girls by the thousand;
> Theirs is a vagabond love, wandering, never at home.
> What can a woman do, when a man is smoother than she is,
> Maybe, for all we know, having more men of his own? (p. 166)

Here, we see that Ovid is not interested in only one-night-stands or temporary gratification. He denounces men who have had "girls by the thousand." This point recalls the observation I made as we begun to look into Ovid. He wants his pupil to "Take some trouble to find the girl whom you really can love" (p. 106).

Ovid then begins to discuss how to win your beloved. Here, parties are a good place. Make eye-contact. "Let your eyes gaze into hers, let the gazing be a confession:/Often the silent glance brings more conviction than words" (p. 123). Favor the food that passes by her:

> Be the first to seize the cup that her lips have been touching,
>   Drink from that edge of the rim which she has touched with her lips,
> Ask her to pass the bread or the fruit she has touched with her fingers;
>   When she passes it on, manage to touch her hand (p. 123).

Ovid cautions his pupil about drinking. Don't drink too much; you need to be aware of your actions at all times. Love is a delicate art that requires our full faculties. But it is alright to pretend you are drunk; in fact, it could help:

> Now, let me give you advice on the limit to put on your drinking:
>   Never let feet or mind either lose track of their place.
> . . . Getting drunk is bad, but pretending to do so
>   Does no harm at all, might, in fact, be a gain.
> Make your cunning tongue stumble and stutter a little,
>   So, if you go too far, people will say, "Oh, he's drunk." (p. 123).

Then there are various tricks that move the hardest hearts. First, tears:

> Tears are a good thing, too; they move the most adamant natures.
> Let her, if possible, see tears on your cheeks, in your eyes.
> This is not easy: sometimes the eyes will not stream at your bidding.
> What can be done about this? — get your hands wet, and apply (p. 125).

In your early wooing, don't come on too strong. Women are likely to be scared off, if we let them know that we intend to win their affections. Take a soft approach. Set her at ease by protesting that all you want is friendship:

> Don't always show in your talk that you know you are going to get her —
> What you are eager to be, tell her, is *Only a friend*.
> I have seen this work, on the most unwilling of women —
> *Only a friend*, who was found more than proficient in bed! (p. 127).

The complexion of a lover is pale. The lover can not sleep, being wound up with passion and is too care-ridden to eat, becoming thin:

> White is a color no sailor should have . . .
> But a pallor is right for the lover, a suitable color: . . .
> Thinness is also good, a proof of sentiment . . .
> Lying awake all night wears down the bodies of lovers,
> All that passion and pain — how can you help but grow lean?
> Be a pitiful sight, if it helps to accomplish your purpose,
> Let anyone who observes say, "The poor fellow's in love" (pp. 127-128).

Ovid suggests Daphnis and Chloe. Chloe is the perfect example of Ovid's lover:

> She took no interest in food, she could not sleep at night, she paid no attention to her flock. One moment she would be laughing, the next she would be crying. Now she would be lying down, now she would be jump-ing up again.[41]

In applying these techniques, be able to adapt; use a variety of approaches; be sensitive to a woman's moods; understand the circumstances in which you are involved and act appropriately. Ovid compares the lover to the Roman god Proteus, who could change his shape into any creature. To show erudition to someone with little education won't work; talking about rock music or a current TV show might be more appropriate. But to someone in your academic department, you may wish to talk about Ovid, himself. Isn't it better to find areas

---

41. Longus, *Daphnis and Chloe* (New York: Penguin Books, 1989), p. 27.

of commonality than to be a bore and attempt to force an appreciation of traits one's partner isn't interested in?

> I was about to conclude, but — the hearts of girls! How they differ!
> Use a thousand means, since there are thousands of ends.
> Earth brings forth varying yield: one soil is good for the olive,
> One for the vine, and a third richly productive in corn.
> Hearts have as many moods as heaven has constellations:
> He who is wise will know how to adapt to the mood.
> Be like the Protean god, a wave, a tree, or a lion . . .
> Some fish are taken with spears, and others by trolling,
> Some rise to the fly, some must be hauled by the net.
> Then there's the question of years, with experience also a factor;
> Wary naive — you must choose which is the method to use.
> If you seem coarse to a prude, or learned to some little lowbrow,
> She will be filled with distrust, made to feel cheap in your eyes,
> So she will run away from an honest man, and go flying
> Off to the embraces of some inferior clown.[42]

Ovid coaches us in finding a lover and winning her over. But couples who have been together for a long period will tell you that a lasting romance takes effort. Ovid says it is not enough to trust nature to keep the flame alive. We must act artfully. We can say and do hurtful things if we allow inappropriate spontaneous reactions to burst forth. Words spoken in anger are difficult to take back. Ovid says that to hold on to love requires as much art as finding love. It is by art that Ovid will pin down the flighty wings of Cupid:

> Give the victory cry, and give it over, and over!
> What I have sought, I have won: give the victory cry!
> Happy, the lover brings green palms to the poem I have written:
> Homer and Hesiod yield, in his opinion, to me.
> . . . Not so fast, young man! Your vessel sails in mid-ocean,
> Far away, still, is the port; harbor and haven are far.
> It is by no means enough to have won your girl through my singing;
> What you have won by my art, art must instruct you to hold.
> Seeking is all very well, but holding requires greater talent:
> Seeking involves some luck; now the demand is for skill.
> Now, if ever, be kind, be gracious, Venus and Cupid,
> Favor my work, O Muse named for the power of love!

---

42. Ovid, *The Art of Love*, pp. 128-129.

> Great is the scope of my plan — to tell how to keep him a captive,
> Love, that vagabond boy, flitting all over the world.
> He has two wings for his flight, he is fickle and light and capricious;
> Pinning his pinions down — that is the problem we face.[43]

Many accuse Ovid of being superficial, but here he shows some depth. He urges his disciples to add distinction of mind to their character. Good looks will not last long, but a noble soul will endure:

> Be a lovable man; a face and figure won't do.
> You might have all the good looks that appealed to the sea-nymphs, or Homer;
> That's not enough, you will find; add some distinction of mind.
> Beauty's a fragile boon, and the years are quick to destroy it,
> Always diminished with time, never enduring too long.
> Violets always fade, and the bloom departs from the lily;
> When the roses are gone, nothing is left but the thorn.
> Look, my handsome young man, gray hairs will come in your lifetime,
> Soon the wrinkles will plough furrows in cheek and in brow,
> So, make a soul to endure, a spirit to go with the body;
> Spirit and soul will abide, up to the ultimate fire.
> Culture is surely worth while, and the liberal arts are a blessing
> ... (p. 133).

Never argue with your beloved. Arguing is better saved for married people. Here Ovid contrasts marriage with his "free love." Love is nurtured by affectionate words:

> Tactfulness, tolerance — these are more than desirable virtues.
> Harshness arouses hate, rancor, resentment, and war.
> Why do we hate the hawk? Because he lives by aggression.
> Why do we hate the wolves, stalking the timorous fold?
> But we set no snares for the swallow, because he is gentle,
> Set no snares for the dove, haunting the eaves of the tower,
> Keep far away, far off, all bitter tongue-lashing quarrels;
> Love is a delicate thing, won with affectionate words.
> Husbands and wives, by right, may harry each other with nagging;
> ... This is all right for wives: the dower of a wife is a quarrel;
> Let your mistress hear nothing but what they desire.
> ... Bring her courtesies, and flattering words, and endearments,

---

43. *Ibid.*, p. 130.

Words that are sweet to the ear; make her be glad you are there
(pp. 134-135).

Ovid contrasts the pure love of a mistress with the legally-enforced attachment of marriage. For him, the love of a mistress is not bound by anything other than love itself. It is free, while marriage is bound by law: "You have not come to bed in the name of the law, but more freely./Love is your warrant and bond, love holds the office of law," (p. 135). Can't we apply the same advice in a marriage? Shouldn't you continue to expend effort to make your married partner "glad you are there"? Perhaps the reason that so many marriages fail these days is that people forget to continue employing their "arts of love" after being together for an extended period of time.

Ovid shows little respect for the institution of marriage. Married people are still free game for other suitors. Ovid even goes so far as to advise one to make friends brazenly with your lover's husband. Your affair will be easier that way. "Also, make it your aim to get her husband to like you;/If you can make him your friend, he will be useful you'll find. . . ." Offer a toast to the lady and her husband, while under your breath you curse the spouse. "Propose 'A health to the lady! A health to the fellow she sleeps with!'/Making your silent toast, 'Damn her husband to hell!' (p. 123).

Ovid emphasizes the effect of gift giving. Nothing moves the heart like gifts. A rich man doesn't need Ovid's teachings: "I do not lecture the rich in my role of professor of loving:/'Here is something for you!' A man who can say that has genius!/I give up, I retire; he can learn nothing from me" (p. 135). For the rest of us, we can give gifts from the heart. We need not spend a lot; the important thing is that our gifts appear to be chosen with care:

> I do not say you should spend great sums of money on gifts for the
>   lady:
> Let them, however small, seem to be chosen with care.
> When the fields are rich, and the boughs droop under their burden,
> Have a boy come to the door, bringing her baskets of fruit.
> Tell her they came from your farm, your little place in the country:
> She would not know, nor suspect fruit stands are easy to find (p. 138).

Ovid suggests simple gifts that seem to show thoughtfulness; but he doesn't have much confidence in poetry as a gift. Money talks even in ancient Rome:

What about sending her poems? A very difficult question.
Poems, I'm sorry to say, aren't worth so much in this town.
Oh, they are praised, to be sure; but the girls want something more
    costly.
Even illiterates please, if they have money to burn.
Ours is a Golden Age, and gold can purchase you honors,
All the "Golden Mean" means is, gold is the end.
Homer himself, if he came attended by all of the Muses,
With no scrip in his purse, would be kicked out of the house
(p. 138).

Ovid's point is well taken. It is quite difficult to survive the early courting days without money. If one is unable to pay for dinner for two, how can one ask someone out? Ovid suggests that we need not spend a lot, if the gift only looks thoughtful. Perhaps inviting a date over for a home-cooked dinner might work. It might even earn more sentimental points than a dinner bought at some restaurant. But in the ordinary modern rituals, just as in ancient Rome, sufficient means make for easier going. It requires a special character to appreciate another person for who he is in the early stages of a relationship. It is naive to suppose that love can conquer all. The dollar has a voice, too.

As you are getting to know your beloved, it is important to stay continually in her sight lest she forget about you:

Always appear in her sight, . . .
Be a presence, on hand all of her nights and days;
Don't stay away, not once, until you are sure she will miss you,
Don't go away until you know she will be sorry you go (pp. 140-141).

Even then, only stay away a short while, or her attention may turn to others. Ovid refers to Helen of Troy in this context, and absolves Helen, and Paris who kidnapped her, of any crime. The fault lies with Menelaus, who left Helen alone with Paris:

Still, a short absence is best: be away too long, she'll forget you:
Hearts are inclined to grow fond, then, of available men.
When Menelaus was gone, and the bed of Helen was lonesome,
Paris and warmth were found in the embrace of the night.
Menelaus, I think, was a fool to go off on a journey,
Leaving his wife and his guest housed in identical walls.
Only a madman would think that the dove was safe with the falcon, . . .

> Helen was not to blame, and neither, so help me, was Paris;
> Given the chance that he had, who would do anything else?
> You were to blame, Menelaus: you gave him the time, the occasion; . . .
> I acquit Helen outright, and put the blame on the husband.
> What did she do but make use of the occasion he gave? (p. 141).

Here, Ovid speaks resoundingly to our society. How often do we find partners accused of not paying enough attention to their beloved? When we become too involved in our work, relationships can suffer. When we fail to show our loved ones that they still have a place in our hearts, they become discontented. Some, as Ovid suggests, look to extramarital affairs for the companionship they don't have in their marriages. Couples forget that love is an art, and requires continual nurture to endure.

Sometimes one needs to adjust for imperfections in one's beloved. What one has can depend on how one views one's beloved. Ovid's general rule is, "If you like what you get, you will get what you like" (p. 149).

> Do not blame a girl for flaws of her nature or person:
> Where's the advantage in that? Better pretend them away.
> . . . Words have a magical power to mitigate many shortcomings:
> If she is blacker than tar, tanned is the term to employ.
> Cross-eyed? She looks like Venus! Albino? Fair as Minerva!
> Thin as a rail? What grace lies in her willowy charm!
> If she's a runt, call her cute; if fat, a full-bodied woman:
> Dialectic can make grace out of any defect (pp. 149, 150).

By sleight of mind, even imperfections can become endearments. All the unique quirks that make up a person become part of the overall character and look we have come to love. A nuance of speech, a tilt of the head, the way someone walks, all of these traits combine and become elements of the person we love. We wouldn't wish away any of these qualities that we have come to identify with our beloved. This is what the rock band had in mind when they wrote, "Every little thing she does is magic."

Having advised men, Ovid's next task is to teach women. "I gave arms to the Greeks against the Amazon forces:/Arms for the Amazons now: turn about is fair play" (p. 153). At one point in his advice to women, Ovid fears that he is giving away secrets that will be used against him:

I must be out of my mind! Here I go, wholly defenseless,
Into the enemy's camp, giving my secrets away.
Even a bird has more sense than to tell where the fowler may find it,
Deer do not teach the pack where the hounds are to run.
Well, never mind: I began, and so I might as well finish, (p. 173).

Ovid's tips to the ladies are mostly about beauty; that is where a woman's art is most essential. Nature properly enhanced by nurture can turn an unexceptional person into a striking beauty. She is the one who attracts the men. While gifts from a man open up a woman's heart, so a beautiful appearance will gain a man's attention. Ovid's teachings are confirmed by the glut of women's magazines, today, which capitalize on the unquenchable thirst to project an appearance of beauty. We all like to think that we are above appearances, but a first impression still starts the game.

Ovid tells women how to wear their hair:

If your face is long, you should part your hair in the middle;
If your features are round, then let your hair be a crown.
Somebody else might look best with the locks falling over each
shoulder; . . .
Still another might try a braid, in the mode of Diana . . .
Every day, so it seems, brings in a different style. . . . (p. 157).

When it comes to make-up, Ovid suggests moderation. Art is best when it doesn't look like art. "Art that dissembles art gives the most happy effect./Who wants to look at a face so smeared with paint that it's dripping, . . ." (p. 159). Ovid tells his lady readers to apply their makeup privately. Men do not need to know the secrets of a woman's beauty. Let them appear like Venus risen from the depths of the ocean fully formed in all her beauty:

While you are fixing your face, let us assume you are sleeping,
Put on the finishing touch privately, out of sight.
Why do I need to know the cause of your lovely complexion?
Shut the studio door, don't give the artist away!
There are a great many things that men would be better not knowing
. . . (p. 160).

As he did with men, Ovid advises women to go out in public. And as with men, here Ovid employs the metaphor of fishing —

> What are good looks, unseen? Nothing is gained if you hide. . .
> So let a beautiful girl display herself to her public
> Out of the many, she'll find, one may appeal to her mind.
> If she is eager to please, let her be a conspicuous pleasure,
> Let her, by every device, draw every eye to her charm.
> Luck has a part in the game: the hook should be forever dangled;
> Where you might least expect there'll be a tug on the line (p. 165).

Ovid also provides a quick list of the same places for women to frequent: open air gathering places such as monuments; temples; theaters, and horse race tracks. In public gatherings, women should know how to display themselves for maximum benefit. Although the man is the pursuer, the woman is the one who attracts:

> Lie on your back, if your face and all of your features are pretty;
> If your posterior's cute, better be seen from behind.
> Milanion used to bear Atlanta's legs on his shoulders;
> If you have beautiful legs, let them be lifted like hers . . .
> If the breasts and the thighs are youthful and lovely to look at,
> Let the man stand and the girl lie on a slant on the bed (p. 177).

When a woman has a suitor, she must take care to find out whether he is serious or merely trifling with her affections. Critics of Ovid miss his underlying claim that he is talking about love. In his advice to women, Ovid advises his pupils to carefully plumb their letters to see if they are from the lover's heart:

> When a man's paving the way with a letter, in wax, on the tablets, . . .
> Study it, give it some thought; you ought to find out from the phrasing
> Whether he's making it up, whether he writes from the heart (p. 167).

Ovid seems to be speaking from contradictory motives. While at times he wants genuine love, at other times he unabashedly advises outright deceit: "Cheat these little cheats, for most of them haven't a scruple — Let them be caught in the net they are so eager to set" (p. 125). Aware of his own ploys, Ovid's advice to women seeks to keep them from being trapped by one of his own male pupils. Men can be sweet-talkers in order to get what they want, particularly if they are writing and have time to think up honeyed words. Women need to carefully consider the words they are hearing and determine whether they are all pretence or whether they are heartfelt.

But he arms women with tricks of their own. Keep the man guessing for a while. Don't be too clear about your affections too soon:

> Answer, after a while: delay is good for a lover —
> Only one bit of advice — don't keep him waiting too long.
> Don't be a reckless girl, too quick with a promise, too easy,
> Don't, on the other hand, absolutely refuse.
> Let him keep hoping and fearing, and when you send him an answer,
> Give him more cause to hope, lessen his reasons for fear (p. 167).

This evil technique has a remarkably effective result. If we men think that we have our fish hooked, we may become complacent. Nothing keeps our interest up like uncertainty. Our tormented hearts keep us working, bringing flowers, writing cards, courting, calling on the phone and worrying about where we stand in our lady's affections.

Summing up his lessons on love, and showing his concern that both sexes find love, Ovid hopes that the sexual experience will be ecstasy for both the lovers and, in the spirit and style of the whole of his poetic work, play.

> Let the woman feel the act of love to her marrow,
> Let the performance bring equal delight to the two. Coax and flatter
>   and tease, with inarticulate murmurs, Even with sexual words, in
>   the excitement of play . . . (p. 177).

But unfortunately, as in some of Ovid's work, pretence finds its way into even this amorous climax —

> And if nature, alas! denies you the final sensation
> Cry out as if you had come, do your best to pretend.
> Really, I pity the girl whose place, let us say, cannot give her
> Pleasure it gives to the man, pleasure she ought to enjoy.
> So, if you have to pretend, be sure the pretence is effective,
> Do your best to convince, prove it by rolling your eyes,
> Prove it by your motions, your moans, your sighs, what a pleasure it
>   gives you.
> Ah, what a shame! (p. 177).

Ovid pities the women who don't reach climax, and sex requires particular sensitivity. Arts are most needed as we try to discover what moves our partners best. Perhaps that is why the Bible refers to sex as "knowing" one's partner.[44]

44

Only by intimately knowing our partners are we able to provide the stimulus that they will respond to, before, during, and after sex. In the act of sex, all the arts of love find their culmination.

It is fitting that Ovid concludes his great manual on loving with a comment on the art of sex, with ecstasy either real or pretended. He has followed his own belief that "love requires art to survive" (p. 154). The happy lover has found someone to love, has won over his or her affections, and has retained them. Then, as is only fitting, one should not forget to honor one's teacher. Ovid appends a final, playful stanza asking his successful pupils to invoke his own name on their "votive spoil" — i.e., their attainment of love. His lofty poetic chariot, drawn by swans, must descend. Grateful lovers bring their coach in this "sport" the laurel wreath.

> So our sport has an end: our swans are tired of their harness:
> Time for their labor to rest, time to step down from our car.
> As the young men did, now let the girls, my disciples,
> Write on the votive spoil, "Ovid showed us the way" (p. 178).

Remedies For Love

One may still fail, despite all of Ovid's arts. What to do with unrequited love? Ovid does not leave his lovers victims to their amorous feelings. He has concluded his work on love in ecstasy. But with a doctor's healing care, Ovid then turned his talents to another book: *The Remedies for Love*.[45] In this work, Ovid provides cures for the wounds of Cupid's arrows,

> So now listen to me young men who have been so deluded,
> Whom, for all your pains, love has completely betrayed.
> I have taught you to love — do you want to know how to recover?
> Mine is the hand that will bring the wounds, and the cure for the
> wound.[46]

The lover must assess his or her chances early on. If you are suspicious of the outcome, get out before you are in too deep:

---

44. "Now Adam knew Eve his wife, and she conceived and bore Cain" (Genesis 4:1).
45. In Ovid, *The Art of Love*, trans. Rolfe Humphries (Indiana: Indiana UP, 1957).
46. Ovid, *The Remedies for Love*, p. 182.

While you still have a chance, and your heart is moved, but not
    deeply,
If you're uncertain at all, never step over the sill.
Crush, before they are grown, the swelling seeds of your passion,
Let your spirited steed never get into full stride . . .
Get your neck from the yoke, if you suspect it will gall.
Fight the disease at the start, for once symptoms develop
Medicine comes too late, losing effect from delay. . . .
I have seen a wound that might have been healed when inflicted
Fester with long delay, aggravated by time.[47]

The first point of advice Ovid brings in getting over unrequited love is to
stay busy. Idleness only makes passion more likely.

. . . shun all leisurely ways.
Idleness tempts you to love, and idleness watches its captives, . . .
Toss your leisure away, and you've broken the arrows of Cupid,
Toss your leisure away, his torch is extinguished and scorned. . . .
So does Venus delight in idleness: keep yourself busy
If you would drive her away; if you are busy, you're safe (pp. 185, 186).

Ovid lists some activities you might want to take up. There is law; you may
need to defend a friend in court. Then there is war — help Caesar against the
Parthians. Farming and country pursuits are good. Just stay busy.

Then there are the psychological weapons one can draw on in order to
escape love. When Ovid discusses these methods, he consistently refers to
getting over women. It would appear that the remedies are for men, only. Some
of Ovid's techniques are so harsh that he has been accused of hating women and
being interested only in their oppression. Ovid would respond that his cures are
harsh, but so are Cupid's arrows. If one wants to be healed, one will endure the
surgeon's steel:

Some may call my advice cruel and hard: I admit it.
Still, if you want to be well, therapy must be endured.
When I was sick myself, I often drank down bitter tonics,
Often denied myself food, fighting the urge of my will.
For your bodily health, you submit to the steel and endure it,
Nor will water's cool slake your feverish thirst.
So, for your mental health, is any treatment too drastic?

---

47. *Ibid.*, pp. 183, 184.

Ailments of mind demand more than placebos to cure (p. 188).

One remedy employs the imagination. When we are falling in love, we use the imagination to make the beloved's imperfections into endearments; now we reverse the process and turn perfections into defects.

> When you possibly can, fool yourself, ever so little,
> Call those attractions of hers defects, or possibly worse.
> If she has full round breasts, call her *fat as a pig*; if she's slender,
> Thin as a rail; if she's dark, black as the ace of spades.
> If she has city ways, label her *stuck-up* and *bitchy*;
> If she is simple and good, call her a *hick from the farm*.

After turning her virtues into defects comes the process of accentuating the actual defects as much as possible:

> Whatever talent she lacks, coax and cajole her to use it:
> If she hasn't a voice, try to persuade her to sing;
> If she trips over her feet, make her dance; if her accent's atrocious,
> Get her to talk; all thumbs? — call for the zither or lyre.
> . . . If her teeth aren't too straight, tell her a comical story; . . .
> Sometimes it works very well to surprise her early some morning,
> Hardly expecting a call, when she's not fixed for the day (p. 191).

Ovid intensifies this process of desensitizing when it comes to the act of lovemaking. In one of the most frightening passages in the work, he counsels his student to make the act of physical love as disgusting as possible. This is sure to quench the flames of passion.

> This I should not say, but I will: adopt a position
> Awkward for her and for you, hardly becoming or fit.
> . . . Open the windows wide, all of them, draw back the curtains,
> Let the light make clear parts that are ugly to see.
> When you have come to an end, and the pleasure is over,
> When your body and mind both are exhausted and spent,
> While you are bored, and you wish you never had touched any
> woman,
> While you haven't the least impulse to touch one again,
> Then note down in your mind every blemish of body,
> Keep your eyes on her faults, memorize every defect.

> Possibly some one will say, and be right, that they're really quite small
>   ones;
> Still, the little things count; all of them come to your aid (pp. 193-194).

These several selections show the general direction Ovid takes in desensitizing a lover from unrequited love. There are others — "Thousands the forms of disease, thousands the methods of cure." But as art guided the lover to his or her conquest, so art will alleviate the wounds of unsuccessful love.

We can enjoy Ovid and learn from him; but some people take real offence at his seemingly manipulative methods. While there is sufficient merit in his text to commend this point, we must also remember that humor is often on a cutting edge of propriety.

In fact, Ovid's lasting contribution is in bringing a robust humor to the institution of love. Is it so serious, after all? Ovid's earthy style anticipates the broad, and at times ribald, comedy of Shakespeare — whom we all read and love. Shakespeare's Romances that end happily are comedies — it was a requirement of the genre in that time period, which may suggest something deeper about loving itself. Some suggest that all of Ovid's machinations amount to no more than a boy whistling as he passes the graveyard. For all his efforts, Ovid knows that he isn't impervious to Love's arrows, after all; so his comedy is a form of irony. The greater and more elaborate the plan of attack, the more deeply the poet acknowledges the danger.

But Ovid's response is not that of Plato. He doesn't attempt to transcend love. Rather, Ovid dives deeply into the dynamics of emotion — loving deeply when that is possible, becoming disgusted with love when it is impossible. Ovid's ongoing interest is in coaching the emotions, and Ovid approaches emotion with gusto, drinking deeply, loving, laughing, cursing, and adoring. For Ovid, the life of love is funny and fun. Hearts may be broken, but we can respond in keeping with Shakespeare's song from *Much Ado About Nothing*:

> Then sigh not so, but let them go,
> And be you blithe and bonny;
> Converting all your sounds of woe
> Into Hey nonny nonny.

Aristotle: How Far Has The Apple Fallen From Plato's Tree?

Aristotle opens Book VIII of his *Nicomachean Ethics* with a remarkably sensitive insight for such a rigorous philosopher. After determining that happiness is the ultimate goal of human existence, he tenderly asks what makes humans happy. No one would be able to live a happy life without friends:

> For nobody would choose to live without friends, although he were in possession of every other good. Nay, it seems that if people are rich and hold official and authoritative positions, they have the greatest need of friends; for what is the good of having this sort of prosperity if one is denied the opportunity of beneficence, which is never so freely or so admirably exercised as towards friends. . . . In poverty and other misfortunes we regard our friends as our only refuge. Again, friends are helpful to us, when we are young, as guarding us from error, and when we are growing old, as taking care of us . . . and when we are in the prime of life, as prompting us to noble actions, . . . for two people have a greater power both of intelligence and of action than either of the two by himself.[48]

The philosopher observes also that friends are not only desirable for happiness in life, but are also noble:

> Nor is friendship indispensable only; it is also noble. We praise people who are fond of their friends, and it is thought to be a noble thing to have many friends, and there are some people who hold that to be a friend is the same thing as to be a good man.[49]

Aristotle was a student of Plato. Although his philosophical method is different, one wonders how far the apple has fallen from the tree. Clearly, Aristotle's description of friendship is rational; but the way Aristotle reasons is different. Plato begins from philosophical principles and deductively reasons his way to logical conclusions. Aristotle, on the other hand, reasons by looking at the world around him. His philosophical conclusions are based on what he sees. He is the first empiricist. His conclusion that friendship is indispensable to a happy life is based on a commonplace observation of human nature, that "nobody would choose to live without friends." He hasn't proved this by argument; rather, he simply assumes that everyone would agree and accept this

---

48. Aristotle, *The Nicomachean Ethics* (Buffalo, New York: Prometheus Books, 1987), p. 253.
49. Aristotle, *The Nichomachean Ethics*, p. 255.

empirical observation. Similarly, speaking about friendship as a noble institution, his "proof" is that "there are some people who hold" — again, observing people around him and concluding his principles from what he sees. And if his empirical observations are sufficient to establish the truth of a fact, it will be enough. "We must begin then with such facts as are known. . . and, if the fact is sufficiently clear, it will not be necessary to go on to ask the reason of it."[50] Aristotle is less interested in philosophical causes than he is in finding observable facts.

But Aristotle is indeed a philosopher. He immediately proceeds to define friendship itself, by looking at what draws us to our friends. He finds three things that draw us to our friends: that which is 1) good in them, or 2) pleasant, or 3) useful.

Aristotle challenges us to question our relationships in the light of these three qualities. The only true form of friendship is virtuous friendship, or friendship that desires what is good. For true friendship, we want what is good for our friend, for our friend's sake, and not for anything we derive from our friend. "We ought to wish our friend's good for his sake, and not for our own." But this well-wishing must be returned, for friendship to thrive:

> If we wish people good in this sense, we are called well-wishers, unless our good wishes are returned; such reciprocal well-wishing is called friendship or love.[51]

Aristotle is careful not to leave out any important detail in his definition. He adds that this mutual well-wishing be known by both parties.

> A person often wishes well to people whom he has not seen, but whom he supposes to be virtuous or useful; and it is possible that one of these persons may entertain the same feeling toward him. Such people then, it is clear, wish well to one another; but they cannot be properly called friends, as their disposition is unknown to each other. It follows that, if they are to be friends, they must be well-disposed to each other, and must wish each other's good . . . and that each of them must know the fact of the other wishing him well (pp. 257-258).

So Aristotle's first definition is philosophical friendship.

---

50. *Ibid.*, p. 14.
51. *Ibid.*, p. 257.

This is a high order to be expected from us. Aristotle also discusses two other forms of friendship that are less demanding: friendships of utility and pleasure. In these two, we are concerned with what we get out of the friendship, and not what we give to the other person.

Friendships of utility are based on some benefit that we get from the other person. These friendships are like business partnerships, where we derive a financial benefit but are not concerned with the actual person him or herself. Aristotle says that for friendships of utility, the friendship is a secondary concern. Our own benefit is our primary concern and "friendship" is a way to get it. This is not true friendship, because our primary concern is not the actual person him or herself. Aristotle says that old people tend to form friendships of utility, because they have more need to be taken care of. We don't even have to like the other person, in a friendship of utility. The "friendship" will endure as long as one derives a benefit from the other. But as soon as the benefit is gone, such a friendship dissolves.

Another form of secondary friendship is friendship that seeks pleasure. Again, we are not interested in the actual person, only the pleasure that we derive from the "friend." We like witty people as long as they make us laugh. At a party, everybody loves everybody as long as the wine flows. But when the wine stops, so does the fun; and everybody goes his own way. All the vows of eternal friendship, all the promises to go golfing together are forgotten the next day. Aristotle says that young people are more likely to form friendships of pleasure, because they live by their emotions. Young people also fall in and out of love quickly, forming friendships of pleasure with their beloved. Friendships of pleasure are closer to philosophical friendship because the friends wish to spend time together — the actual person providing the pleasure.

Aristotle's philosophical friendship is based on virtue. Both friends possess virtue, and love the virtue in the other. This is an enduring friendship because, for Aristotle, virtue is a permanent quality. One begins to practice virtue at a young age, and after years of character training, one comes to love the virtuous life. One has made virtue a permanent part of one's character. One is courageous, temperate, generous, a philanthropist, self-respecting, gentle, friendly, truthful, witty, and just. These virtues become second nature; one enjoys living a virtuous life. These are what philosophical friends look for in each other.

Aristotle employs an ancient Greek proverb to describe the way one forms philosophical friendships — it doesn't happen overnight. You don't have a friend until you have eaten a bushel of salt with him or her.[52] (Each time we eat with a friend, we sprinkle a little salt on our food. We each test the other for virtue, all along the way; by the time this salt adds up to a bushel, and we have determined that our friend is virtuous and loyal, only then can one say that one has a true friend.)

In today's fast-paced society, many people make friends prematurely. We think that friendship, like everything else in our lives, can be instantaneous. The consequences can be disappointment or a broken heart. Aristotle's philosophical friendships are impervious to envy or slander, because friends have been tested and we know firsthand that they can be trusted — with intimacy and our hearts.

> It is only the friendship of the good which cannot be destroyed by cal-umnies. For it is not easy to believe what anyone says about a person whom we have tested ourselves for many years, and found to be good. The friend-ship of the good too realizes confidence, and the assurance that neither of the two friends will do injury to the other . . . (p. 262).

In a remarkable passage, Aristotle claims that friendships of virtue are possible between men and women. This claim is remarkable because, in Classical Greece, women held little power and were esteemed as little more than possessions. Aristotle is progressive in the way he explains the relationships between husband and wife. As is typical of Aristotle's general empirical method, he looks at marriage as a function of nature:

> But the love of husband and wife seems to be a natural law, as man is naturally more inclined to contract marriage than to constitute a state . . . and the procreation of children is the more universal function of animals (p. 281).

Bearing children is the limit of animals' association in Aristotle. But humans render aid to one another according to the division of labor within a household:

> As soon as a man and a woman unite, a distribution of functions takes place. Some are proper to the husband and others to the wife; hence they supply one another's needs, each contributing his special gifts to the com-mon stock (pp. 281-282).

---

52. Although clearly Aristotle is referring primarily to men when he discusses friendships, as we will see later, he includes women in his discussion of friendships of virtue.

So far, Aristotle has identified friendships of utility and pleasure in marriage. Supplying one another's needs is utility, and sex is friendship of pleasure. But in a striking statement, Aristotle states that women possess virtue, and can enter friendships of virtue with their husbands:

> It is thus that utility and pleasure seem alike to be found in this friendship; but its basis will be virtue too, if the husband and wife are virtuous, as each of them has his or her proper virtue, and they will both delight in what is virtuous (p. 282).

True friends delight in each other's company. Friendship, for Aristotle, is an activity. It is shared time together. If friends are separated by sleep or long distance, the friendship is strained. In our mobile society, friendship can suffer. We are no longer able to enjoy spending time with our friends. While distance may make the heart grow fonder, too much distance over too long a period of time may cause the friendship to dissolve. Aristotle quotes an unknown source in this regard — "Many a friendship is dissolved by lack of converse" (p. 264).

Friendships are best among equals. When there is inequality in a friendship, special consideration is required. Can we be friends with our bosses? Can a rich person be friends with a poor person? In a society like that of the United States, where we witness so much social mobility and changes in fortune, these are significant questions. If one comes into a fortune, can one remain friends with one's poorer schoolmates? Will other rich people accept one into friendship, or will he or she be branded "nouveau riche" and be excluded? If a wife or husband goes on to earn a Ph.D. while the other partner continues to work, can the couple stay together? Aristotle says that where the difference in station is too great, friendship cannot be sustained:

> For persons so widely different cease to be friends; they do not even affect to be friends. . . . It is clear too in the case of kings; for people who are greatly inferior to them do not expect to be their friends. Nor again do worthless people expect to be friends of the best or wisest of mankind (p. 269).

In general, Aristotle says that some form of equalization is needed, if the two people are at different levels. Balance can be achieved by measuring on various scales, so that prestige, wealth, or power may be weighed against intellect or beauty or other forms of success. Mutual respect can then be equal.

Courting practices today bring these questions to the fore. In initiating and maintaining a romance, chivalry and some adherence to the traditional roles and rules of the hunt still work, but the economic inequality between men and women that used to be assumed and that still, largely, prevails, is now countered by stringent efforts toward economic and other forms of equality. Women want (and anyway, in many cases are forced into) self sufficiency, and they expect to be treated as competent adults, equal to men. This may make friendships more equal between the sexes, but our culture has not found a way to allow for what used to be accepted courtesies between the sexes.

It may be understood that the superior party in an unequal relationship might receive more affection, in return. If the man pays for dinner out and a movie, can the woman accept these benefits and say goodnight with a handshake? Our culture is in conflict over this question. Can a man open a door for a woman, without being branded chauvinistic? Can he not open the door, and expect the woman to feel that she is respected and cherished, anyway? If a woman is earning more money than a man, who should pay the dinner check? Can a man stay home and be supported by his wife without being considered a slacker? Can men and women compete with one another for jobs in the work place and yet keep chivalry alive in their personal lives?

From Aristotle's point of view, one would conclude that equality will make for better friendships. But in order to achieve total equality between the sexes, many time-honored cultural practices will need to be revised or abandoned. Meanwhile, considerable friction between the sexes is probably inevitable as our culture sorts through its courting traditions.

Aristotle raises the religious question about the ultimate inequality — the relationship between humans and God. For Aristotle, the distinction makes friendship impossible. "Where there is a great distinction, as between God and man, it ceases to be" (p. 269). In the Greek tradition, humans supplicated their gods by sacrifice, hoping for favor from the all-powerful deities.

But Christianity (and certain Eastern religions) raises theological issues relating to our theme. The idea of incarnation, where God takes on human form, is one way in which the infinite can approach the finite. In the Christian Gospel of John, we find perhaps one of the most remarkable instances of incarnation. In the other Gospels, Jesus indeed walks among humanity as God in human form. But in John's Gospel, friendship is emphasized; Jesus calls his disciples friends:

> You are my friends if you do what I command you. No longer do I call you servants, for the servant does not know what his master is doing; but I have called you friends, for all that I have heard from my father I have made known to you.[53]

The Greek word used in this passage is the same one used by Aristotle — *philos*. In John, union with God — "Abide in me, and I in you"[54] — is the overriding theological point of the incarnation. God has come to humans, and humans are lifted into union with God.

Aristotle discusses the popular topic of loving oneself. In our society, that concept receives much press. Almost every talk show and pop psychologist stresses that, in order to love someone else, one must first love oneself. What does Aristotle have to say on this issue? Yes, and no. In determining whether people ought to love themselves, their character must be considered. Wicked people not only should not love themselves, they cannot.

Aristotle's analysis of wicked people is telling: wicked people live by their passions. Here, we see Plato's influence. Wicked people indulge the "irrational" part of the soul. They "gratify their desires and emotions generally, or in other words, the irrational part of the soul."[55] When we act on our emotions, we are inconsistent. Emotions do not have the stability that long practice of virtue has. Indulging emotions and seeking pleasure may result in a divided self. Acting on the impulse of emotion may cause us to indulge in harmful actions. And without virtue, one may lack the resolve necessary to choose good over bad.

> . . . such people are at variance with themselves, and while desiring one set of things, wish for something else. They are e.g. incontinent people; they choose, not what seems to themselves good, but what is pleasant, although it is injurious, or they are so cowardly and lazy that they abstain from doing what they think to be best for themselves . . . for their soul is divided against itself, one part pained — so vicious is it — at abstaining from certain things, and the other part pleased, one part pulling this way, and the other that way, as if they would tear the man asunder. . . .[56]

We can all understand this observation. Perhaps we eat too much, when we like the food; but we don't enjoy the indigestion we feel later, or the struggle

---

53. John 15:14-15 (RSV).
54. John 15:4 (RSV).
55. Aristotle, *Nichomachean Ethics*, p. 308.
56. *Ibid.*, pp. 300, 301.

to lose those extra pounds. In the case of an alcoholic, which part of the individual is the true person — the one who cannot resist having a few drinks, or the one who makes up his mind (over and over again!) never to take another drink? This person is clearly divided. Which part of himself or herself should such a person love? Aristotle carries this reasoning to individuals who are actually criminal. There are "people whose moral depravity has led them to commit terrible crimes, and they hate and shun life and put an end to themselves" (p. 300). Such people do not seek friends to give their love to, but to escape themselves:

> Vicious people seek companions to spend their days with and try to escape from themselves; for when they are alone, there are many disagreeable things which they recall, and others which they anticipate, but when they are in the company of other people, they forget them (p. 300).

Aristotle is severe in his judgment about confirmed criminals. "There is nothing lovable in them, and therefore they have no feeling of love for themselves . . ." (pp. 300-301).

Good people, on the other hand, are interested in their rational capacity. "He therefore wishes what is good or what appears to be good for himself, . . . does so for his own sake, i.e. for the sake of the intellectual part of his nature . . ." (p. 299). Following Plato, Aristotle goes so far as to claim that the thinking faculty is our true self. "[T]he thinking faculty is the man's true self, or more nearly his true self than anything else is" (p. 299). When one acts rationally, one acts according to human nature. Aristotle in another place has defined humanity as "the rational animal."

Also, it is when we act most rationally that we are held in the truest sense to have acted as ourselves, and to have acted voluntarily.

> It is perfectly clear then that it is the rational part of a man which is the man himself . . . (p. 309).

Only virtuous people can be at one with themselves. This is because they have a character that they have learned from continual exercise of virtue. These people want the same thing always and can love the virtue they have acquired, "for the virtuous man is at unity with himself, and desires the same things with his whole heart" (pp. 298-299).

Wicked people want more than what is appropriate for themselves. When it is carried to an inappropriate level, self-love is wrong, and the term can be used as an insult: "self-absorbed," "self-interested," or just "selfish." "When people use it as a term of reproach, they give the name 'lovers of self' to people who assign themselves a larger share of money, honours, and bodily pleasures than belongs to them" (p. 308).

On the other hand, virtuous people are noble and want what is just. That being their character, no one would look down on them as lovers of self in the negative sense:

> . . . if a person would set his heart always on preeminence in doing what is just or temperate or virtuous in any other respect, and were always and by all means to reserve to himself the noble part, nobody would accuse him of self-love or censure him for it (p. 309).

Aristotle concludes his discussion on self-love by arguing that a virtuous person ought to love him or her self, and the vicious person should not:

> We conclude then that a good man ought to be a lover of self, as by his noble deeds he will benefit himself and serve others, but that the wicked man ought not to be a lover of self, as he will injure himself and others too by following his evil passions (p. 310).

Students of Aristotle often miss Aristotle's criticism of the wicked person. I attribute this misreading to our media, which rarely gives voice to Aristotle's caution that wicked persons harm themselves and others by loving themselves. Yet his observation seems to make sense. Aristotle's philosophy of self-love speaks to the issue of how whole a person is. Is the person at one with him or herself? Has the individual found completeness in his or her character? Only a person who has attained a level of virtue by continual practice is at one with himself. Only such a person can love him or herself without internal contradiction.

One wonders, though, whether Aristotle has provided an acceptable definition of the virtuous individual. How many of us would agree that we live best when we are rational? Has Aristotle denied us a primary part of our whole person, in denying us an emotional life? Can we truly be friends without involving our emotions to a large extent? Aristotle is quite clear — his wicked people "gratify their desires and emotions" (p. 308). Has he left his virtuous people with a sterile life? How far from Plato is he?

Aristotle challenges us in several ways to scrutinize our friendships. Are we deceived into thinking we have friendships of virtue when instead we have only friends by utility or pleasure? Do our friends want what is good for us for our own sake, or are they after something? Do we want what is good for our friends, for their own sake?

I think that, largely, we form mixed friendships. Aristotle's categories are meant to be taken in degrees. A friendship may tend toward one of his definitions, but it is unlikely to be purely one or the other. I may like a witty person for his personality and still care about him or her, to some degree. Certainly, there are some people whom we are likely to care about more deeply than others. The only real problem arises when we are not clear as to which form of friendship we are involved in.

We need to know what type of friendship we are entering into. We can become disillusioned and hurt if we think that we are in a friendship of virtue when we are, in fact, in a friendship of pleasure. We need to know if we are exchanging pleasure for pleasure, utility for utility, or mutual care for one another. If we know what quality our friendship is, we will function well and involve ourselves with the proper proportion of interest.

We can come away from Aristotle with one moral lesson. We need to be clear, ourselves (if we can be), when we are involved with someone else. Friendships can spring up in any area of life. We can be open to genuine care where it presents itself. In other areas, we need to let our acquaintances know the extent of the emotional contract into which we are entering. Some people are careful to call their superiors (in any regard) by their titles, in order to remind themselves and the others that there is an imbalance in the relationship. They might grow friendly, but there is a limit on the degree of friendship that is possible as long as, for example, one party will ultimately be judging and promoting, paying or firing the other.

Those who are closest emotionally usually are closest also in status and mutual caring, and then is when it makes the best sense to use first names. Even in a world as mixed as twenty-first century America, one can care for the good of someone else for his own sake. At least Aristotle gives us something to strive for.

CHAPTER III. EROS AND THE BIBLE: ROMANTIC SCRIPTURES, AMBIGUOUS INTERPRETATIONS, AND GREGORY OF NYSSA'S PLATONIC BIBLICAL ALLEGORIES

Despite its vastness, in the Bible there are relatively few passages that speak about love. Consequently the Church has had to get as much mileage as possible from the few passages that exist. Objectively speaking, one may question the enormity of the theological monuments that have been erected upon such a slight footing. Much of the West's religious literature concerning love is based on tradition, reasoning, and the authority of Church Fathers. They have sometimes founded their doctrines on Bible quotations — but not always. Some of the theological issues raised by the Bible involve power dynamics between men and women, procreation, marriage as an institution, celibacy and finally, the experience of love itself.

The issue of love is raised in the very first chapter of the very first book of the Bible. The treatment in Genesis 1, though, is different than in Genesis 2-3, so we need to consider those two sections separately.

In Genesis 1:26-28, man and woman are created together:

> Then God said, "Let us make man in our image, in our likeness" ... So God created man in his own image, in the image of God he created him; male and female he created them. God blessed them and said to them, "Be fruitful and increase in number; fill the Earth and subdue it."[57]

---

57. New International Version (Grand Rapids, Michigan: Zondervan Bible Publishers, 1979).

Consider the implications of this simple statement! In the Genesis 1 account, man and woman are on equal footing — created together. Furthermore, the passage reads, "in the image of God created he him; male and female he created them." This means that we are made in God's image. There is a relationship between what we are and what God is. This is a staggering thought. Somehow we are like God; God is like us. But what may be even more staggering is the clear implication that both man and woman are created in God's image. If man and woman together reflect Godhood, then God contains both a masculine and a feminine quality. Although many are accustomed to think of God as "Father," the implication of Genesis 1:27 is that we need to include a feminine consideration in our reflection about what God is.

Genesis 1:26-28 also includes the injunction to "Be fruitful and increase in number." While it may seem obvious that having children is part of the relationship between men and women, it may not seem apparent how necessary it is. Catholic theologians hold that Genesis 1:28 means that the intention of having children is essential in the man-woman relationship: that relations between men and women are valid only in the context of family. This is the source of Catholicism's inflexible position on birth control. Since the only justification for sexual relations in Catholicism is the intent of producing children, any act that interferes with the possibility of procreation makes sexuality illicit.

The Puritans also emphasized procreation, albeit less strictly. They saw the family unit as the basic building block of society, and called the family a "little commonwealth." To the Israelites of the Old Testament, having children was almost the primary purpose of marriage. Abraham was allowed to have sexual relations with his Egyptian servant because his wife Sarah was unable to conceive.

Relations between the sexes are presented somewhat differently in Genesis 2-3. There, the Garden of Eden is described, and in this account Adam is created first:

> "And the LORD God formed man from the dust of the ground and breathed into his nostrils the breath of life, and man became a living being."[58]

Eve is then created out of Adam:

---

58. Genesis 2:7 (NIV). All following Bible passages are from the New International Version.

But for Adam no suitable helper was found. So the LORD God caused the man to fall into a deep sleep; and while he was sleeping, he took one of the man's ribs and closed up the place with flesh. Then the LORD God made a woman from the rib he had taken out of the man, and he brought her to the man.

> The man said,
> "This is now bone of my bones
> and flesh of my flesh;
> She shall be called 'woman,'
> for she was taken out of man."[59]

A beautiful passage about spiritual marriage comes from the Genesis 2 account. The Bible says that the intimacy between married people is so close that they are one flesh; their spiritual union becoming physical unity in the sex act:

> For this reason a man will leave his father and mother and be united to his wife, and they will become one flesh.
> The man and his wife were both naked, and they felt no shame.[60]

The Genesis 2 account argues for the purity of sexuality without the necessity of childbirth. Adam and Eve are unashamed of their nakedness, and they are said to become one flesh. The Bible does not say that their souls will become one, but rather that their flesh will. And in this account, no mention is made of children. This is the passage that Jesus refers to when he is questioned about divorce.

> "But at the beginning of creation God 'made them male and female.' 'For this reason a man will leave his father and mother and be united to his wife, and the two will become one flesh.' So they are no longer two, but one."[61]

Jesus proclaims that husband and wife are joined together by God — "Therefore what God has joined together, let not man separate."[62] By these words, Jesus asserts that marriage is not merely civil; it is a spiritual union formed by God. As with Daphnis and Chloe, for Jesus, married love is a gift of God.[63]

---

59. Genesis 2:20-23.
60. Genesis 2:24, 25.
61. Mark 10:7-8.
62. Mark 10:9.

Some consider that the Genesis 2 account implies a difference in status between man and woman. Since woman was created second, some interpret her status as secondary to man's. Furthermore, she is said to be made from the man's body — "bone of my bones and flesh of my flesh" — implying dependence on men. Subservience to men is outright proclaimed in Genesis 3. This is a condition imposed on the sexes because of their first sin, after they are expelled from the Garden of Eden. "Your desire will be for your husband, and he will rule over you."[64] While we were in Eden, sexual equality appears to have existed. But after the Fall, by way of punishment, Genesis 3 holds that the husband will rule over his wife.

Unfortunately, the Church, being largely a male-run organization, has historically emphasized the account of Genesis 2-3 over the account of Genesis 1. Christians have buttressed the account of Genesis 2-3 with a passage from Paul's letters in the New Testament. Although somewhat milder, Ephesians 5 contains the doctrine that women are subject to men. The model of the Christian family is like the relationship of the God to the Church. Just as God is the head of the Church, so the husband is the head of the family. The passage in Ephesians relies on the Genesis 3 passage that considers woman to be made from man's body. However, the power dynamic is somewhat softened by the Christian injunction of love:

> Wives, submit to your husbands as to the Lord. For the husband is the head of the wife as Christ is the head of the Church, his body, of which he is the savior. Now as the Church submits to Christ, so also wives should submit to their husbands in everything.
>
> Husbands, love your wives, just as Christ loved the Church and gave himself up to her to make her holy.... In this same way, husbands ought to love their wives as their own bodies. He who loves his wife loves himself. After all, no one hates his own body, but he feeds and cares for it, just as Christ does the Church — for we are all members of his body.... However,

---

63. In Matthew 5:32, Jesus allows divorce if the other party commits adultery. But Catholicism, drawing on a different Biblical tradition, forbids divorce altogether. In order to arrive at their doctrines about the inviolability of marriage, Catholicism draws on those Bible passages in which Christ's eternal bond with the Church is compared to a marriage (Ephesians 5). Since Christ's bond with the Church is eternal, so the marriage bond must be inseparable in this world (see below, pp. 80-82).

64. Genesis 3:16.

each one of you also must love his wife as he loves himself, and the wife must respect her husband.[65]

The passages from Genesis 2-3 and this one from Ephesians 5 continue to work against the ethic of equality between the sexes. To this day certain Christians and Orthodox Jews maintain the power of men over women, denying to women certain occupations, roles, and other rights of power considered the exclusive domain of men. Here we can see how traditions have selected certain passages over others — in this case Genesis 2-3 over Genesis 1 — to decide religious doctrines. The Biblical texts themselves argue for and against equality between the sexes. Feminist and liberation theologians are laboring hard to reform the weight of history and to institute equality.[66]

The Genesis 2 passage is used in most wedding ceremonies to show that marriage is a religious institution created by God. This brings up the theological idea of "sacrament." "Sacrament" means that there is something sacred about the subject. We have already observed that the union between husband and wife is God-given. There are several Bible selections that can be added to this Genesis passage which reinforce the religious nature of marriage. Marriage between man and wife is compared to the relationship between God and the Church in Ephesians 5. Other comparisons like this can be found in the Bible, and such passages can be collected to add support to the idea that marriage is ordained by God.

The High Anglican Church does this in a magnificent way. The wedding ceremony in the 17th-century edition of the *Book of Common Prayer* contains a charming passage (it has been rewritten today, but its modern language loses some of the impact of the 17th century text).

> Dearly beloved, we are gathered together here in the sight of God, and in the face of this congregation, to join together this Man and this Woman in holy Matrimony; which is an honourable estate, instituted of God in the time of man's innocency, signifying unto us the mystical union that is betwixt Christ and his Church; which holy estate Christ adorned and beautified with his presence, and first miracle he wrought, in Cana of Gali-

---

65. Ephesians 5:22-23.

66. David Matzko McCarthy does a masterful job of showing that the Ephesians 5 passage does not represent the whole theology of the New Testament. He thoroughly searches the whole New Testament and shows that women have a great variety of power relations and roles, often possessing outright equality with men. See *Sex and Love in the Home* (London: SCM Press, 2001), pp. 191-196.

lee; and is commended of Saint Paul to be honourable among all men: and therefore is not by any to be enterprised, nor taken in hand, unadvisedly, lightly, or wantonly, to satisfy men's carnal lusts and appetites, like brute beasts that have no understanding; but reverently, discreetly, advisedly, soberly, and in the fear of God. . . .[67]

The first doctrine mentioned in this solemn selection from the *Book of Common Prayer* is that marriage was "instituted of God in the time of man's innocency." This is a reference to the Genesis 2 passage that we looked at already — "For this reason a man will leave his father and mother and be united to his wife, and they will become one flesh." Marriage was thus instituted in Eden, "the time of man's innocency."

Next, the *Book of Common Prayer* alludes to the "mystical union that is betwixt Christ and his Church." In several Bible passages, the relationship between God and the Church is compared to a marriage. Although the *Book of Common Prayer* mentions the Christian relationship between Christ and the Church, the symbolism is also developed in the Old Testament.

In Jeremiah 31, God speaks of a covenant of love that God will form between the Israelites and Himself. In this covenant, the Law will be written on their hearts and God refers to himself as Israel's husband: "They broke my covenant though I was a husband to them."[68] The prophet Hosea develops this metaphor at even greater length. The first three chapters of his book develop the metaphor of adultery and reconciliation to illustrate Israel's abandoning the laws of God and turning back to the Law. God begins by chastising Israel for turning to foreign gods by using the metaphor of adultery. "Rebuke your mother, rebuke her, for she is not my wife, and I am not her husband. Let her remove the adulterous look from her face and the unfaithfulness from between her breasts."[69] God then says that he will "lure" his adulterous "wife" back from her lovers and "betroth" her again to himself.

> "Therefore I am going to allure her
> I will lead her into the desert
> And speak tenderly to her. . . .
> "In that day," declares the LORD,
> "you will call me 'my husband';

---

67. *The Book of Common Prayer* (New York: Henry Holt and Company, 1992), p. 308.
68. Jeremiah 31:32.
69. Hosea 2:2.

you will no longer call me 'my master.'
"I will remove the names of the Baals from her lips;
no longer will their names be invoked. . . .
"I will betroth you to me forever;
I will betroth you in righteousness and justice,
in love and compassion.
"I will betroth you in faithfulness,
And you will acknowledge the LORD."[70]

In the New Testament, several passages continue this comparison between God's relationship to the Church and marriage. In the Gospels, Jesus is asked why his disciples do not fast, while the followers of John the Baptist and the Pharisees do. Jesus responds with a wedding metaphor: "How can the guests of the bridegroom mourn while he is with them."[71] This statement is duplicated in Mark 2:19 and Luke 5:34. In another place, John the Baptist uses a wedding metaphor to describe those who follow Jesus: "The bride belongs to the bridegroom. The friend who attends the bridegroom waits and listens for him, and is full of joy when he hears the bridegroom's voice."[72] In an apocalyptic passage in Matthew, the second coming of the Son of Man is compared to virgins waiting to meet the bridegroom.[73] In the Ephesians 5 passage, Genesis 2:24 is quoted and used to speak of the mystery of Christ's union with the Church:

> After all, no one ever hated his own body, but he feeds it and cares for it, just as Christ does the Church — for we are members of his body. "For this reason a man will leave his father and mother and be united to his wife, and the two will become one flesh." This is a profound mystery — but I am talking about Christ and the Church.[74]

A marriage feast is used to symbolize the relationship between Christ (as the lamb of God) and the Church in a visionary passage in Revelation. The saints of the Church are the bride wearing fine linen:

> For the wedding of the Lamb has come,
> and his bride has made herself ready.
> Fine linen, bright and clean,
> was given her to wear."

---

70. Hosea 2:14, 16-17, 19-20.
71. Matthew 9:15.
72. John 3:29.
73. Matthew 24:30-25:13.
74. Ephesians 5:29-32.

(Fine linen stands for the righteous acts of the saints.)

Then the angel said to me, "Write: 'Blessed are those who are invited to the wedding supper of the Lamb!'"[75]

Finally, in the book of Revelation the Evangelist sees the spiritual New Jerusalem coming down from heaven dressed like a bride. She is then given to the Lamb of God as his wife:

Then I saw a new heaven and a new Earth, for the first heaven and the first Earth had passed away, and there was no longer any sea. I saw the Holy City, the new Jerusalem, coming down out of heaven from God, prepared as a bride beautifully dressed for her husband. . . .

One of the seven angels who had the seven bowls full of the seven last plagues came and said to me, "Come, I will show you the bride, the wife of the lamb." And he carried me away in the Spirit to a mountain great and high, and showed me the Holy City, Jerusalem, coming down out of heaven from God.[76]

From these passages, Catholic theologians deduce that the relationship between God and the Church instills a mystical power into the marriage ceremony. They call this power "grace." Grace makes the wedded couple's actions holy. Those who do not have the grace of the marriage ceremony cannot act in a similarly holy manner. Although two couples may perform the same act (intercourse, for instance), a married couple does it in a state of grace while the unmarried couple does it without grace. Hence, for Catholics any sexual relations outside of marriage are not holy because they lack the grace given by the marriage ceremony. This doctrine illuminates another interesting note about Catholic marriage doctrine. Since Christ is forever united with His Church and never separates from it, so the married couple, who are a symbol of Christ's union with the Church, also cannot ever be separated.

Catholics, according to this doctrine, do not allow divorce. In recent times, they allow an annulment — but annulment means that the couple did not have sufficient knowledge to intend marriage. Since the intent of marriage wasn't there, the marriage never actually happened no matter how long the couple

---

75. Revelation 19:7-9.
76. Revelation 21:1-2, 9-10

thought that they had been married. This may raise questions about the legitimacy of children born of such a marriage. In an unusual cooperation with secular law, the Catholic Church affirms the legitimacy of such children. Even though a sacramental union hasn't taken place between the couple, a civil marriage has occurred and by civil law, the children are legitimate and so they are in the eyes of the Catholic Church. This whole doctrine leaves unresolved the question of what status the couple's sexual relations had during the marriage that never happened, but this issue is too involved to enter into at this point.

Whether marriage is actually a sacrament or is a holy institution that falls just short of actual sacramental status is a question that divides most Protestants from Catholics. Catholics, as we have just seen, hold that marriage is a sacrament. Luther, on the other hand, does not consider marriage to be a sacrament, but a "rite." Exactly how Luther considered marriage will be looked at in a later chapter; but for now, we can say that since Jesus never performed a marriage ceremony, Luther doesn't consider it a sacrament. Episcopalians have constructed a doctrine that balances between Protestants and Catholics. They call marriage a "sacramental rite."

The *Book of Common Prayer* calls our attention to another Bible passage that treats the nature of marriage. The wording of *The Book of Common Prayer* is extremely careful. It states that "Christ adorned and beautified [marriage] with his presence, and the first miracle that he wrought, . . ." (The reference is to the Gospel of John, Chapter 2, wherein Jesus performs his first miracle by turning water into wine at a wedding festival in Cana.) Some take this as a divine blessing on the estate of marriage. In arguments about marriage versus celibacy, proponents of marriage refer to this passage as an instance of Christ favoring the married estate. But just how much to make of Jesus' contribution could hardly have been more carefully stated: Christ "adorned and beautified" the wedding. Christ did contribute something to the marriage, but He didn't actually perform the ceremony. By wording the prayer book so, the Anglican Church can maintain the holiness of marriage but keep it just shy of actual sacrament.

The Book of Common Prayer continues with a reference to Saint Paul. Marriage "is commended of Saint Paul to be honourable among all men." This is clearly a reference to 1 Corinthians 7. This moderate passage among Paul's letters brings up the virulent issue of celibacy versus marriage. Paul's passage is quite even-handed and there are only two other extremely vague passages relating to the subject of celibacy; but proponents of either view can argue with fervent passion, hurling these three passages back and forth, emphasizing one part of the whole over another part of the whole. Reasoning, authority from ancient traditions, and all other convenient ammunition are added to these Biblical passages in order to favor one side or another.

The Anglican Church interprets Paul's passage to say that marriage is "commended . . . to be honourable among *all* men." Does Paul, in fact say this? To be fair to Paul, we need to quote the whole section dealing with the subjects of marriage and celibacy, and to keep in mind, as we read it, that Paul himself was celibate.

> Now for the matters you wrote about: It is good for a man not to marry. But since there is so much immorality, each man should have his own wife, and each woman her own husband. The husband should fulfill his marital duty to his wife, and likewise the wife to her husband. In the same way, the husband's body does not belong to him alone but also to his wife. Do not deprive each other except by mutual consent and for a time, so that you may devote yourselves to prayer. Then come together again so that Satan will not tempt you because of your lack of self-control. I say this as a concession, not as a command. I wish that all men were as I am. But each man has his own gift from God; one has this gift, another has that.
>
> Now to the unmarried and the widows I say: it is good for them to stay unmarried, as I am. But if they cannot control themselves, they should marry, for it is better to marry than to burn with passion.[77]

This selection is quite moderate. Paul does say that he wishes that "all men were as I am" — meaning celibate. He also says that, "It is good for a man not to marry." However, he adds, "But each man has his own gift from God; one has this gift, another has that." This would mean that some have the gift of celibacy, others the gift for marriage. Paul is concerned with the issue of sexual immorality and, since people have such a tendency for sexual indulgence, Paul suggests that marriage is the best solution for those unable to remain celibate. This is also the motivation behind the language about fulfilling the marital duty. This means that married partners should have sex if one of the two wants it. That is the "marital duty." Paul speaks about a period of time when they may deny one another for the sake of prayer. In Hebrew as well as Greek traditions, sometimes during holy festivals and times of religious observance, priests and sometimes all the others were expected to remain celibate. For instance, before God came down to Mount Sinai, the people were told to abstain from sexual relations. Paul carries this tradition on in his letter to ordinary people; but note

---

77. 1 Corinthians 7:1-9.

that he insists that the period of abstinence should be by mutual consent, and of limited duration lest "Satan . . . tempt you because of your lack of self control." Paul's continual fear is about the power of the sex drive.

But later in the same letter, Paul confesses that his instructions about marriage and celibacy are not God-given, but practical considerations he has made up. He reiterates his advice with an important qualifier: "Now about virgins: I have no command from the Lord, but I give a judgement as one who by the Lord's mercy is trustworthy."[78] In this reappraisal, Paul's concern is that Christ will be making his Second Coming very soon. Therefore no drastic change should be made.

> Because of the present crisis, I think that it is good for you to remain as you are. Are you married? Do not seek a divorce. Are you unmarried? Do not look for a wife. But if you do marry, you have not sinned; and if a virgin marries, she has not sinned. But those who marry will face many troubles in this life, and I want to spare you this.
> What I mean, brothers, is the time is short. . . . For this world in its present form is passing away.[79]

One can see how selective reading could turn this even-handed treatment into a battle cry for one position. When Luther seizes this passage, he claims that Paul commands marriage for those who can't keep themselves celibate.

Two other New Testament passages are used in the argument about celibacy. Both of them are vague. The first comes from the Gospel of Matthew. It is one of those strange sayings that sometimes appear in the New Testament without a context to explain its meaning. The general context of the passage in question is indeed about marriage. Jesus has just told his disciples that the only just cause for divorce is "unchastity." The disciples respond that, "If such is the case of a man with his wife, it is not expedient to marry." Then Jesus responds with the passage we are interested in:

> Not all men can receive this saying, but only those to whom it is given. For there are eunuchs who have been so from birth, and there are eunuchs who have been made eunuchs by men, and there are eunuchs who have made themselves eunuchs for the sake of the kingdom of heaven. He who is able to receive this, let him receive it.[80]

---

78. 1 Corinthians 7:25.
79. 1 Corinthians 7:25-29.
80. Matthew 19:11-12.

Receive what? What is Jesus saying here? There are three kinds of eunuchs. The third was for the sake of the kingdom of heaven. Is Jesus enjoining this? Is Jesus saying that one *should* make oneself into a eunuch for the sake of the kingdom? To proponents of celibacy, this is a clear statement that Jesus has proclaimed celibacy to be essential for the kingdom of heaven. He does indeed say that there are those who have made themselves eunuchs for the sake of the kingdom of heaven, but is he saying that they were correct in doing this, and has he said that it is essential?

The final passage brought into the discussion about celibacy is a little tricky. Jesus appears to say that people don't marry, in heaven; but his answer is in response to a trick question posed by the Sadducees, who employed Jewish marriage laws to prove there is no life after death. They posed an imaginary problem about a man who dies without leaving a son to carry on the family name. Jewish law requires the man's brother to marry the deceased man's wife and try to have a child by her. The Sadducees thought up the ingenious case of several brothers who all, one after the other, married a widow. If there is a life after death, they asked, who would she be married to? They thought that they had proved she would end up a polygamist, since everyone would be alive in the next life and she had married them all. Jesus' response is that no one is given to someone else by forced consent to fulfill traditions about the necessity of childbirth. Then, after settling the question about marriage, Jesus immediately returns to the real issue of life after death. Using the story of Moses and the burning bush, Jesus asserts that the patriarchs (Abraham, Isaac and Jacob) were alive in heaven when Moses met with God in the burning bush; so the whole issue is not really about marriage, but about life after death. The text is as follows:

> Now there were seven brothers. The first one married and died without leaving any children. The second married the widow, but he also died, leaving no child. It was the same with the third. In fact, none of the seven left any children. Last of all, the woman died too. At the resurrection whose wife will she be, since the seven were married to her?
>
> Jesus replied, "Are you not in error because you do not know the Scriptures or the power of God? When the dead rise, they will neither marry nor be given in marriage; they will be like the angels in heaven. Now about the dead rising — have you not read in the book of Moses, in the account of the bush, how God said to him, 'I am the God of Abraham, the God of Isaac, and the God of Jacob'? He is not the God of the dead, but of the living. You are badly mistaken.[81]

Those who favor celibacy read this passage as a clear statement that in heaven no one is married. Thus marriage is strictly an earthly accommodation to be shucked off in heaven. Others read this passage more as a statement about life after death, marriage being really a side issue.

The entire Biblical argument for celibacy is almost completely summed up in these three passages: Paul's moderate discussion in 1 Corinthians 7; the vague passage about eunuchs in Matthew 19; and the trick question in Mark 12. There are a few other passages in the Old Testament that enjoin a period of abstention from sexual relations before a holy festival or event. The bulk of the Christian argument for celibacy is summed up in the three passages we have looked at. Whether these passages are sufficient, I will leave up to the reader.

We have looked at every passage in the New Testament that deals with the subject of love and marriage: Ephesians 5, 1 Corinthians 7, Matthew 19, Mark 12, Jesus' first miracle at the wedding in Cana (John 2), and the symbolic passages in which marriage is compared to God's relation to the Church. That is about all we have, when we look for passages dealing with sexual love. Other passages can be produced that speak about general love of one's neighbor, but our interest is specifically in love between "lovers." There isn't much material to go on if we wish to build a theology about love from New Testament materials.

We are helped by only a few more passages from the Old Testament. We have already looked at Genesis 1-3 and the passages from Jeremiah and Hosea which compare God's relationship to Israel as a marriage bond. Just two more stories from the patriarchs complete the study. They are brief, but quite poignant. The first patriarch is Abraham; his wife is Sarah. The story of Abraham and Sarah is dominated by the tensions between the two sons of Abraham, Ishmael and Isaac. For our purposes, Abraham doesn't contribute to a discussion of love. But the story of his son Isaac and Isaac's bride Rebekah contains remarkably tender elements, considering the time period in which the story was written.

To find a bride for his son Isaac, Abraham sends his servant into Mesopotamia, his home country. The servant goes to a well in Mesopotamia where the women come to draw water for their families. He prays to God to help him pick a suitable wife for Isaac. "May it be that when I say to a girl, 'Please let down your jar that I may have a drink,' and she says, 'drink, and I'll water your camels too' — let her be the one you have chosen for your servant Isaac."[82]

---

81. Mark 12:20-27.

Rebekah soon appears, and responds just as Abraham's servant asked. She's the one, chosen by God. This is further emphasized in the way Rebekah's father responds to the servant's story. "[L]et her become the wife of your master's son, as the LORD has directed" (Genesis 24:51). God is the source of love in this story, as he was in *Daphnis and Chloe*. Abraham's servant goes to Rebekah's home and asks her father to give her in marriage to Isaac. The father's response is remarkable. Men had exclusive control over women in those days, and women were often considered no more than property, like servants and cattle. Men could marry off their daughters as they willed; yet, in the case of Rebekah, everybody asks her what she wants to do.

> Then they said, "Let's call the girl and ask her about it." So they called Rebekah and asked her, "Will you go with this man?"
> "I will go," she said.[83]

Rebekah returns with Abraham's servant and is married to Isaac. Then, in a striking comment, we find one of the most poignant statements in the Old Testament about love. "So she became his wife, and he loved her."[84] In all the marriages and all the families in the Old Testament, nowhere do we find such a simple, concise statement about married love.

Only in the story of Isaac's son Jacob do we find a passage rivaling this simple, tender statement. Jacob falls in love with Rachel, and asks for her hand in marriage. Rachel's father Laban agrees to give Jacob his daughter — in exchange for seven years of servitude. Jacob agrees, and works for Laban for seven years. But in another striking, simple statement, we are shown the nature of Jacob's love: "So Jacob served seven years to get Rachel, but they seemed like only a few days to him because of his love for her."[85] Under the influence of love, time disappears. Such is the testimony of the patriarch Jacob.

I suppose no perusal of love stories in the Bible would be complete without considering the two great epic stories of the darker side of love: Samson and Delilah, and David and Bathsheba. These stories do little to inform us about spirituality and love. They rarely if ever appear in theological discussions about love; but they are important stories not to be passed over completely.

---

82. Genesis 24:14.
83. Genesis 24:58.
84. Genesis 24:67.
85. Genesis 29:20.

Samson and Delilah is a story about emotional manipulation and betrayal. Though manipulation rarely becomes deadly (one would hope), the kind of tactics used by Delilah can be recognized today. Delilah's main manipulative device is the common plaint, "How can you say, 'I love you,' when you won't confide in me."[86] (In other words, if you love me, you will do what I want you to do.) A spy for the Philistines, Delilah tries to make the hero tell her the secret of his great strength. He gives her three false reasons, which she then employs to weaken him. They don't work; Delilah persistently accuses him of not loving her. In an acutely accurate sentence, the Bible captures the experience of being relentlessly dogged for something. "With such nagging she prodded him day after day until he was tired to death."[87] Samson finally relents under tireless pressure and tells Delilah the real source of his great strength: his long hair. Delilah lulls him to sleep; the Philistines rush in, cut his hair, blind Samson, and send him to prison. But Samson gets his revenge. The rulers of the Philistines are all assembled in a temple and they summon Samson to entertain them. But in prison, Samson's hair has grown back. He pushes down the central support pillars of the temple, bringing it down to crush all the leaders of the Philistines (along with himself).

This tale illustrates the worst kind of emotional manipulation that can occur in couples. Delilah acted deceitfully and with malice, pretending to love Samson. She manipulated him by accusing him of not loving her. Her manipulations are opposed to the spirit of actual love. Love perishes when either party seeks to dominate and manipulate. The health of a relationship is measured by the freedom each partner allows the other. It requires trust and emotional security to relinquish control and to allow one's partner freedom; but without freedom one experiences the uncomfortable feeling of constraint and seeks to relieve one's bonds. To manipulate by claiming that love requires abject obedience is the sign of insecurity or, in this case, a relationship contrived on the basis of utility, with a complete disregard for the good of the other.

David's love for Bathsheba illustrates the havoc wreaked by powerful officials with base inclinations. Our society is no stranger to the abuse of power exhibited by King David in his lust for Bathsheba. As he is walking around the roof of his royal palace, David spies Bathsheba, the wife of Uriah,[88] bathing down below. He covets her, and has his way with her. To get rid of Uriah, David

---

86. Judges 16:15.
87. Judges 16:16.
88. Uriah is a soldier in King David's army.

sends him to the front lines in the war with the Philistines. Uriah is killed, and David marries Bathsheba. But the monarchy in Israel was balanced by the role of the prophet. The prophet was a check on the power of the king. The prophet remained in the outskirts of society, appearing at court to remind the king that God's laws still applied — even to the king. The prophet Nathan tells David a parable that relates to David's relations with Bathsheba. Nathan's tale is so skillfully constructed that David's righteous indignation falls on the king's own head.

> The LORD sent Nathan to David. When he came to him, he said, "There were two men in a certain town, one rich and the other poor. The rich man had a very large number of sheep and cattle, but the poor man had nothing except one little ewe lamb he had bought. He raised it, and it grew up with him and his children. It shared his food, drank from his cup and even slept in his arms. It was like a daughter to him.
>
> "Now a traveler came to the rich man, but the rich man refrained from taking one of his own sheep and cattle to prepare a meal for the traveler who had come to him. Instead, he took the ewe lamb that belonged to the poor man and prepared it for the one who had come to him."
>
> David burned with anger against the man and said to Nathan, "As surely as the LORD lives, the man who did this deserves to die! He must pay for that lamb four times over, because he did such a thing and had no pity."
>
> Then Nathan said to David, "You are the man!"[89]

This dramatic statement — "You are the man!" — is almost unparalleled in the history of Western literature. By that one statement the powerful king accused himself, and was able to see the sin he had committed with Bathsheba.

Our society is weary with the sexual indiscretions of our leaders. Some of the most severe abuses of power are when a powerful official commits a sexual indiscretion with a subordinate — be it an intern or altar boy, or anyone else. The closest thing we have to a prophet is the press, which is often all too ready to pounce upon a particularly juicy story. But news stories do not put the fear of God into anyone's heart the way Nathan was able to do for David. Our culture has become desensitized to sexual indiscretions. The abuses of power have ancient roots, as the story of Bathsheba and David shows; what our culture lacks is the office of the prophet to keep the powerful in check.

---

89. 2 Samuel 12:1-7.

We have looked at the passages in the Bible that usually arise in discussions of sexual love. There aren't many. For this reason, some theologians do not consider sexual love itself to be a theological topic. In fact, very few theological treatises are devoted to the subject. Usually, theologians are more interested in discussions of neighborly love, or what the Greeks call *agape*. *Agape* love is directed to the whole human race. The kind of love that is directed to a particular person — such as friendship (*philos*) or interpersonal love (*eros*) — doesn't find much discussion by theologians, but the subject is valuable to most people; poetry and literature are our culture's primary sources for spiritual nurture when it comes to these forms of love.

There is, however, one book of the Bible that is exclusively devoted to the subject of erotic love. It is considered a highly problematic book — probably for that very reason. To lovers, this is a stimulating endorsement of passion; to Christian mystics, it is a problem to overcome. The book in question is called by several names: *Song of Songs*, *Song of Solomon*, or *Canticles*.

The *Song of Songs* is a short book, but it is intense in its erotic language and imagery. It is so rich in eroticism some wonder why it is in the Bible at all. The text is somewhat disjointed. The lines in it do not flow like a narrative. It isn't a story. It is, rather, a number of lyric poems strung together. The book is essentially a dialogue between a lover and his beloved. By nature imagery similar to what we saw in *Daphnis and Chloe*, the two lovers praise each other's beauty and express their desire for one another. The nature imagery is that of pastoral Judah. The lover lists the alluring parts of his beloved's body:

> How beautiful you are, my darling!
> Oh, how beautiful!
> Your eyes behind your veil are doves.
> Your hair is like a flock of goats.
> descending from Mount Giliad.
> Your teeth are like a flock of sheep just shorn,
> coming up from the washing . . .
> Your lips are like a scarlet ribbon;
> your mouth is lovely.
> Your temples behind your veil
> are like the halves of a pomegranate.
> Your neck is like the tower of David,
> built with elegance . . .
> Your two breasts are like two fawns . . .
> All beautiful you are, my darling;
> there is no flaw in you.[90]

The beloved praises the body of her lover in a similar manner:

> My lover is radiant and ruddy,
> outstanding among ten thousand.
> His head is purest gold;
> his hair is wavy
> and black as a raven.
> His eyes are like doves
> by the water streams,
> washed in milk,
> mounted like jewels.
> His cheeks are like beds of spice
> yielding perfume.
> His lips are like lilies
> dripping with myrrh.
> His arms are like rods of gold
> set with chrysolite.
> His body is like polished ivory
> decorated with sapphires.
> His legs are like pillars of marble
> set on bases of pure gold. . . .
> His mouth is sweetness itself;
> he is altogether lovely.[91]

In this remarkable book, expressions of sexuality are explicit. The very first verses are amorous:

> Let him kiss me with the kisses of his mouth —
> for your love is more delightful than wine.
> Pleasing is the fragrance of your perfumes;
> your name is like perfume poured out.[92]

Some of the erotic passages are breathtaking. The beloved speaks to her lover:

> Like an apple tree among the trees of the forest
> is my lover among the young men.
> I delight to sit in his shade,
> and his fruit is sweet to my taste.

---

90. Song of Songs 4:1-2, 3-4, 5, 7.
91. Song of Songs 5:10-16.
92. Song of Songs 1:2-3.

> He has taken me to his banquet hall,
> and his banner over me is love.
> Strengthen me with raisins
> refresh me with apples,
> for I am faint with love.
> His left arm is under my head,
> and his right arm embraces me.[93]

Another passage speaks with great depth and lyricism about the intensity of erotic love:

> Place me like a seal over your heart,
> like a seal over your arm;
> For love is strong as death,
> its ardor unyielding as the grave.
> It burns like blazing fire,
> like a mighty flame.
> Many waters cannot quench love;
> rivers cannot wash it away.
> If one were to give
> all the wealth of his house for love,
> it would be utterly scorned.[94]

The lover responds with a highly sensual rhapsody of love, expressed in terms of vision, taste, and smell:

> You have stolen my heart, my sister my bride;
> you have stolen my heart
> With one glance of your eyes,
> with one jewel of your necklace.
> How delightful is your love, my sister, my bride!
> how much more pleasing is your love than wine,
> and the fragrance of your perfume than any spice!
> Your lips drop sweetness as the honeycomb, my bride;
> milk and honey are under your tongue.
> The fragrance of your garments is like that of Lebanon.[95]

The love between the two is apparently consummate. Several passages suggest this. They share a bed: "How handsome you are, my lover!/Oh, how

---

93. Song of Songs 2:3-6.
94. Song of Songs 8:6-7.
95. Song of Songs 4:9-11.

charming!/And our bed is verdant."[96] In another passage rich in metaphor, the lover speaks of symbolically "consuming" his beloved, comparing physical expressions of love to enjoying fruit and drink:

> How beautiful you are and how pleasing,
> Oh love, with your delights!
> Your stature is like that of the palm,
> and your breasts like clusters of fruit.
> I said, "I will climb the palm tree;
> I will take hold of its fruit."
> May your breasts be like clusters of the vine,
> the fragrance of your breath like apples,
> and your mouth like the best wine.[97]

In this glorious celebration, one finds a statement that all lovers feel. They belong to each other in a special way: "I am my lover's and my lover is mine."[98] This sense of mutual belonging is repeated in 7:10. "I belong to my lover,/and his desire is for me."

As passionate, sensitive, and sensual as the text of *Song of Songs* is, one is not likely to find selections from it in theological essays, sermons, or even in wedding texts. It is as if theologians would like the issue of erotic love to go away. But the Bible preserves these wondrous lines of love, inviting readers of the Holy Scriptures to enter the world of Romantic Love. *Song of Songs* carries the divine blessing of its place in sacred scriptures, and so sanctifies the experience of Romantic Love. Its ecstatic verses lift the consciousness of its readers into a world of intimate passion and religious purity. Even as the text of *Song of Songs* remains in the Holy Bible, so the experience of Romantic Love remains a part of the religious life.

Gregory of Nyssa: The Song of Songs becomes a Platonic Journey

The Church needed to revise drastically the literal meaning of these passionate lyrics in order to accept them. One popular way of revising them was to read them allegorically. The desire for the lover and beloved is considered a

---

96. Song of Songs 1:16.
97. Song of Songs 7:6-9.
98. Song of Songs 6:3.

symbol for the relationship between the worshipper and God. This makes the desire safely holy and not sexual at all. One such allegorical revision is found in the writings of Gregory of Nyssa, a remarkable Christian mystic who was born in 355 CE into a remarkable family. His name was Gregory of Nyssa. His sister Makrina and his brother Basil were both canonized. Gregory himself earned the title of "Father of Fathers," due to his mystical teachings. Gregory was educated in Athens, and there he was steeped in the philosophy of Plato and Aristotle. He was directly influenced by another Church Father named Origen, an early Christian commentator on the Bible who was also deeply influenced by Greek philosophy. Origen found Platonism in the Jewish theologian Philo, in the Christian mystic Clement of Alexandria, and directly in the writings of Plotinus.

Gregory applies his Platonism to the *Song of Songs*. His method of interpretation owes much to Origen. Origen was pioneering in that he saw a meaning beyond the Bible's literal words. He derived Church doctrines by reading Bible passages symbolically. Gregory follows Origen in his interpretation of the *Song of Songs*. Gregory's Platonic Christian interpretation turns the lovely lyrics of the *Song of Songs* into a "philosophy of divine things by means of chaste concepts."[99] In Gregory, we see basic Platonic doctrines embraced in a Christian form. We find a fear of passion, a strict duality between the world of "becoming" here on Earth and the world of "Being." This duality is now between Earth and heaven. Gregory even uses Plato's exact terminology. He uses the word "archetype," which is the Platonic term for the Ideal Forms, and this archetype is of "the Beautiful," which is now understood as the image of God. All of these ideas can be traced back to Plato's *Symposium*, his *Phaedrus*, and the *Timaeus*, which we looked at in Chapter One.

Gregory defends his method of symbolic interpretation by citing several passages of Paul in which Paul interprets the Old Testament allegorically. He then brings in a familiar Pauline passage contrasting the spirit with the flesh. For Gregory, the literal sense of scripture is like the flesh, while the allegorical meaning is like the spirit. In his opening apology for his allegorical method, Gregory introduces the Platonic emphasis on reason. He shucks off the "merely human" elements of scripture by suggesting that the spiritual sense of scripture is perceived by mind, or the "intelligent" element of the soul:

---

99. Gregory of Nyssa, *Commentary on the Song of Songs* (Brookline, MA: Hellenic College Press, 1987), p. 50.

In all these different expressions and names of contemplation Paul is teaching us an important lesson: we must pass to a spiritual and intelligent investigation of scripture so that considerations of the merely human element might be changed into something perceived by the mind once the more fleshly sense of the words has been shaken off like dust. For this reason Paul says, "the letter kills, but the spirit gives life" [2 Cor 3.6].[100]

Gregory's own interpretation follows this metaphor as he systematically takes out all the meanings that relate to Romance. Gregory translates into passionless Platonic Christian mysticism the very erotic passages that we looked at above as a valorization of Romantic Love. All the breathless passages that we saw in Song of Songs are read by Gregory according to the "spirit," and become purged of passion. In explaining this process, Gregory alludes to the Platonic ideas that the spiritual nature is invisible to the material senses and that it consists in intellectual Beauty:

> The most acute physical pleasure (I mean erotic passion) is used as a symbol in the exposition of this doctrine of love. It teaches us of the need for the soul to reach out to the divine nature's invisible beauty and to love it as much as the body is inclined to love what is akin to itself. The soul must transform passion into passionlessness so that when every corporeal affection has been quenched, our mind may seethe with passion for the spirit alone and be warmed by that fire which the Lord came to cast upon the Earth [Lk 12.49].[101]

In another passage explaining his method, Gregory invites his readers to approach the text as if they were dead to the body. In a typically Platonic way, purity is understood to be passionless, while the body is identified with passion and desire. In this curious passage, we learn that Christ has no passions. Gregory's interpretation actually denies fleshly life altogether:

> Let us now listen to the Song's words as if we were dead according to the body and not attracted by words with a carnal meaning. For the person dead to both passion and desire transfers the outward meaning of the Song's words to that which is pure and undefiled. Being unmindful of lowly, earthly affairs, he sets his mind on things above where Christ, in whom there is no passion, is seated at the Father's right hand in glory

---

100. Gregory of Nyssa, *Commentary on the Song of Songs*, p. 36.
101. *Commentary on the Song of Songs*, p. 49.

[Col 3.1]. . . . Let us listen as if we had no share in the nature of flesh and blood and had been transferred into the spiritual realm.[102]

In his allegorical methodology, Gregory frequently alludes to the passage we looked at above from Ephesians 5. There, Paul compares human sexuality to the mystical union of Christ and the Church. Gregory can translate language of sexuality into symbols of the soul's desire for union with God. God is then understood as the bridegroom and the Church is understood as the bride. *Song of Songs* becomes a mystical text about the soul's love for God instead of a lyrical celebration of human sexuality.

> Thus the text of the Song exhorts us, even if we now live in the flesh, not to turn to it in our thoughts; rather we should only regard the soul and attribute all manifestations of affection in the text to the surpassing good-ness of God as pure, undefiled offerings. For God alone is truly sweet, desir-able and worthy of love.[103]

Most of Gregory's spiritual interpretations are quite a stretch. In order to reinterpret several of the most explicit sexual passages, their sexual meanings are "translated out" by a train of associations in which one word leads to another word, and ultimately the sexual language is applied to some relationship between God and the soul. The very first chapter of the *Song of Songs*, which opens with the line, "Let him kiss me with the kisses of his mouth," follows an association of words that have at their core the image of the mouth. Words proceed from the mouth, so God's words — which are eternal life — proceed from his mouth. Then Gregory follows the image of the mouth to drinking from a fountain. When one drinks from a fountain, one must apply one's own mouth to the mouth of the fountain. According the Gospel of John, God is the fountain of spiritual life, so drawing eternal life from God is compared to the kiss in *Song of Songs*:

> . . . since the Lord himself is a fountain as he says: "If anyone thirsts, let him come to me and drink" [Jn 7.37], so the thirsting soul wishes to bring its mouth to the mouth that springs up with life and says: "Let him kiss me with the kisses of his mouth" [1.2] (p. 51).

---

102. *Ibid.*, p. 171.
103. *Ibid.*, p. 50.

Likewise, the bed shared between the lovers becomes a symbol for Christ's union with the Church. Gregory makes this association by referring again to Paul (Ephesians 5:31-32), where Paul describes human sexual union as the mystical union of Christ and the Church.

The bride uses the term "bed" to interpret in a figurative sense the blending of human nature with the divine. In the same way, the great apostle Paul joins us as virgins to Christ and acts as an escort for the bride. He says that the clinging together of two persons in the union of one body is a great mystery of Christ's union with the Church. For he said: "The two shall be one flesh," and then he added: "This is a great mystery with reference to Christ and the Church" [Eph 5.31-32].

Because of this mystery, the virgin soul names the union with God a "bed" (p. 94). Gregory is really challenged by the erotic passage found in chapter 4, vs. 10-15 of *Song of Songs*:

> 10. How beautiful are your breasts, my sister, my spouse!
> How much more beautiful are your breasts than wine,
> And the scent of your ointments than all spices!
>
> 11. Your lips drop a honeycomb, my spouse . . .
> And the scent of your garments is as
> The scent of frankincense.
>
> 12. My sister, my spouse, is a garden enclosed;
> A garden enclosed, a fountain sealed.
>
> 13. Your shoots are a garden of pomegranates
> With the fruit of choice berries;
> Henna with nard:
>
> 14. Nard, and saffron, calamus and cinnamon;
> With all the woods of Lebanon:
> Myrrh, aloes, with all the chief spices.
>
> 15. A fountain of gardens, and a well of living water
> Springing from Lebanon.

Gregory dismisses the breasts rather summarily. They are good doctrines: "She would not have been adorned by the fountains of good doctrines signified by her breasts unless she had first made herself a sister of the Lord through good works" (p. 172). However the scent of her ointments requires an especially convoluted chain of associations. We smell spices, and sacrifices to God smell sweet to God, so the scent of the beloved's ointments leads Gregory to a consideration of Old Testament sacrifice:

> Every good smelling spice is sweet to our sense of smell. Noah offered such a sacrifice to God, and "the Lord smelled a good odor" [Gen 8.21]. Sacrifice, therefore, is a good odor to God, as were many propitiatory sacrifices — thanksgiving sacrifices, sacrifices for salvation, purification and sin. All these are spices, holocausts, whole burnt offerings, and parts of votive offerings of things consecrated to God . . . (p. 173).

Gregory interprets the Old Testament sacrifices according to Platonic philosophy. Old Testament sacrifice symbolizes that we must sacrifice our passions. Gregory buttresses his interpretation with a passage from the Psalms:

> Animal sacrifices were many and frequent. If any lesson can be gained, it is enjoined upon you in mystery, that is, the necessity of sacrificing your own passions. "A sacrifice to God is a contrite heart. A contrite and humble heart God will not spurn" [Ps 50.19] (p. 173).

The passage that refers to the bride's lips that drop a honeycomb requires a similarly convoluted chain of associations. First, the nature of the honeycomb is considered, and the labor of the bees that create it. Like bees, one flies over Church doctrines and builds up a "honeycomb" of Church doctrines in one's memory. From doctrines one builds up the various virtues in our soul:

> . . . by flying over the fields of divinely inspired words, we are to gather something from each one for the creation of wisdom. We mold within ourselves a honeycomb, so to speak, storing up in our hearts this labor of love as in a hive. The various doctrines create in our memory storehouses like the different cells in wax which are unable to be destroyed. By imitating that wise bee whose honeycomb is sweet and whose sting does not prick, we are always busy about the noble task of acquiring virtues (p. 174).

Then, when one has become a "honeycomb" of virtue, one speaks from one's virtuous heart. One's lips, then, "drop a honeycomb" of words from the heart's virtues.

> The manifold divisions of spiritual graces are in proportion to the zeal of those who strive after them. Thus the bridegroom says to his bride: "Your heart has become a honeycomb full of every kind of instruction. From your

heart's treasure come your words. They are honeyed drops that the Word may be blended with milk and honey. 'Your lips drop a honeycomb, my spouse; honey and milk are under your tongue'" [4.11] (p. 174).

The sweet lips of the beloved have become virtuous words of religious instruction.

Gregory's explanation of the scent of the bride's garments is based again on the Platonic doctrine that true virtue is passionless. Passionless wisdom also reflects Plato's "transcendent" world of the Ideal Forms for Gregory. He then applies these Platonic ideas to the beloved's garments, reading them as the many virtues in the soul —

> The end of a virtuous life is likeness to God. Because of this, purity of soul and freedom from the disturbance of passion is exercised by attention to the virtues so that a certain form of the transcendent nature might become present in them due to their more refined way of life. Since the life (*politeia*) of virtue is neither uniform nor the same, it is like the art of skill-fully making a garment by weaving various threads: some threads are pulled straight and others drawn crossways against them. Therefore, it is necessary to have many elements concur to create a virtuous life. The divine Apostle enumerates the various strands constituting the texture of good works — love, joy, peace, long suffering, goodness, etc. [Gal 5.22] (p. 175).

Having established a symbolic interpretation for the garments, Gregory then explains the scent of frankincense which the garments effuse. The scent of frankincense becomes the Platonic state of freedom from passion and a suggestion of the transcendent realm of the Ideal Forms:

> Frankincense is used strictly as incense in worship of God. It is better than all spices and is worthy as the one spice dedicated to God. Our under-standing of this mystery is as follows: The garment of your virtues, my bride, imitates the divine blessedness and resembles the transcendent divine nature by your purity and freedom from passion (pp. 175-176).

The bride's garden becomes an emblem for the Platonic virtue of reason which the soul uses to quiet passions. Recall that in Plato's *Phaedrus* the soul is compared to a charioteer driving two winged horses. One horse is disobedient and wild while the other is obedient and tame. The driver of the chariot is the rational faculty in the soul and the wild horse represents passions. The tame horse is noble affections for honor and the good. In his own inimitable way,

Gregory turns the garden of the *Song* into this Platonic metaphor. Gregory thinks that this substitution of rationality for the garden is obvious.

> "You are a garden enclosed, a fountain sealed" [4.12]. The book of Proverbs symbolically teaches us about this fountain: "Let your fountain of water be for you alone, and let no stranger partake of it" [Pr 5.17]. The song testifies to this by saying "sealed," that is, guarded. In my opinion this clearly means that our soul's rational faculty swells up and always flows over. . . .
>
> Because a seal protects the inviolability of whatever it guards, it scares off thieves; everything not stolen remains unharmed for the master. Praise of the bride in the Song would then testify to her excellence in virtue because her mind remains safe from enemies and is guarded for her Lord in purity and tranquility (p. 177).

Gregory's Platonic praise of the intellect continues in a discussion of the cinnamon which grows in the bride's garden. He begins his symbolic interpretation with a rather strange fact about the power of cinnamon: "It is said that if cinnamon is put in the mouth of a sleeping person, he will not withold his answer to a question, but will remain asleep and give a sober, articulate answer" (p. 181). Gregory then applies this unique property of cinnamon to the soul's rational faculty and its battle with passion:

> When a person teems with desire or burns with rage, he uses reason to quench the passions. It is the same with the sleep of this present life: if you place the sober cinnamon of reason in your mouth, you will clearly and accurately bring forth the meaning it contains. . . . Thus you can say that cinnamon swells up from your mouth to quench passion's fire and any seething rage in your heart; as a result, reason purifies the dream-like fantasy and confusion of this present life (182).

Finally, the *Song* compares the bride to a fountain. Again, Gregory recalls the passage in John in which Jesus says that he gives living water, like a fountain. Thus the bride who is a fountain is compared to Jesus himself, also a fountain. Comparing the human soul to Jesus follows the mystical teachings of Clement of Alexandria. According to Clement, and his disciple Gregory, our souls can merge with Godhood even as Plato taught (in the *Symposium*) that we can merge with Absolute Beauty by contemplation. In his concluding paragraph, Gregory even employs the Platonic philosophical term "archetype" — the Greek term usually translated in English as "Ideal Form." The bride is compared to Jesus, who is identified with the archetype of beauty. Gregory thus concludes Homily Nine with a final Platonic flourish —

> Who can worthily comprehend the wonders applied to the bride? It seems that she has no further to reach once she has been compared to beauty's archetype. She closely imitates her bridegroom's fountain by one of her own; his life by hers and his water by her water. . . . The bride contains his inflow of water within the well of her soul and becomes a treasure house of that living water flowing from Lebanon, rather, rushing, as the text says. We become partakers of God by possessing that well, . . . We do this in Christ Jesus our Lord, to Whom be glory forever and ever. Amen (p. 184).

The next homily in Gregory's commentary on *Song of Songs* is more concerned with Plato's doctrine of two worlds. The real world is the world of Being, where the Ideal Forms reside in unchanging eternity. This world is grasped by reason alone, with the passions quiet. The world of Earth is the world of becoming because here things come into the world by birth and pass out of it in death. This world is perceived by our bodily senses. Gregory applies this Platonic world view to heaven and Earth, or the soul and body. In a discussion of a phrase from the *Song*, Gregory describes heaven in Platonic terms and ideas. Heaven appears to the extent that our worldly senses are quieted. The vision of heaven that Gregory describes is akin to the doctrine of Ideal Beauty that we saw in Plato's *Symposium*. The phrase from the *Song* that occasions Gregory's Platonic mysticism is "I sleep but my heart is awake."[104] For Gregory, this refers to the sleep of the physical senses during philosophic contemplation when the mind and reason look at spiritual realities. Here, the body is contrasted with the soul:

> As long as the mind lives alone and untroubled by the senses, it is as though the body were overcome by sleep and torpor. . . . Despising all such wonders through the contemplation of true goodness, the body's eyes become tired, and the more perfect soul is not attracted to anything visible . . . Hearing, too, is dead and does not function, . . . The soul keeps far away from our more animal sensations as if they were a foul stench; I mean the sense of smell which enjoys perfumes, the sense of taste which is subservient to the stomach, and the vulgar sense of touch . . . Once all these sense have been put to sleep and are gripped by inaction, the heart's action is pure; reason looks above while it remains undisturbed and free from the senses' movement.[105]

---

104. Song of Songs 5:2.

The Platonic ideas are clear in this passage, as a glance at Plato's *Phaedo* will disclose. In that work, Plato says that the soul which desires true knowledge will shun the senses, and draw into herself. By relying on reason, the soul can understand true reality, which is invisible:

> The lovers of knowledge, I repeat, know that philosophy takes the soul when she is in this condition, and gently encourages her, and strives to release her from her captivity, showing her that the senses are full of deceit, and persuading her to stand aloof from the senses and to use them only when she must, and exhorting her to rally and gather herself together, and to trust only to herself and to the real existence which she of her own self apprehends, and to believe nothing which is subject to change, and which she perceives by other faculties, has any truth, for such things are visible and sensible, while what she herself sees is apprehended by reason and invisible.[106]

Gregory accepts this Platonic doctrine that true reality is invisible and apprehended by our reason alone. The reasoning mind, in Gregory, aims at the transcendent world of Plato's Ideal Forms which are grasped by reason, not bodily senses. "[T]hrough the contemplation of true goodness, the body's eye becomes tired, and the more perfect soul is not attracted to anything visible; with the mind it regards only what transcends visible objects."[107] This regard for objects that transcend the visible sight echoes Plato's *Symposium* — "the Beautiful itself, absolute, pure, unmixed, not polluted by human flesh or colors or any other great nonsense of mortality."[108]

Gregory follows Plato's world view by explaining that the object of non-sensory contemplation is true Being, while the senses perceive only the world of becoming (in which objects come into being and go out of being). The body perceives the world of becoming, but the soul perceives the world of Being. The Platonic realm of Being is now identified with God. Thus Platonic Being becomes Christianized into God.

> If a person pays attention to the senses and is drawn by pleasure in the body, he will live his life without tasting the divine joy, since the good can be overshadowed by what is inferior. For those who desire God, a good not shadowed over by anything awaits them; they realize that what enters the

---

105. Gregory of Nyssa, *Commentary on the Song of Songs*, p. 104.
106. Plato, *Phaedo* (Indianapolis: Bobbs-Merrill Educational Publishing, 1978), p. 33.
107. Gregory of Nyssa, *Commentary on the Song of Songs*, p. 195.
108. Plato, *Symposium* (Indianapolis: Hackett Publishing Company, 1989), pp. 58, 59.

senses must be avoided. Therefore when the soul enjoys only the contemplation of Being, it will not arise for those things which effect sensual pleasure. It puts to rest all bodily movement, and by naked, pure insight, the soul will see God in a divine watchfulness.[109]

Plato's discussion of the two worlds — the world of Being and the world of becoming — comes fairly early in his *Timaeus*. This text is clearly what Gregory has in mind when he refers to God as Being. In Plato, the world of Being is unchanging and apprehensible by reason alone, completely devoid of the body's senses. "Irrational sensation" perceives only the world of becoming.

> We must in my opinion begin by distinguishing between that which always is [Being] and never becomes from that which is always becoming and never is [becoming]. The one is apprehensible by intelligence with the aid of reasoning, being eternally the same, the other is the object of opinion and irrational sensation, coming to be and ceasing to be, but never fully real.[110]

This description of the two worlds is also clearly stated in Plato's *Symposium*, as we saw in Chapter One of this book: "First, it always *is* and neither comes to be nor passes away, neither waxes nor wanes. . . ."[111] Gregory's understanding of spiritual realities follows Plato's descriptions of the world of Ideal Forms since his apprehension of God involves a putting to rest of "all bodily movement" and the vision of God is given by "pure insight."[112]

In Gregory's remarkable commentary, the most erotic book in the Bible is transformed into a Platonic journey of the soul away from everything related to the body and human sexuality. All the bodily senses are to be transcended so that reason may grasp the archetype of Beauty called God and Being. Plato's concepts have crept into Christianity by Gregory's interpretation of the *Song of Songs*.

Gregory was not the first Christian mystic to import Plato into Christianity. Clement of Alexandria, before him, had done so, and Philo of Alexandria had imported Platonism and Stoicism into Judaism before Clement. What interests us in Gregory is his use of erotic materials as a symbol for Platonic transcendence. Other Christian mystics (notably Bernard of Clairvaux

---

109. Gregory of Nyssa, *Commentary on the Song of Songs*, p. 195.
110. Plato, *Timaeus and Critias* (London: Penguin Books, 1977), p. 40.
111. Plato, *Symposium*, p. 58.
112. Gregory of Nyssa, *Commentary on the Song of Songs*, p. 195.

in the Middle Ages) would follow Gregory in turning the eroticism of *Song of Songs* into allegorical interpretations about Church doctrine and the soul's search for God. Gregory's methods and doctrines derived from the huge popularity of Plato among thinkers in the fourth century CE. Although Plato had died 800 years past, convicted as a capital criminal, his ideas continued to influence the Mediterranean thought world. His ideas acquired a new life as they were imported into Christianity by Clement of Alexandria, Origen, and Gregory of Nyssa, to name a few. In the following chapter, we will look at other Church Fathers who continued to follow Platonic ideas. Plato's struggle with erotic passion now becomes a Christian issue.

CHAPTER IV. BAD NEWS FOR LOVERS: SAINT JOHN CHRYSOSTOM, SAINT JEROME, AND SAINT AUGUSTINE

The writers discussed in this chapter are shocking to readers today. They have to be read to be believed.

It is hard to imagine that anyone could have come up with such ideas. One could understand a religious argument against sexual immorality; but these powerful theologians argue against marriage itself, which is universally considered to be a holy institution in Christianity. And what is striking in their reasoning is that at times they blur the line between healthy expressions of sexuality and unhealthy sexual expression. They lump it all together and then denounce it.

These texts surprising in their own right, and because the Fathers are all saints, they have powerfully influenced the development of Christianity. Luther had to deal with Saint Jerome's text. Thomas Aquinas accepts many of Augustine's theological presuppositions, as does contemporary Catholicism. Chrysostom and Augustine owe much to Plato. Jerome bases his theology of celibacy mostly on the Bible, referring to the passage from Paul that we looked at in the last chapter (1 Corinthians 7) and a passage from the book of Revelation. These writers are not speaking to a select audience of monks or priests; they are writing to the general (educated) public.

I will let them speak for themselves.

Saint John Chrysostom

Saint John Chrysostom can use very vivid language when he is trying to persuade his audience to espouse the celibate life and turn from erotic love:

> Since if one were to see a soldier returning from the war, stained with gore and blood and brains, he will not loathe him nor turn from him on this account, but will even admire him the more. So let us do, when we see any-one returning, covered with blood after the slaughter of his evil desire, let us the more admire him and become partakers of his battle and victory, and say to those who indulge this wild love, "show us the pleasure you derive from lust; for the continent hath that which comes of his victory, but thou none from any quarter.[113]

Chrysostom unleashes his cleverly reasoned diatribes against all sexuality in his commentaries on 1 Corinthians. He relies mainly on reason and rational arguments to make his case, rather than on Bible quotes and the tradition of the Church Fathers. In making his arguments, the clear presence of Plato stands forth.

In his commentary on 1 Corinthians 7, Chrysostom makes a clearly Platonic statement. He contrasts slavery to the life of a free man. This becomes a metaphor for slavery to passion, that most Platonic of subjects: "For tell me, what profit is it when, though not in bondage to a man, thou liest down in subjection to thy passions.[114] Chrysostom's embrace of Plato colors his interpretation of the Bible. In the previous chapter we considered Paul's moderate treatment of sexuality in 1 Corinthians 7. Chrysostom claims that Paul clearly prefers virginity. The only excuse for marriage, in Chrysostom's analysis, is human infirmity. He severely slants Paul's moderate treatment into a pointed ringing endorsement of celibacy, claiming that Paul calls it "the excellent and greatly superior course."

> "For if," says he, "thou enquire what is the excellent and greatly supe-rior course, it is better not to have any connection whatever with a woman: but if you ask what is safe and helpful to thine own infirmity, be connected by marriage.[115]

---

113. Saint John Chrysostom, "Homily XXXVII on 1 Corinthians 14:34," http://ccel.org/fathers/NPNF1-12/Chrysostom/Homilies1/t38.htm. 2/17/2000, [6].

114. Saint John Chrysostom, "Homily XIX on 1 Corinthians 7:1,2," http://ccel.org/fathers/NPNF1-12/Chrysostom/Homilies1/t20.htm. 2/17/2000. [6].

115. Saint John Chrysostom, Homily XIX on 1 Corinthians 7:1, 2, [1].

Marriage is an accommodation to infirmity. In Chrysostom's age, few Christians could read. Thus when they heard Chrysostom preach, they couldn't check his treatment of Paul with the writings of the Apostle himself; they had to take his word for it. It was abuses of this sort that led Luther to urge his followers to read the Bible themselves and to base theology *sola scriptura* or solely on scripture. By characterizing marriage as an indulgence of infirmity, doesn't Chrysostom rob the institution of spiritual dignity? In another passage, Chrysostom seeks to remove his listeners from the married estate. He argues that even if we are married on Earth, we should look forward to our heavenly condition where angels "neither marry nor are given in marriage." This is a reference to the trick question the Sadducees asked Jesus in Mark 12:25. Chrysostom makes his point by bringing in another quote from 1 Corinthians 7, "From now on those who have wives should live as if they had none" (1 Corinthians 7:29). And why burden oneself with trouble, in marriage, if one has to live as if one weren't married anyway?

> And yet even although marriage had no troubles, even so we ought to press on towards things to come. But when it hath affliction too, what need to draw on one's self an additional burden. What occasion to take up such a load, when even after taking it you must use it as having it not? For "those even that have wives must be," he saith, "as though they had none.[116]

Chrysostom appeals to all strata of society in his commentary on Paul. He claims that Paul is not addressing only priests or monks, but intends all men to strive for continence. Celibacy is a mandate "of universal application." Chrysostom claims that Paul's concession to human infirmity is an attempt to "guide men to continence":

> Some indeed say that this discourse was addressed by him to priests. But I, judging from what follows, could not affirm that it was so: since he would not have given his advice in general terms. For if he were writing these things only for the priests, he would have said, "It is good for the teacher not to touch a woman." But now he has made it of universal application, saying, "It is good for a man;" not for priest only. . . . And in saying, "Because of fornications, let every man have his own wife" by the very cause alleged for the concession he guides men to continence.[117]

---

116. Saint John Chrysostom, "Homily XIX on 1 Corinthians 7:12," [7].
117. *Ibid.*, [1].

One can understand a religious complaint about sexual immorality, but why is Chrysostom so upset with marriage? The answer to this question lies in Chrysostom's Platonism. In "Homily XXXVII on 1 Corinthians 14:34," Chrysostom attempts to show that passion disturbs the individual to such an extent that one can find peace only in virginity. In this text, Chrysostom uses graphic imagery, narrative, and strong language. He begins calmly, like a gentle breeze before a storm. Referring to Platonic ideas, Chrysostom claims that the right way to live is under the guidance of reason, not passion:

> Neither let us then destroy our order, not place the head below and the feet above: now this is done when we cast down right reason, and set our lusts, passions, and pleasure, over the rational part: whence violent are the billows, and great the confusion, and intolerable the tempest, all things being wrapt in darkness.[118]

Having graphically denounced passion, Chrysostom makes a simple statement against Romantic Love, "Wherefore they who have no passionate love at all are in more pleasure than any lovers."[119] The rest of this Homily will be a defense of this point.

Chrysostom's first defense is taken from common experience. He claims that one will love another person better if one is spurned rather than if one achieves the object of his or her affections. Chrysostom holds that we honor those who most look down upon us. And the one doing the looking down enjoys greater pleasure, due to the honor he or she gets from those whom he looks down upon. This defense is somewhat Ovidian. Ovid did counsel his feminine reader to leave a man guessing for a while, but he added that she must all the while hold out hope. In making his first defense about his position on love, Chrysostom, like Ovid, concludes his argument with metaphors drawn from the military and hunting.

> . . . of which woman would a man be more enamored; one that easily submits and gives herself up to him, or one that denies, and gives him trouble? Evidently the last; since hereby the longing is more vehemently kindled. Of course then in the woman's case also exactly the same thing will happen. And him will they honor and admire more who looks down upon them. But if this be true, so likewise is the other, that he enjoys greater pleasure who is more honored and beloved. Since the general too lets alone

---

118. Saint John Chrysostom, "Homily XXXVII on 1 Corinthians 14:34," [4].
119. *Ibid.*

94

the city that has been once taken, but that which stands out and maintains the struggle he besets with all diligence: and the hunter, when the animal is caught, keeps it shut up in darkness as the harlet doth her lover, but pursues that which flies from him.[120]

Chrysostom continues to bring up observations from the general lover's condition to defend his statement that the continent enjoys more pleasure than the lover. His discussion now turns to the act of intercourse itself. In his argument, Chrysostom does not distinguish between married love and simple fornication. He is arguing against intercourse itself, and he is not concerned with how that act comes about. Chrysostom denies that the time lovers spend together is delightful; he makes his case as if sexual intercourse were the only good thing to come of love. And his description of love is a list of abuses. In this passage, Chrysostom claims that war has more truces in it than the relations between lovers. He also appears to take on a degree of woman-hatred, since all the evils that come to lovers are from women:

> But I shall be told, "the one enjoys his desire, the other not so." But freedom from disgrace, and from being a slave under her tyrannical commands, the not being led and dragged about by her as a drudge, beaten, spit upon, pitched head foremost; dost thou consider this to be a small pleasure, tell me? Nay, if one would accurately examine these things, and were able to gather into one their insults, complaints, everlasting quarrels, some arising from their tempers, others from their wantonness, their enmities, and all the rest, such as they only that feel them know; — he will find that there is no war but hath more truces than this wretched life of theirs. What pleasure meanest thou, tell me? The temporary and brief enjoyment of intercourse? But this speedily doth strife overtake, and storms, and rage, and the same madness again.[121]

Chrysostom next analyzes the state of mind of the continent versus the lover. Again, he is comparing the pleasure of sexual intercourse with the difficulty of maintaining a celibate life. Chrysostom claims that the celibate continually subdues his passions and so reaps a stable reward that one buffeted by passion can never know. Among the rewards of the continent is a clean conscience. It would appear that sexual passion of any kind — married or not — will leave conscience disturbed. Again, Chrysostom blurs the line between sacred and profane love. It is all passionate and a distress to the soul. The lover's

---

120. *Ibid.*, [5].
121. *Ibid.*

soul is like a storm at sea and like the mad mind of the deamon-possessed. But the continent wins a trophy like a noble champion for his efforts. Chrysostom relies more on lively rhetoric and rich metaphor than reasoning to make his point:

> "But intercourse hath a certain pleasure"; for this they are continually repeating: "while the continent continually suffers pain contending with the tyranny of nature." Nay, but one shall find just the contrary result. For this violence and tumult is present with the unchaste rather: there being in his body a violent tempest, and no sea in a storm so grievously vexed as he; never withstanding his passion, but ever receiving blows from it; as the possessed and they that are continually rent in the midst by evil spirits. Whereas the temperate like a noble champion continually giving blows to it, reaps the best of pleasures, and sweeter than ten thousand of that kind; and this victory and his good conscience, and those illustrous trophies, are ornaments for him continually to deck himself withal.[122]

Next, Chrysostom introduces the familiar Platonic metaphor of the unruly horse. Recall that Plato's *Phaedrus* compared the soul to a charioteer driving two horses: one obedient and the other unruly. The noble horse represents heroic emotions like courage and fortitude, while the unruly horse represents our passions. The true philosopher pulls so hard on the reins of the unruly horse that the jaws of the horse bleed from the bit and the beast is drawn down on his haunches. Those who did not subdue the unruly horse were dragged down from heaven to this Earth. In Chrysostom's passage, the continent keeps his horse under command while the lover lets the wild horse drag him around.

> As to the other, if after his intercourse he hath a little respite, it must be counted nothing. For again the storm comes on, and again there are waves. But he that commands himself doth not suffer this tumult to lay hold of him at all, nor the sea to arise, nor the wild beast to roar. And even if he endure some violence in restraining such an impulse, yet so doth the other also, continually receiving blows and stabs, and unable to endure the sting: and it is like as if there were a wild horse furious and struggling, and one should check with the bridle, and hold him with all skill: while another giving him the rein to escape the trouble, were dragged along by him and carried hither and thither.[123]

---

122. *Ibid.*, [6].
123. *Ibid.*

In the previous arguments, Chrysostom attempts to show that the continent enjoys a greater pleasure than the lover. His true genius shows in his concluding arguments. Chrysostom argues that one actually doesn't feel pleasure at all in sexual intercourse. Now Chrysostom's language has cleverly shifted. He drops the neutral term "intercourse" and now uses the term "lust." Sexuality then shifts into religious evil, and he refers to intercourse as an "evil desire." His metaphors also become more graphic. The one who has succeeded in subduing lust should be honored like a soldier returning from battle, covered with gore:

> . . . when we see anyone returning, covered with blood after the slaughter of his evil desire, let us the more admire him and become partakers of his battle and victory, and say to those who indulge this wild love, "show us the pleasure you derive from lust. . . ."[124]

The so-called pleasure of sex is so brief that it is hardly noticeable, but the continent holds on to a long-enduring state. Here we see Aristotle's conception of the rational man keeping his virtue over a long period, while the base man is at variance with his own soul, always subject to passions that often conflict. This Aristotlean reference is butressed with another metaphor from Plato. Again alluding to the *Phaedrus*, Chrysostom claims that the continent man gives his soul wings. Again employing deprecating language, sex is now "the criminal act."

> But if ye should mention that which is connected with the criminal act, yet the other is more manifest and satisfactory. For thou hast from the enjoyment something brief and hardly apparent; but he from his conscience, hath both a greater and an enduring and a sweeter joy. The company of woman hath surely no such power as self-command, to preserve the soul and give it wings.[125]

Chrysostom then musters all his forces and shows that neither before, during, nor after sex is there any actual pleasure.

> For what dost thou consider the moment of pleasure? That before the criminal action? Nay, it is not so, for it is a time of madness and delirium and frenzy: to grind the teeth and be beside one's self is not any pleasure: and if it were pleasure, it would not produce the same effects on you which

---

124. *Ibid.*
125. *Ibid.*

they who are in pain endure. For they who strike with their fists and are stricken grind their teeth, and women in travail distracted with pains do the same. So that this is no pleasure, but frenzy rather, and confusion, and tumult. Shall we say then, the time after the action? Nay, neither is this. For neither could we say that a woman just delivered is in pleasure, but in release from certain pains. But this is by no means pleasure, but weakness rather and falling away: and there is a great difference between these two. What then is the time of pleasure, tell me? There is none. But if there be any, it is so brief as not even to be apparent. At least, having zealously sought in a great many ways to detect and apprehend it, we have not been able. But the time of the chaste man's pleasure is not such, rather it is wider and evident to all. Or rather, all his life is in pleasure, his conscience crowned, the waves laid, no disturbance from any quarter arising within him.[126]

Having now referred to sexuality as lust, a criminal act, and an evil act, Chrysostom finishes his Homily by referring to it as licentiousness. Again, no distinction is made between sacred and profane love. All expressions of sexuality are condemned. Marriage and fornication are placed in the same category. Chrysostom is not urging his readers to sexual morality but to an asexual life; and he is addressing all people, not specifically priests and monks. His final words are that the celibate enjoys more pleasure than the lover, so all should become continent. He implies that only the continent will enjoy "the good things to come," i.e., heaven.

Since then this man's life is more in pleasure, while the life spent in love of pleasure is in dejection and disquiets; let us flee from licentiousness, let us keep hold on continence, that we may obtain the good things to come, through the grace and mercy, &c., &c.[127]

Saint Jerome

One of Saint Jerome's opponents accused him of arguing his point by devious means:

"Do not," you say, "attack unexpectedly or wound by a side-thrust. Strike straight at your opponent. You should be ashamed to resort to feints instead of force."[128]

126. *Ibid.*
127. *Ibid.*

Jerome does not deny that he uses craftiness in his arguments. In fact, he carries on the metaphor of sword fighting and says that it is better to use trickery during a sword fight than to strike straight at one's opponent: "As if it were not the perfection of fighting to menace one part and to strike another."[129] Then he relies on the tradition of the Church Fathers who came before him, praising them for their subtlety in arguing against the heretics. "Origen, Methodius, Eusebius, and Apollinaris write at great length against Celsus and Porphyry. Consider how subtle are the arguments, how insidious the engines with which they overthrow what the spirit of the devil has wrought."[130] One needs to be equally subtle when reading Jerome. One will need to carefully consider what he ends up saying by innuendo, suggestion, and other methods of subtlety.

Jerome's text is a defense of two books that he has written against a certain Jovinian. Jovinian argues that marriage is equal to virginity. Jerome disagrees and wants to make the case that virginity is superior to marriage. But Jerome's readers thought that he went too far and ended up actually denouncing marriage.

> Certain persons find fault with me because in the books which I have written against Jovinian I have been excessive (so they say) in praise of virginity and in deprecation of marriage; and they affirm that to preach up chastity till no comparison is left between a wife and a virgin is equivalent to a condemnation of matrimony.[131]

Jerome clearly considers virginity superior to marriage; but in his early remarks, he seems to dignify marriage, too. He compares the one to gold, and the other to silver. "While we allow marriage, we prefer virginity which springs from it. Gold is more precious than silver, but is silver on that account the less silver?"[132] The connotations are fairly positive at this point in his argument.

Jerome soon adds into his consideration the condition of widowhood. It is better than marriage, because in it one has tasted the pleasures of marriage but now must do without them. That life is harder, so it is better. In making this

---

128. Saint Jerome, "Letter XLVIII to Pammachius, http://ccel.org/ccel/schaff/npnf206.v.XLVIII.html. 9/5/2003. N. 13.

129. *Ibid.*

130. *Ibid.*

131. *Ibid.*, N. 2.

132. *Ibid.*

argument, Jerome refers to the Gospel story about the sower who sowed seeds on different soil. When the seeds fell on good soil, the crop came up thirty-fold, sixty-fold, and one hundred-fold. This story becomes a metaphor for the three conditions of life: marriage, widowhood, and virginity:

> Yields of one hundredfold, of sixtyfold, and of thirtyfold may all come from one soil and from one sowing, yet they differ widely in quality. The yield thirtyfold signifies wedlock, . . . The yield sixtyfold refers to widows who are placed in a position of distress and tribulation. . . . for, as it is extremely trying when one has once tasted pleasure to abstain from its enticements, so the reward of doing this is proportionately great. More-over, a hundredfold . . . indicates the crown of virginity.[133]

Jerome begins to cast aspersions on marriage in the further development of his argument. He states that touching a woman is dangerous. He refers, as so many other disputants do, to the familiar passage from 1 Corinthians 7.

> "Hence, also, the apostle says: 'It is good for a man not to touch' a wife or 'a woman,' as if there were danger in the contact which he who should so touch one could not escape."[134]

Jerome begins to become more subtle in his criticism of marriage as his argument proceeds. "The difference between marriage and virginity is as great as that between not doing evil and doing good."[135] Where does his gold and silver argument stand now? Is Jerome, here, saying that virginity is doing good, but marriage is not? This suggestion is pressed further, as Jerome comments on the same passage from Paul. When he is urging people to virginity, Paul claims that he is acting from the spirit of God, but when allowing marriage, he does not claim the spirit of God:

> "Thus, where he urges men to continence he appeals not to human authority, but to the spirit of God; but when he gives them permission to marry he does not mention the spirit of God, but allows prudential consid-erations to turn the balance, relaxing the strictness of his code in favor of individuals according to their several needs."[136]

---

133. *Ibid.*
134. *Ibid.*, N. 4.
135. *Ibid.*, N. 7.
136. *Ibid.*, N. 8.

Jerome seems to be suggesting that marriage is not an institution ordained by God, but only made by humans for fear of sin; then Jerome says some remarkable things. Immediately following this argument, he claims that marriages are not desirable — they are only excusable.

> "As marriages are permitted to virgins by reason of the danger of forni-cation, and as what is not desirable is thus made excusable, so by reason of the same danger widows are permitted to marry a second time."[137]

Then, Jerome refers to marriage as a form of prostitution:

> For it is better that a woman should know one man (though he should be a second husband or a third) than that she should know several. In other words, it is preferable that she should prostitute herself to one rather than to many."[138]

Mixing the idea of marriage with prostitution damages the sacredness of the marital institution; but Jerome goes even farther. He concludes this part of his argument by associating marriage with whoredom. He does not actually call it that, but he treats the re-married the same as he would a penitent whore-monger. In this section of the text, his controlling Biblical text is that some things are lawful but not expedient:

> "All things are lawful, but all things are not expedient." I do not con-demn digamists nor yet trigamists, nor even, to put an extreme case, octo-mists. I will make a still greater concession: I am ready to receive even a whore-monger, if penitent.[139]

What does Jerome gain by including whore-mongers in a discussion of marriage? Whore-mongers represent illicit sexuality, while marriage is supposed to be holy. This way of reasoning is a kind of guilt by association. Marriage is just as allowable as penitent whore-mongers. Now it would appear that the silver to which marriage was originally compared is tarnished. The crafty Jerome now claims that by allowing whore-mongers, he must certainly allow marriages; but what he is really doing is bringing down the sanctity of marriage by associating it with illicit forms of sexuality.

---

137. *Ibid.*
138. *Ibid.*
139. *Ibid.*

The silver of marriage receives more tarnish still. Marriage is not even considered meritorious. "Not to condemn is one thing, to commend is another. I may concede a practice as allowable and yet not praise it as meritorious"[140]. Marriage is plainly contrasted with virtue: "They [marriages] are permitted, it is true, even under the Gospel; but it is one thing to concede an indulgence to what is a weakness and quite another to promise a reward to what is a virtue."[141]

Jerome has now set up a disparity between the permission of marriage and the virtue of virginity. He then proceeds to call sexuality bad, relying again on Paul's statement from 1 Corinthians 7:

> "If 'it is good for a man not to touch a woman,' then it is bad for him to touch one, for bad, and bad only, is the opposite of good."[142]

Anyone who indulges in sex is defiled, for Jerome. Talking to men about Revelation 7:4, he says,

> "Again, in discussing the one hundred and forty-four thousand sealed virgins who were not defiled with women, I have tried to show that all who have not remained virgins are reckoned as defiled when compared with the perfect chastity of the angels and of our Lord Jesus Christ."[143]

Clearly the comparison of the perfect chastity of virgins with those defiled by sex with women is no longer a comparison of gold to silver.

Jerome's most devastating argument is that marriage denies the couple the body of Christ. This means that married people are cut off from salvation. Only those who are received into the body of Christ are saved. Jerome's text is 1 Corinthians 7.

> "I ask you, what kind of good thing is that which forbids a man to pray, and which prevents him from receiving the body of Christ?" . . . "But if we are always to pray we must never yield to the claims of wedlock, for, as often as I render her due to my wife, I incapacitate myself for prayer." When I spoke thus it is clear that I relied on the words of the apostle: Defraud ye not one the other, except it be with consent for a time, that ye may give yourselves to . . . prayer." The Apostle Paul tells us that when we

---

140. *Ibid.*, N. 9.
141. *Ibid.*, N. 10.
142. *Ibid.*, N. 14.
143. *Ibid.*

have intercourse with our wives we cannot pray. If, then, sexual intercourse prevents what is less important — that is prayer — how much more does it prevent what is more important — that is, the reception of the body of Christ?[144]

Jerome means it literally when he states that marriage cuts one off from the body of Christ. His concluding image is a comparison between heaven and hell. Referring to the New Testament story of the rich man and Lazarus (the love of wealth landed the rich man in hell, while Lazarus was received into heaven), Jerome compares the enjoyment of married love to the rich man, while he compares the virgins to Lazarus. The implication is that hell is for the married while heaven is for virgins. Jerome states outright that only virgins and widows reign with Christ.

> Why do we delude ourselves and feel vexed if while we are continually straining after sexual indulgence, we find the palm of chastity denied to us? We wish to fare sumptuously, and to enjoy the embraces of our wives, yet at the same time we desire to reign with Christ among virgins and widows. Shall there be but one reward, then, for hunger and for excess, for filth and for finery, for sackcloth and for silk? Lazarus, in his lifetime, received evil things, and the rich man, clothed in purple, fat and sleek, while he lived enjoyed the good things of the flesh but, now that they are dead, they occupy different positions. Misery has given place to satisfaction, and satisfaction to misery. And it rests with us whether we will follow Lazarus or the rich man.[145]

Is Jerome's essay a condemnation of matrimony? Does marriage remain silver while virginity is gold?

Saint Augustine

Saint Augustine was one of the greatest theologians in Christian history. His works reveal profound intelligence and extremely deep learning. His works have had a lasting and powerful influence on the development of Christianity. For that reason, his ideas on love and sexuality have influenced practically every Christian theologian up until the Reformation and even after it. Augustine still influences Catholic doctrine. But despite his powerful influence, intelligence,

---

144. *Ibid.*, N. 15.
145. *Ibid.*, N. 21.

and learning, we must not be afraid to hold up his ideas to modern scrutiny. An honest appraisal of his ideas about love may prove revealing.

Augustine wrote a book that describes his conversion to mystical Christianity. It is a remarkably open and honest narration of his life. In it he describes his tortuous wrestling with sexual passion. Ultimately, Augustine gave up Romantic Love for a life of celibacy. Since he has so openly detailed the course of his journey away from Romantic Love, his work has become a powerful promotion of the celibate life. Augustine's writings would probably be less powerful had he not been such a passionate lover before his conversion to monastic Christianity; but he openly and graphically admits that in his youth he indulged in sexual promiscuity.

Augustine's professional career began in the city of Carthage. There he undertook a course of studies in liberal arts with the intention of imbibing the Classical culture of the time. He describes Carthage as a seething pool of unholy loves: "I came to Carthage, and all around my ears were the sizzling and frying of unholy loves."[146] He graphically describes his promiscuity in Carthage, and in describing his sexual excesses he contrasts his sexual passion with Aristotle's philosophical friendship of mind only.

> And what was it that delighted me? Only this — to love and be loved. But I could not keep that true measure of love, from one mind to another mind, which marks the bright and glad area of friendship. Instead I was among the foggy exhalations which proceed from the muddy cravings of the flesh and the bubblings of first manhood. These so clouded over my heart and darkened it that I was unable to distinguish between the clear calm of love and the swirling mists of lust. I was storm-tossed by a confused mixture of the two and, in my weak unstable age, swept over the precipices of desire and thrust into the whirlpools of vice. . . . I was tossed here and there, spilled on the ground, scattered abroad; I boiled over in my fornications.[147]

The unholy loves that Augustine describes were not only sexual. He also saw rhetoric, theatre, poetry, and the other sensual aspects of Classical culture as seductions away from God. Augustine's father thought that the young scholar might be ripe for marriage when he noticed Augustine's bodily maturity in a Roman bath. But his father's idea occasions a remark by Augustine against

---

146. Saint Augustine, *The Confessions of Saint Augustine* (New York: Mentor Books, the New American Library, 1963), p. 52.

147. Saint Augustine, *The Confessions of Saint Augustine*, pp. 40-41.

family life. He calls his father "drugged" by worldly interests, since in Augustine's theology the soul should strive for God only. Anything but God is a fixation on Plato's world of becoming.

> In fact when my father saw me at the baths and noticed that I was growing toward manhood and showing the signs of burgeoning youth he told my mother of it with great pleasure, as though he were already confident of having grandchildren; but his pleasure proceeded from that kind of drunkenness in which the world forgets you, its creator, and falls in love with your creature instead with you; so drugged it is with the invisible wine of a perverse self-will, bent upon the lowest objects.[148]

Already we can see Augustine's low opinion of marriage. To him, it is a fixation on creatures instead of the creator. His mother opposed marriage for fear that a wife would interfere with his future career in literature.

In Carthage, Augustine fell in love. Since Augustine writes of this experience after he converted to monastic Christianity, he uses vivid language to denounce marriage. Romantic Love is again compared unfavorably to philosophical friendship. As in Chrysostom, Augustine lists the negative aspects of love such as jealousy, fear, and quarrels, as chastening rods from God. One can see Augustine's Platonic roots as he declaims all the objects of sensation.

> [M]y soul was in poor health; it burst out into feverish spots which brought the wretched longing to be scratched by contact with the objects of sense. Yet if these had no soul, they certainly could not be loved. It was a sweet thing to me both to love and to be loved, and more sweet still when I was able to enjoy the body of my lover.
> And so I muddied the clear spring of friendship with the dirt of physical desire and clouded over its brightness with the dark hell of lust. . . . Desiring to be captivated in this way, I fell headlong into love. My God and my mercy, how good you were to me in sprinkling so much bitterness over that sweetness! For I was loved myself, and I reached the point where we met together to enjoy our love, and there I was fettered happily in bonds of misery so that I might be beaten with rods of red-hot iron — the rods of jealousy and suspicions, and fears and angers and quarrels.[149]

---

148. *Ibid.*, p. 43.
149. *Ibid.*, pp. 52-53.

In Augustine's theology, as in Plato's philosophy, bodily pleasure is to be overcome. And as in Plato's *Phaedrus*, souls can be loved. So for Augustine, one turns from bodies to God, but one loves souls *in* God.

> If bodies please you, praise God for them and turn your love back from them to their maker, lest you should displease Him in being pleased by them. If souls please you, love them in God, because by themselves they are subject to change, but in Him they are established firm. . . .[150]

The narrative ultimately turns to an account of how Augustine gave up his desire for sex. The love for sex is part of the entire worldly life that Augustine was to renounce. Augustine precedes his conversion by stating that he was bound up in a desire for marriage. He invokes 1 Corinthians 7 and interprets the passage to mean that Paul prefers celibacy over marriage:

> But I was still closely bound by my need of woman. Not that the apostle forbade me to marry, although he might recommend something better, his great wish being that all men should be as he was.[151]

When Augustine begins to narrate his abstinence from sex, he includes with it a renunciation of his worldly career: "Now, Lord, my helper and redeemer, I shall tell and confess to your name how it was that you freed me from the bondage of my desire for sex, in which I was so closely fettered, and from my slavery to the affairs of this world."[152] Augustine was moved to question his attachment to sexuality and worldliness by a story he heard from a certain Ponticianus. In the story, two members of the emperor's court decided to renounce their positions and join a monastery. This story is remarkable in that both of these courtiers were engaged to be married. When they told their fiancées about their decision, both of the women "dedicated their virginity" to God and joined a convent. This is an important story element, because it suggests that conversion to Christianity requires a renunciation of civil life and also a relinquishment of marriage itself — not only of fornication.

It may indeed have been difficult to practice Christianity in the Classical culture of the fifth century; but since then our society has become largely Christianized and we don't confront the prevailing culture that Greco-Roman

---

150. *Ibid.*, p. 81.
151. *Ibid.*, p. 161.
152. *Ibid.*, p. 169.

society presented; but Augustine carries so much theological weight that his words are held to still be instructive.

Augustine vividly describes tug of war that occurred in his soul about giving up his civil life and sexuality, and converting to monastic Christianity. He paints a beautiful picture of celibacy:

> In the direction toward which I had turned my face and still trembled to take the last step, I could see the chaste dignity of Continence; she was calm and serene, cheerful without wantonness, and it was in truth and honor that she was enticing me to come to her without hesitation, stretching out to receive and to embrace me with those holy hands of hers, full of such multitudes of good examples.[153]

But Augustine himself felt unclean and wretched: "I could see how foul a sight I was — crooked, filthy, spotted, and ulcerous. I saw and I was horrified, and I had nowhere to go to escape from myself."[154] To Augustine, his sex organs were unclean. The voice of Continence urged him to overcome his unclean organs, as they were against the law of God:

And again she seemed to be speaking: "Stop your ears against those unclean members of yours, so that they may be mortified. They tell you of delights, but not of such delights as the law of the Lord your God tells."[155]

When Augustine finally converted to monastic Christianity, he gave up not only lust but marriage and "any other worldly hope." "For you converted me to you in such a way that I no longer sought a wife nor any other worldly hope."[156] In this conversion we can detect a Platonic doctrine that the real world is beyond this physical one. Augustine retrospectively saw his previous life as complete corruption:

> Who am I and what am I? Is there any evil that I have not done in my acts, in my words, or, if not in my words, in my will? But you, Lord, are good and merciful; your right hand had regard for the profundity of my death, and from the bottom of my heart you dragged up that abysmal load of corruption.[157]

---

153. *Ibid.*, p. 181.
154. *Ibid.*, p. 173.
155. *Ibid.*, p. 181.
156. *Ibid.*, p. 183.
157. *Ibid.*, p. 184.

In his *Confessions*, Augustine's writing style is narrative. In *The City of God*, his style is theological exposition; there, one finds a discussion of sexuality and love. Readers will not believe this author's description unless I provide an extensive quote, which I will therefore give.

Augustine's theology of sexuality is explained in an informal discussion which includes argument and scriptural reference. He does not develop his ideas methodically, but in a conversational, informal way. My task will be to pull out his primary arguments and arrange them into a logical order.

Augustine, like Plato, believes that the sex organs are shameful. Recall that Plato thought that the sex organs were located at the bottom of the torso so that they could be as far away as possible from the reasoning mind. Augustine actually calls the sex organs indecent, and the passion that arouses them for Augustine is always lust.

> We see then that there are lusts for many things, and yet when lust is mentioned without the specification of its object the only thing that normally occurs to the mind is the lust that excites the indecent parts of the body.[158]

Augustine also calls the sex organs "parts of shame." "It is right, therefore, to be ashamed of this lust, and it is right that the members which it moves . . . should be called *pudenda* ('parts of shame')."[159]

Augustine's main problem with sexual passion is Platonic. Sexual pleasure is so intense that it extinguishes reason. To a Platonist, reason is of paramount import in grasping the Ideal Forms; therefore there must be something wrong with the passion that results in the loss of reason. Even a married man would prefer to beget children without sexual passion. He would prefer to use his sex organs "in holiness and honour," not in the "sickness of desire."

> This lust assumes power not only over the whole body, and not only from the outside, but also internally; it disturbs the whole man, when the mental emotion combines and mingles with the physical craving, resulting in a pleasure surpassing all physical delights. So intense is the pleasure that when it reaches its climax there is an almost total extinction of mental alertness; the intellectual sentries, as it were, are overwhelmed. Now surely a friend of wisdom [philosopher] and holy joy who lives a married life but

---

158. Saint Augustine, *Concerning the City of God against the Pagans* (New York: Penguin Books, 1981) p. 577.

159. Saint Augustine, *Concerning the City of God against the Pagans*, p. 578.

knows the words of the Apostle's warning, 'how to possess his bodily instrument in holiness and honour, not in the sickness of desire, like the Gentiles who have no knowledge of God' — surely such a man would prefer, if possible, to beget children without lust of this kind. . . . They would begin their activity at the bidding of the will, instead of being stirred up by the ferment of lust.[160]

There are several problems with lust. One is that it won't obey the will, as an arm or a hand does. When one wants to move one's hand, one wills to move it and it moves. Not so, the sex organs. Sometimes when we want them to respond, they don't cooperate — even when our mind is filled with desire. Thus, lust is a lawless drive.

> In fact, not even lovers of this kind of pleasure are moved, either to conjugal intercourse or to the impure indulgences of vice, just when they have so willed. Sometimes the impulse is an unwanted intruder, sometimes it abandons the eager lover, and desire cools off in the body while it is boiling heat in the mind. Thus strangely does lust refuse to be a servant not only to the will to beget but even to the lust for lascivious indulgence; and although on the whole it is totally opposed to the mind's control, it is quite often divided against itself. It arouses the mind, but does not follow its own lead by arousing the body.[161]

Another problem with lust is that it is shameful. Augustine does not distinguish between married sex and sex outside the institution of marriage. In fact, he makes a point of including marriage in his discussion of sexual desire. The sex act causes shame, either way. Augustine's proof for this assertion is that sex requires privacy. All noble deeds seek public recognition, but sex shuns public expression. Thus, those who indulge in sex must be ashamed, married or not.

> Fornication, in fact, is called a depravity even by those who are depraved themselves; and, fond as they are of it, they dare not display it in public. But what of conjugal intercourse, whose purpose is, according to the prescriptions of the marriage contract, the procreation of children? It is lawful and respectable certainly; but does it not require a private room and the absence of witnesses? . . . Now, a certain 'author supreme of Roman eloquence' asserts that all right actions desire to be set in the full daylight, that is to say, they long to get themselves known. So this right action longs to be known; and yet it blushes to be seen. For everyone knows what act is per-

---

160. *Ibid.*, p. 577.
161. *Ibid.*

formed by the married pair for the procreation of children. . . . Nevertheless, when this act is being performed, with a view to the birth of children, not even the children who have already been born as the result of such an act are permitted to witness it. . . .

A man would be less put out by a crowd of spectators watching him visit his anger unjustly upon another man than by one person observing him when he is having lawful intercourse with his wife.[162]

It is passion itself (or lust, to use Augustine's language), that causes this embarrassment. The genitals have become the exclusive property of lust.

But the genital organs have become as it were the private property of lust, which has brought them so completely under its sway that they have no power of movement if this passion fails, if it has not arisen spontaneously or in response to a stimulus. It is this that arouses shame; it is this that makes us shun the eyes of beholders in embarrassment.[163]

Augustine then buttresses his argument with a discussion of the Platonists, "who approached the truth more nearly than other philosophers." He states precisely the same doctrines that we looked at in Chapter One. "Anger and lust are perverted elements in man's character, or soul, . . . and therefore they need the control of intelligence and reason."[164] The rational faculty is set above these passions and is protected from their influence if one truly practices philosophy.

This third rational division of the soul is located by them in a kind of citadel, to rule the other elements, so that with the rational element in command and the others subordinate, justice may be preserved in the relation between all the parts of man's soul.[165]

As a philosopher. Augustine had to account for the problem of lust. Why, he asks, since God told Adam and Eve to "be fruitful and multiply," does the act that gives birth to children occur by passion? Surely a good God wouldn't give us something so obviously wrong as passion in order to bear children. Augustine comes up with an answer. Sexual passion is punishment for disobedience in the Garden of Eden. "What can be the reason for this, if it is not that something by

---

162. *Ibid.*, pp. 579, 580, 581.
163. *Ibid.*, p. 581.
164. *Ibid.*, p. 580.
165. *Ibid.*

nature right and proper is effected in such a way as to be accompanied by a feeling of shame, by way of punishment?"[166] We move all our other body parts by willing them into action. Why shouldn't the sex organs also be capable of being willed into action without the shameful passion of lust? For Augustine, lust is punishment for disobeying God and eating of the Tree of Good and Evil.

> Then why should we not believe that the sexual organs could have been the obedient servants of mankind, at the bidding of the will, in the same way as the other [organs], if there had been no lust, which came in as the retribution for the sin of disobedience?[167]

Hence, the conclusion remains that if we had not sinned by disobeying God in Eden, our sex organs would have responded to the will whenever we wanted to have children — without any lust.

> Then (had there been no sin) the man would have sowed the seed and the woman would have conceived the child when their sexual organs had been aroused by the will, at the appropriate time and in the necessary degree, and had not been excited by lust.[168]

It is impossible to overestimate the influence of Saint Augustine on the development of Christian doctrine. Thomas Aquinas accepts this explanation of sexuality without modification. Even in Chaucer, who wrote for general audiences, the problem of sexual pleasure follows Augustine's doctrines. In Dante's *Divine Comedy*, heaven is peopled only with celibate Christians, mostly from monasteries. For Dante, sexual desire is the first level in hell, and the last level in purgatory. Sexual passion leads people into hell, and only after souls are purged of their sexual passion are they admitted into heaven. Martin Luther, who tried to put celibacy on a level with marriage, was accused of the heresy of "Jovinianism," the very theologian that Jerome directs his two books against.

What strikes me most in the theologians we have considered in this chapter is that no distinction is made between married sex or unmarried sex. Either way, sex is a problem, for all of them. Chrysostom called it a criminal act. Jerome compared married sexuality to the rich man in the New Testament who ended up in hell. Whenever marriage is conceded, it is deemed allowable only as

---

166. *Ibid.*
167. *Ibid.*, p. 585.
168. *Ibid.*, p. 587.

a concession lest the greater evil of fornication or adultery tempt frail humanity into sin.

But in treating sexuality as they do, don't these Fathers make all sexuality basically wrong? Can one feel good about love and sexuality, in the light of what these writers have to say about it? Worse still, what incentive does one have to seek marriage over fornication, since both are equally denounced? Haven't these theologians said that lust is lust, be it married or unmarried? If one commits wrong no matter how one enjoys sexuality, can marriage be better than fornication? Have these three theologians robbed marriage of its glory and holiness? In the light of Chrysostom, Jerome and Augustine, can one still consider marriage sacred, or the institution a sacrament?

CHAPTER V. KNIGHTS AND LADIES VERSUS THE MONKS: CHIVALRIC ROMANCE AND ASCETIC DISCIPLINE

In twelfth-century France, a wondrous new style of literature emerged out of the warrior tales of the Dark Ages. For the first time since the Classical age, love became the subject of literature. The earliest form of this love literature was the song. Composers and singers called "troubadours" began to fashion lyrics about the love between courtiers and ladies. This form of love lyric soon spread outside of France into Germany, Italy, Spain, Portugal, and England.

Under the patronage of Marie of Champagne, this style of love literature developed into stories called Romances. It is probably no accident that Romance stories began under the patronage of a lady — women are the most avid consumers of love stories. Without the influence of Marie of Champagne, it is doubtful that the exceedingly refined manners and courtesy of the chevaliers would have become such an important aspect of the code of the knight; but the Romance tale had something for everyone. For men, there was the element of prowess and battle; for the women there was the element of love and "courtoisie."

The first known author of Romance tales was Chretien de Troyes; he invented the character of Sir Lancelot, among others. His stories proclaimed and championed the code of chivalry, and formed the models for all the Romancers who followed.

The Romance tales are concerned foremost with the relationship between knight and lady, although kings and barons appear as well. Before the twelfth century, knights were only warriors. But by then, the order of knighthood was considered a spiritual discipline by its practitioners. Knighthood was a "secular virtue."[169] An elaborate ceremony filled with religious symbolism went into the dubbing of knights. First, the initiate bathed (symbolizing baptism). Then he was brought to a bed, which signified the rest in paradise which a knight would win through chivalry. He was given a red cloak symbolizing his duty to shed blood in defense of the Church. Then his waist was bound by a white belt, which admonished the knight to shun lust. Gold spurs were put on his feet to signify that the knight must be swift to follow God's commands. Finally, he was girt with his sword and solemnly instructed to follow the order of knighthood.

The order of knighthood contained four charges. First, the knight would not consent to false witness or treason. Second, he would honor all women and damsels and be ready to aid them. Third, he would hear mass every day. Fourth, he would fast every Friday in remembrance of Christ's passion. The spiritual nature of knighthood was felt so deeply that one writer compared the order of knighthood to the order of monks — "we poor soldiers will save our souls in arms just as well as we might by living in contemplation upon a diet of roots."[170]

But no knight had honor unless he had a lady. And the inclusion of the lady into this new form of fiction added considerable tension to the story line. Certainly, the power of the knight was important. A knight's primary function was to defend his king, his lady, or the Church. But power was not enough. The knight was also known by his manners. Even if a knight lost a tournament, if he showed honor in his loss he still had that precious quality — "courtoisie." This quality of courtoisie made him suitable for a lady's love. Here, the knight experienced considerable tension. While he was a source of power by his use of arms, he submitted to a lady's love. Society granted ladies little explicit power, but through her knight's devotion she acquired power over the knight and hence over society through him.

Society was extremely unstable at the time when the Chivalric Romances were written. Power was diffuse in the complex system of feudal society. Most knights held their land as a gift, called a fief, from a nobleman of higher social rank than himself — a baron, a lord, a king or even another knight. Some imagine the feudal age as an orderly organizational chart with power funneled down from the king to the baron to the knight in a tight system. Nothing could be further from the truth. A knight might hold several fiefs from different overlords

---

169. Maurice Keen, *Chivalry* (New Haven: Yale UP, 1984), p. 177.
170. Jean de Buil, in Keen, p. 70.

with conflicting allegiances. Then, there were noblemen who wanted territory that belonged to another nobleman. They would simply attack and try to gain the other's territory. Landholders of the same country had as much to fear from each other as from foreign attackers. Kings held only localized areas of power, and had to appease their noblemen in order to keep peace in their lands.

Marriage was also a problem. Royalty sought marriage with other members of the royalty. Class lines were strictly maintained. Often, marriages were made for political reasons or in order to increase land holdings or wealth. This put love in tension with marriage, and often love was expressed independently of the institution of marriage.

All these dynamics generated a rich literature in which violence appears perilously close to intimacy and love. Warfare and brotherhood can be closely juxtaposed. Death, love, marriage, pageantry, class distinctions, gentility, the sword and the heart all mix to form the material of Chivalric Romance.

But the rise of Chivalric Romance was accompanied by a tremendous upsurge in the monastic movement; and the monastic orders were dead set against the ideals of chivalry. Tournaments were forbidden by priests and monks. Love was challenged. During this time period, the Church taught that salvation could be won only through monastic Christianity. Even priests who preached in a diocese were considered relatively worldly. They were tainted by their involvement with the world outside the monastery wall. The monastic orders were quite astute in their preachings. They founded an order of warrior-monks — the famous Knights Templars. These were half monk, half knight and devoted exclusively to the service of Christ.

In his unceasing attempts to convert regular knights to his form of monastic knighthood, Bernard of Clairvaux denounces ordinary knighthood as "knavery," "frivolous," "pomp," "mortal sin," and other spiritually deadly practices:

> What, then, is the end or fruit of this knighthood, or rather knavery, as I should call it? What if not the mortal sin of the victor and the eternal death of the vanquished?
>
> What, then, O knights, is this monstrous error and what is this unbearable urge which bids you to fight with such pomp and labor, and all to no other purpose except death and sin? . . .
>
> Above all, there is that terrible insecurity of conscience, in spite of all your armor, since you have dared to undertake such dangerous business on such light and frivolous grounds. . . . It is certainly not safe to kill or to be killed for such causes as these.[171]

Having denounced ordinary knighthood, Bernard then extols the virtues of the monastic order of knights that the Church has recently inaugurated:

> But the knights of Christ may safely fight the battles of their Lord, fearing neither sin if they fight the enemy, nor danger at their own death; since to inflict death or to die for Christ is no sin, but rather an abundant claim to glory. . . .
> The knight of Christ, I say, may strike with confidence and die more confidently, for he serves Christ when he strikes, and serves himself when he falls. Neither does he bear the sword in vain, for he is God's minister, . . . if he kills he is not a mankiller, but, if I may so put it, a killer of evil. . . . Should he be killed himself, we know that he has not perished, but has come safely home to port. When he inflicts death it is to Christ's profit, and when he suffers death, it is for his own gain.[172]

Today, one reads this teaching about holy warfare warily. We have seen firsthand the terrible results of holy war. Mixing religion with killing and guaranteeing heaven for the killer now appears as fanaticism of the worst kind. When one recognizes this form of fanaticism in other cultures, its depravity is easy to recognize. It is harder to recognize, closer to home, but we need to remember that in the Middle Ages, killing in the name of Jesus was taught almost universally by the Church.

As an attempt to enlist all of Europe into the ranks of the monastery, a remarkable piece of literature was written by a Cistercian monk story about the Quest of the Holy Grail (*Queste del Saint Graal*).[173] The story tells about a holy quest to find the grail that caught Christ's blood when he was crucified. The *Tale of the Holy Grail* was adapted by the greatest English writer of Arthurian Romances, Sir Thomas Malory. Most of Malory's works valorize knightly prowess and the love of knights and ladies, but the Quest champions the ideals of celibacy and virginity. Thus the *Tale of the Holy Grail* severely undercuts the ideals of Courtly Love. All the character virtues that have given Lancelot the appellation "the flower of chivalry" are used against him in this monastic story; yet Malory considers this story to be "one of the truest and one of the holiest that

---

171. Bernard of Clairvaux, *The Works of Bernard of Clairvaux*, Treatises III. *In Praise of the New Knighthood* (Kalamazoo: Cistercian Publications, Inc., 1977), p. 132, 133.

172. Bernard of Clairvaux, *In Praise of the New Knighthood*, p. 134.

173. *The Quest of the Holy Grail*, trans. P. M. Matarasso (New York: Penguin Books, 1986).

is in this world." Including the *Tale of the Holy Grail* in Malory's *Works* illustrates the tension between the Platonic approach to love (now Christianized) and the Romantic approach; the significance is considerable. Showing the celibate life accepted by a popular author as the holiest life means that celibacy is not reserved for monks only; it is considered the holiest life by the ordinary population. Even the greatest "worldly" knight, Lancelot, is judged according to monastic values.

In *The Tale of the Holy Grail*, all the conventions of traditional knighthood are replaced with monastic ideals. The hero is a celibate knight who is aided by a nun-like lady. In this story, Lancelot, the greatest knight of all, is denounced for pride, for his love of Guinevere, and for his general worldliness. Since Malory included it in his Romance tales, this piece of monastic propaganda was transmitted to the secular world. The anonymous Cistercian monk who wrote the *Queste* apparently had his victory.

Chivalric Romance

Sir Thomas Malory, in the voice of the fair lady Isolde, says "there be within this londe but four lovers, and that is sir Launcelot and dame Gwenyver, and sir Trystrames and quene Isode."[174] If such a great romancer as Malory thinks that the greatest lovers are Tristan and Isolde, and Lancelot and Guinevere, we should probably pay attention. These two tales have captured the hearts of lovers for centuries. Wagner composed a magnificent opera about Tristan and Isolde, and countless versions of Lancelot and Guinevere have appeared since the first telling by Chretien de Troyes in the twelfth century. Most recently, the story of Lancelot and Guinevere was made into the musical "Camelot," by Lerner and Loewe, basing the storyline on T.H. White's Once and Future King.

But both of these couples are adulterers. The case of Tristan and Isolde is easier to reconcile, because their love was due to their accidental drinking of a love potion. That lets them off the hook, to some degree. Lancelot and Guinevere have no extenuating circumstances to make their love palatable to conventional society; yet Malory holds their love up as a model for other lovers:

---

174. Sir Thomas Malory, *Works* (Oxford: Oxford UP, 1983), p. 267.

And therefore all ye that be lovers, calle unto youre remembraunce the monethe of May, lyke as ded quene Gwenyver, for whom I make here a lytyll mencion, that while she lyved she was a trew lover, and therefore she had a good ende.[175]

The love of both these couples is perhaps best understood in the light of their times. Marriage then, at their social level, was less connected with love than it generally is today. Marriage was often a political arrangement made to keep royal lines intact or to extend property. Kings needed to marry royalty; other nobles needed to marry within their class. Love was considered a destabilizing force in society as it challenged the integrity of institutional marriages. Some clergy preached against love altogether.

Tristan and Isolde

The oldest Romance of Tristan and Idolde that remains to us now is by a French author named Beroul. His *Romance of Tristan* was collated from several sources, making the text somewhat fragmented. Some critics, notably Denis de Rougemont,[176] consider Beroul to have bastardized the original text. Beroul's account has the love of Tristan and Yseut (Beroul's spelling of the heroine) consummate. De Rougemont thinks that their love was Platonic, and symbolic of a Christian mystery tradition. Whatever its origins, Beroul's text is the oldest available edition and served to propagate the story through the course of time.

It is a highly provocative story. It seems to pit pure love against the enforced constraints of the civil institution of marriage.

The Romance of Tristan contains elements that we saw in Ovid. Tristan and Yseut are devious in the way they express their love for one another. Recall that for Ovid, any number of tricks were allowed to fulfill one's desire, particularly when pursuing another's wife or husband. Both Tristan and Yseut are consummate artisans, recalling Ovid's teaching that love is an art. Tristan is trained in the arts of battle, hunting, music, or, as Beroul's reconstructed text puts it, "all the warlike and peaceful arts."[177] Yseut was possessed of all the healing arts. Both were children of royalty. In every way, they were exceptional nobles. The reconstruction that introduces Beroul's text states of Tristan that

---

175. Malory, *Works*, p. 649.
176. Denis de Rougemont, *Love in the Western World* (New York: Harper and Row, 1974)
177. Beroul, *The Romance of Tristan* (New York: Penguin Books, 1970), p. 39.

"his prowess and his accomplishments made him stand out above the rest."[178] The characters of Chivalric Romance are usually superlative. This is the case with Tristan and Yseut.

The *Romance of Tristan* pits violence and love perilously close to one another from the very beginning. The tale opens in Cornwall, where a certain knight named Morholt demands a tribute of Cornish citizens to serve as slaves for his home in Ireland. He offers to do battle with any Cornish knight who wants to contest the tribute, but all are too afraid to take up his challenge. Enter young Tristan. He asks his uncle, the Cornish King Mark, to knight him and allow him to do battle with Morholt. King Mark knights Tristan, who then challenges Morholt. In the course of battle, Tristan cuts into Morholt's head, and a fragment of his sword breaks off and remains lodged there. Morholt dies on his return voyage to Ireland.

All of Tristan's wounds heal except one from Morholt's poisoned spear. Trusting in God, Tristan drifts away in a boat and comes to the land of Yseut. There, Yseut's healing arts restore Tristan to health and he returns to Cornwall. At this point, Yseut does not know that Tristan was the knight who slew Morholt. (This is good for Tristan, since Morholt is Yseut's uncle.)

The time comes for King Mark to seek a queen. Tristan sets out to Ireland to find Mark a suitable mate. The knight discovers that the land is being ravaged by a dragon and that the king of Ireland is offering his daughter as a prize for whoever slays the dragon. Notice that Yseut has no choice in this matter. Marriage serves the social institutions of the time. Ireland needs a protector and Cornwall needs a lady of royal blood for the king. Tristan slays the dragon and takes Yseut back to Cornwall with him for King Mark.

Before they leave for Cornwall, Yseut's mother prepares a love potion for her daughter to drink on her wedding day. One can already see the tension between love and marriage: Yseut's mother recognizes the difficulty her daughter will have leaving her relatives, going to a strange land, and being wed to a man about whom she has no previous knowledge. In fact, poor King Mark is made out to be somewhat of a dolt, and unworthy of the love of Yseut.

> "Hit is pite," sayde sir Lameroke, "that ony suche a false kynge cowarde as kynge Marke is shulde me macched with suche a fayre lady and a good as

---

178. Beroul, *The Romance of Tristan*, p. 39.

La Beall Isode is, for all the wo[r]lde of hym spekyth shame, and of her grete worshyp as ony quene may have."[179]

But a fatal accident happens on the voyage. Tristan and Yseut drink the love potion, mistaking it for ordinary wine. They fall fatally in love with one another.

The narrator of this tale maintains a strong voice, repeatedly interjecting his own opinions about plot elements. Nowhere is this more telling than in the relationship between Tristan and Yseut and King Mark's court. Beroul takes the side of Tristan and Yseut against King Mark, even though Yseut does marry the King and remains his queen. What is even more interesting is that we are told many times that God favors the lovers. Apparently God is on the side of love, not necessarily marriage. This strikes a modern reader as rather strange, since we would not normally think of God favoring adultery.

At times, honesty is preserved by verbal tricks. For instance, in one occasion Tristan and Yseut meet at night to enjoy each other's love. But they see King Mark hiding in a tree, and keep their talk non-sexual. At one point in their dialogue, Yseut says, "But before God I swear I have been loyal [to King Mark]: may He scourge me if anyone has ever had my love except the man who had me as a maiden."[180] Now, this is true, since Tristan and Yseut tricked King Mark on his wedding night. In the darkness they substituted Yseut's maid for Yseut (who had already consummated her love for Tristan). After sex with the maid, Mark fell asleep; then Yseut herself came back to bed.

God's favor on the couple is proclaimed several times by the author. For instance, after this meeting between Tristan and Yseut, Yseut's maid Brangain claims that God was protecting the lovers:

> "Yseut, my lady, God is always true. He has been very kind to us when he let you finish your conversation without doing anything else, so that the king saw nothing that cannot be easily explained. God has really worked a miracle for you. He is a true father, and he will not harm those who are loyal and good."[181]

Apparently, the loyalty that God values is the loyalty lovers (Tristan and Yseut) have for each other.

---

179. Malory, *Works*, p. 355.
180. Beroul, *The Romance of Tristan*, p. 48.
181. I*Ibid.*, p. 55.

Buttressing this are many authorial denunciations of the courtiers who stir up trouble for the lovers. There were three barons in King Mark's court who knew about the love affair, and out of jealousy they tried to tell King Mark about it. These squealers get no end of criticism from Beroul — "At Mark's court there were three barons — you never saw more wicked men!"[182] They enlist the aid of a hunchbacked dwarf in order to catch the couple in the act. In regard to this plot, the dwarf receives his curse from the author:

> "Sire send for the prophetic dwarf. There is no doubt that he is very clever, and a plan will soon be made. Send for the dwarf, then everything will be settled."
> And he came very quickly (cursed be the hunchback!). One of the barons embraced him, and the king revealed why they had sent for him. Now hear what treachery and corruption this dwarf Frocin proposed to the king. (Cursed be all such magicians! Whoever would have thought of such wickedness as this dwarf did? May God curse him!)[183]

The attempt to catch the adulterers is called treachery and corruption. It is indeed treachery against love, which seems to be the main measure of morality in this story. The actions of Tristan and Yseut are clearly treachery against the king. If a child were born of their love, that bastard offspring would be a pretender to the throne.

The plan to catch Tristan and Yseut succeeds. The couple is bound and brought to a pyre to be burned at the stake. As they are paraded before the city, all the residents weep for the lovers.

> Old and young wept and said to each other: "Alas, we have much to weep for! Alas Tristan, noble knight! What a shame these wretches have had you taken by treachery. Noble, honoured queen, in what land will a king's daughter be born who is your equal? Dwarf, your magic has done this! If anyone finds the dwarf anywhere and does not pass his sword through his body, may he never see the face of God!"[184]

By the grace of God, Tristan and Yseut escape from King Mark and flee into the forest. This opens up an important chapter in the *Romance of Tristan*. Now, their love can live free and unimpeded. This part of the narrative contrasts the

---

182. *Ibid.*, p. 60.
183. *Ibid.*, p. 61.
184. *Ibid.*, p. 66.

constraints of civilization with the freedom of humans in a state of nature, and recalls the tale of *Daphnis and Chloe* who met and found love in nature. Perhaps the tale of Tristan reinforces the assumption that society interferes with the natural development of love. Although Tristan and Yseut were raised in the court and accustomed to luxury, their love for one another made their life in the forest mild: "They were leading a rough and hard life, but they loved each other with such true love that neither felt any hardship because of the other."[185]

During their stay in the forest, an important episode occurs that causes us to recall Denis de Rougemont's theory that the original tale was about Platonic mysticism and the quest for Ideal love. The love of Tristan, for de Rougement, is symbolic of the soul's yearning for union with God. In the forest, at one point, Tristan and Yseut lie down together in their bower made of leaves. But on this occasion they remained clothed and Tristan places his sword between them. De Rougemont makes much of this one incident, claiming that it represents the older version of the Tristan legend. He claims that, all along, the two remained examples of a pure divine love that shunned physical intimacy. To de Rougemont, making the love between Tristan and Yseut sexual reduced a mystical myth to the level of carnal Romance. Another teller of the Tristan tale makes much of this scene in his story. Gottfried von Strassburg describes Tristan and Yseut's bower by imagery that suggests a medieval cathedral. The "grotto" in which they lie is a temple to the goddess of love:

> The story tells us that this grotto was round, broad, high, and perpen-dicular, snow-white, smooth, and even, throughout its whole circumfer-ence. Above, its vault was finely keyed, and on the cornerstone there was a crown most beautifully adorned with goldsmiths' work and encrusted with precious stones. Below, the pavement was of smooth, rich, shining marble, as green as grass. At the center there was a bed most perfectly cut from a slab of crystal, broad, high, well raised from the ground, and engraved along its sides with letters, announcing that the bed was dedi-cated to the Goddess of Love. In the upper part of the grotto some small windows had been hewn out to let in the light, and these shone in several places.[186]

The holiness of the love between Tristan and Yseut is underscored by this description of the temple. In Gottfried's account, the mysticism of their love is even more heightened since he claims that the lovers do not need food — they

---

185. *Ibid.*, p. 78.
186. Gottfried von Strassburg, *Tristan* (New York: Penguin Books, 1982), p. 261.

feed on love itself. Beroul attempts to explain the position of the lovers in mundane terms. He claims that Tristan was tired from hunting and wanted to sleep. Nevertheless, the image of the two lovers fully clothed, lying with a sword between them, is a powerful picture in itself. De Rougement suggests the original tale was one of wholly Platonized Christian mysticism derived from Manichaeism and Muslim Sufi imagery. In all accounts of the tale, King Mark discovers the lovers when they are fully clothed and is convinced that their love is not illicit.

The time approaches when the love potion wears off. This occasions a strange repentance in Tristan. He begins to feel sorry for all the hardships he has caused himself and Yseut in depriving themselves of court life. What is striking is that he never repents on religious grounds. He remains quite worldly when he questions what his relationship with Yseut has meant for both of them.

> God, I have had so much hardship! For fully three years today there has not been a moment when I was not suffering, either on a feast-day or a week-day. I have forgotten chivalry and the life of a knight at court. I am an exile in this country and there is nothing left of the light and grey furs I had. I am not in the company of the knights at court. God, how dearly my uncle would love me if I had not caused him so much distress. God, how badly things are going for me! I ought now be at the court of a king with a hundred squires in attendance, preparing to win their spurs and enter my service. I ought to go to another land where I could fight battles to win rewards. And it grieves me to think of the queen. I give her a bower of leaves in place of a curtained room. She is in the wood, and she could be living with her servants in fine rooms hung with silken cloths. For my sake she has erred in following this way of life.[187]

For counsel, the couple visits a holy hermit named Ogrin, who is also living in the woods. He denounces love itself and the hardship it has caused them. He doesn't phrase his counsel in terms of adultery, but in terms of love. "Exiles, what great suffering love forces on you! How long will this madness last?"[188] His curious position on the subject of love seems to follow the extreme doctrines that we looked at in the previous chapters. There we saw that the Church Fathers denounced all sexual passion — even married passion. When the hermit Ogrin counsels the couple to repent, he calls love a sin and doesn't even mention adultery: "When a man and woman sin, if they have first loved each other and

---

187. Beroul, *The Romance of Tristan*, p. 96.
188. *Ibid.*, p. 99.

then given up their sin, and if they have become penitent and make true repentance, God will pardon their misdeed, however horrible or ugly it is."[189]

The counsel he continues to give is even more strange. In order "to cover up the wrong" that the couple has done, the hermit decides to "think of some suitable falsehoods." This monk is ready to lie in order to help the adulterers regain their status at court.

Tristan's repentance seems suspect, since he is concerned more with material gain than any religious conviction or sense of sin. The development of this segment of the story causes even more suspicion. Initially, the reader was told that the love potion was to blame for Tristan and Yseut's love. In this respect their love was accidental. But now the love potion has worn off; the couple, accordingly, should no longer be in love. But their love continues! Tristan pours out his heart on the eve of their departure from the forest and their impending return to court:

> "God," said Tristan, "what sorrow it is to part! How unhappy is the man who loses his beloved! But it must be done to make up for all the suffering you have endured on my account; you need suffer no longer. When the time comes to take leave of each other I will pledge my love to you and you shall pledge yours to me."[190]

Yseut indeed pledges her love to Tristan:

> "Tristan, my love, I have a ring with a green jasper mounted: fair friend, for my sake wear this ring on your finger. And if you wish to send a messenger to me, I assure you I shall believe nothing unless I see this ring. No king will forbid me, once I see this ring, from doing whatever I am asked to, whether it be wisdom or folly, by the man who bears this ring; provided only that it is to our honour. This I promise you in true love."[191]

Tristan returns Yseut to court and lies about his past three years. In those days, claims of truth or falsehood were settled on the battlefield, and Tristan, powerful knight that he was, asserted his innocence and offered to do battle with anyone who would challenge him. Once again, Tristan does not demur from bringing God's name in to his claim of innocence:

---

189. *Ibid.*, p. 100.
190. *Ibid.*, p. 107.
191. *Ibid.*, pp. 107-108.

"King, I hereby restore to you the noble Yseut. No man ever made better restitution. I see the men of your land here: in their hearing I want to request you to allow me to clear myself and make my defense in your court. Never at any time did she or I love each other wickedly. You have been led to believe lies; but, as God gives me joy and happiness, they never put it to the test in a combat on foot or otherwise. If I agree to this taking place in your court, then burn me in sulphur if I am found guilty!"[192]

No one takes up Tristan's challenge. Yseut is received back at court, but Tristan is banished. Before Tristan departs, he shares with a trusted courtier his true intentions: "Tristan said that he had parted from a lovely woman and swore that one day he would have her with him again, although the king would not allow this."[193]

Before the story concludes, there is another occasion for the couple to trick the court and lie in God's name. King Mark's wicked and jealous courtiers stir up doubt again about Yseut's innocence. This time she is to swear on holy relics that she is guiltless. In order to make good on this vow, she arranges a humorous encounter with Tristan. The trial is to take place on the far side of a river. The river has a low, wooden bridge over it. Dressed like a leper, Tristan watches the Queen approach from a distance. The Queen asks the leper to come to her and carry her across the bridge. She mounts Tristan piggy-back style and he carries her across the bridge. No one recognizes Tristan. When the relics are brought forth, the Queen boldly makes her claim of innocence, swearing by all the relics that are in the world:

> "My lords," she said, "by the mercy of God I see holy relics here before me. Listen now to what I swear, and may it reassure the king: so help me God and St. Hilary, and by these relics, this holy place, the relics that are not here and all the relics that there are in the world, I swear that no man ever came between my thighs except the leper who carried me on his back across the ford and my husband, king Mark. . . . The leper was between my legs" [as everyone who was watching could see].[194]

In Gottfried von Strassburg's account of this ordeal the stakes are much higher. Yseut is to grasp a red-hot iron poker to test her innocence. If she remains unburned, she is innocent, but if the poker burns her, she is guilty. The

192. *Ibid.*, p. 111.
193. *Ibid.*, p. 113.
194. *Ibid.*, pp. 141-142.

same plot plays out, with Tristan in leper's clothing. Yseut grasps the firebrand and is not burned. But this occasions a rather cynical remark from Gottfried:

> Thus it was made manifest and confirmed to all the world that Christ in His great virtue is pliant as a windblown sleeve. He falls into place and clings, whichever way you try Him, closely and smoothly, as He is bound to do. He is at the beck of every heart for honest deeds or fraud. Be it deadly earnest or a game, He is just as you would have Him. This was amply revealed in the facile Queen. She was saved by her guile and by the doctored oath that went flying up to God, with the result that she redeemed her honour and was again much beloved of her lord Mark, and was praised, lauded, and esteemed among the people.[195]

The story of Tristan and Yseut is a tragedy and the couple never reunites. All the trickery and deceit recall Ovid's *Art of Love,* which enjoyed great popularity in the time of Chivalric Romance. The fact that God's name is so often brought in on the side of the lovers is quite curious. A brief theological reflection may help reconcile the tension between marriage and love as it evolves in the tale of *Tristan.*

The problem is where to locate the holy. In the fractured culture of the Middle Ages, the holy can be located in two distinct areas. One would be the ceremony of marriage, conducted by the Church — the explicit symbol of holiness. The other area would be in love itself, which found little sanction in the Church of the Middle Ages. Writers in the medieval period could hardly turn to the Church for uplifting messages of sexual love. Recall that in the story of Tristan, the hermit Ogrin preached that love itself was the cause of the lovers' suffering. "Exiles, what great suffering love forces on you! How long will this madness last?"[196]

This duality of loci for the holy is illuminated by Paul Tillich, who identifies two opposing forms of culture; one is called "theonomous," the other, "heteronomous." The theonomous culture is open to spiritual depth, to spirituality; and this generates cultural forms infused with meaning and religious significance. "Religion is the life-blood, the inner power, the ultimate meaning of all life. The 'sacred' or 'holy' inflames, imbues, inspires, all reality and all aspects of existence."[197] In such a culture,

---

195. Gottfried von Strassburg, *Tristan,* p. 248.
196. Beroul, *The Romance of Tristan,* p. 99.
197. Paul Tillich, *The Protestant Era* (Chicago: UP of Chicago, 1957), p. 43.

> . . . the gap between religion and culture is filled: religion is more than a
> system of special symbols, rites and emotions, directed to a highest being;
> religion is ultimate concern; it is the state of being grasped by something
> unconditional, holy, absolute. As such it gives meaning, seriousness, and
> depth to all culture and creates out of cultural material a religious culture
> of its own.[198]

Put another way, "Religion is the substance of culture and culture is the
form of religion."[199] Religion in a theonomous culture is all around a person in
culture and is also inside him or her as the depth of their personality. "Theonomy
asserts that the superior law is, at the same time, the innermost law of man
himself, rooted in the divine ground which is man's own ground."[200]

By contrast, a heteronomous culture loses contact with its spiritual depth.
This occurs when culture "becomes emptier, more formalistic, or more factual
and is driven toward skepticism and cynicism, toward the loss of meaning and
purpose."[201] Then external authority is imposed on humanity's actions. One
loses touch with the inner depths of one's own soul.

> Heteronomy imposes an alien law, religious or secular on man's mind....
> It destroys the honesty and truth and the dignity of the moral personality.
> It undermines creative freedom and the humanity of man.[202]

A theonomous marriage is the kind we saw in Daphnis and Chloe. The
marriage ceremony occurs at the end of the tale as the culmination of the intense
love that has overtaken the couple. The nature gods were revered by the couple
and acted to preserve their love; and their love was called forth by the god of love
himself, Eros. It was a marriage in which the full depth of love between the
couple was opened to the divine.

But marriage in the time of Tristan and Isolde was often a heteronomous
institution. It was an external law imposed by the Church and subject to social
rules that sought to preserve class lines. Kings, like Mark, were forced by their
culture to marry the children of kings and queens. And Yseut was compelled by
her culture, by an external law, to leave her homeland and kin and sail off to

---

198. Paul Tillich, *The Protestant Era*, p. 59.
199. *Ibid.*, p. 57.
200. *Ibid.*, pp. 56-57.
201. *Ibid.*, p. 46.
202. *Ibid.*

Cornwall to marry a king she had never met. Gottfried von Strassburg embellishes on Beroul's bare outline of this sad event. "She wept and she lamented amid her tears that she was leaving all her friends in this fashion, and was sailing away with strangers, she neither knew whither nor how."[203] Clearly in this culture, we see marriage as precisely that "alien law" imposed on Yseut by the norms preserving royal bloodlines in a highly stratified social structure. In short, the marriage between King Mark and Yseut lacks the inner depth and openness to the divine that we saw in Daphnis and Chloe.

Thus, in the Middle Ages, the depth of love and the institution of marriage were often split. The author of *Tristan* senses the holiness and depth of love, and accordingly puts God on the side of love, not on the side of a barren social ritual, even if endorsed by the external law of the Church.

The story of Tristan is an example of pure love unencumbered by the complicated political demands of the marriage ceremony. It is no coincidence that they enjoyed their love in the forest, far away from the complications of the court. In this, they were like Daphnis and Chloe, who refused to enter city life after their marriage but stayed in the hills with their flocks to love each other freely in a state of nature. Perhaps the author of Tristan felt he needed to rebel against the institutions of his day to paint the experience of love as purely as he could. God favors love, Beroul seems to say — a statement he couldn't find in the Church of his day, or in the institutions of marriage as they were often practiced.

This is not to say that love and marriage were never united in Chivalric Romance Literature. There are also stories in which marriage is the consummation of love, most notably the story of *Cliges* by Chretien de Troyes. But I think that people did not associate the two institutions (love and marriage) as commonly as we might today — or do we? Perhaps the best image we can take from this story is Gottfried's image of the "grotto of love." There, in a temple resembling a medieval cathedral which is devoted to the goddess of love, the couple enjoys mutual love, subsisting on love alone.

The Quest of the Holy Grail: The Undoing of Chivalry

We have seen above that Queen Isolde claimed that in England only herself and Tristan and Lancelot and Guinevere were true lovers; and Malory

---

203. Gottfried von Strassburg, *Tristan*, p. 193.

editorializes that Guinevere had a good end because she a true lover. We have looked at Tristan and Yseut, and now we turn to Lancelot and Guinevere.

Their reputation as an ideal Chivalric couple is severely undermined by the story of the Holy Grail. In Malory's *Works* there are seven stories about heroic and noble knights and their ladies, a celebration of the ideals of Chivalry, and one story of the Holy Grail — which challenges all these values. The ideals found in the Grail story are those of celibacy, virginity, and monastic Christianity, ideals that parallel the efforts of the Cistercian monastics. Even as Malory included a story about monastic ideals in his collection of knightly stories, so the Cistercian monks sought to convert all of the population of Europe into monastic Christianity. They particularly exerted their efforts on knights. Saint Bernard, the most successful propagandist of the Cistercians, preached that all should be converted to monastic discipline as the best way to heaven:

> Bernard also worked a well-worn theme in preaching that the cloister provided the only sure route to salvation. For the individual there was only one sort of conversion, and that was to the monastic life; and the call was imperative to cleric and layman alike.[204]

Bernard taught a form of mystical Christianity that roundly echoes Plato's ladder of love. For Bernard, we begin in the flesh and climb upward away from the body into the realm of pure spirit which is God. As with the Church Fathers, sex is denounced as "concupiscence." In making this ascent, one puts off all that has to do with the flesh:

> Since we are carnal and born of concupiscence of the flesh, our cupidity or love must begin with the flesh, and when this is set in order, our love advances by fixed degrees, led on by grace, until it is consummated in the spirit . . . In some wondrous way he forgets himself, he passes entirely into God and adhering to him, he becomes one with him in spirit . . . he would have to cast off all the infirmities of the flesh so that he would no longer have to think of the flesh, but wholly in the spirit he would be mindful of God's justice alone.[205]

In making this ascent, as we saw in Plato, all human feelings are stripped away leaving the devotee in a contemplation of a transcendental reality:

---

204. C. H. Lawrence, *Medieval Monasticism* (New York: Longman, 1984), p.154.

205. Bernard of Clairvaux, *The Works of Bernard of Clairvaux*, Treatises II. *On Loving God* (Kalamazoo: Cistercian Publications, Inc., 1974), pp. 130, 131.

As a drop of water seems to disappear completely in a big quantity of wine, even assuming the wine's taste and color; . . . so it is necessary for the saints that all human feelings melt in a mysterious way and flow into the will of God. Otherwise, how will God be all in all if something human survives in man.[206]

Bernard of Clairvaux was not alone in his preaching — "In his wake there was a throng of lesser writers, men whose talents had been fertilized by his torrential literary genius."[207]

Bernard and his colleagues seem to have been successful. Malory thought that the Grail story was "one of the trewest and of the holyest that ys in thys worlde."[208] In the Grail story, the conflicting values of mystical perfection and Chivalric Romance can be seen in mortal battle. The monastic ideals of the Grail story dramatically reverse the status that Lancelot has achieved in Malory's previous stories. (The Malory text that I will be quoting is in an older form of English; by reading the "misspelled" words aloud, the meaning becomes clear. A modern paraphrase is provided in the footnotes.)

Before the story of the Grail, Malory is at pains to develop Lancelot into the greatest knight of Arthur's court for his prowess, courtly manners, and as a lover. Lancelot's prowess as a knight is shown early on at a grand joust at King Arthur's court to which the greatest knights were invited:

> Sone aftir that kynge Arthure was com from Rome into Ingelonde, than all the knyghtys of the Rounde Table resorted unto the kynge and made many joustys and turnements. And som there were that were but knights encresed in armys and worshyp that passed all other of her felowys in prouesse and noble dedys, and that was well proved on many.
>
> But in especiall hit was prevyd on sir Launcelot de Lake, for in all turnements, justys, and dedys of armys, both for lyff and deth, he passed all other knyghtes, and at no tyme was he ovircom but yf hit were by treson other inchauntement. So this sir Launcelot encresed so mervaylously in worship and honoure; . . . Wherefore quene Gwenyvere had hym in grete favoure aboven all other knyghtys, and so he loved the quene agayne aboven all other ladyes dayes of his lyff, and for hir he dud many dedys of armys and saved her frome the fyre thorow his noble chivalry.[209]

---

206. Bernard of Clairvaux, *On Loving God*, p. 120.
207. C. H. Lawrence, *Medieval Monasticism*, p. 152.
208. Malory, *Works*, p. 608.

It was not only in tournaments that Launcelot excelled, but also in the many challenges that arise for knights-errant as they wander through wild forests seeking adventure. In his itinerate wanderings under unfamiliar armor, Lancelot is repeatedly attacked and is repeatedly victorious. He secures a pledge from his vanquished opponents for them to go to King Arthur's court and submit themselves to Queen Gwenyver's service. The tale concludes with all the vanquished knights assembled at Arthur's court just before Pentecost, and all of them extol the prowess of Lancelot. By the tale's conclusion, Lancelot has overcome three knights with one spear, overcome a certain Sir Terquyn, said to be "the strongest knyght that ever he saw;" three score knights all testify to Lancelot's prowess. So many knights were victims to Launcelot's prowess that his armor became widely recognized and no one would engage him in battle for fear of shame and dishonor. In a humorous passage concluding Malory's Tale of Sir Launcelot, the ignoble Sir Kay puts on Launcelot's armor and rides home in "Goddys pece [God's peace]." Malory concludes this book with a superlative accolade for Launcelot:

> "And by Jesu," said sir Kay, "sir Launcelot toke my harneyse [armor] and lefte me his, and I rode in Goddys pece and no man wolde have ado with me."
> And so at that tyme sir Launcelot had the grettyste name of ony knyght of the worlde, and moste he was honoured of hyghe and lowe.[210]

Malory holds up the legendary love between Launcelot and Gwinevere as an ideal for his readers to reflect upon:

> And therefore all ye that be lovers, calle unto youre remembraunce the monethe of May, lyke as ded quene Gwenyvere, for whom I make here a

---

209. *Ibid.*, p. 149. Soon after King Arthur came from Rome into England, then all the knights of the Round Table came unto the king and made many jousts and tournaments. And some there were who increased in arms and worship [honor] who passed all of their fellows in prowess and noble deeds, and were well-proven on many. But especially proved was Launcelot of the Lake, for in all tournaments, jousts, and deeds of arms, both for life and death, he passed all other knights, and at no time was he overcome except by treason or enchantment. So this Sir Launcelot increased so marvelously in worship and honor; . . . wherefore Queen Guinevere held him in great favor above all other knights, and so he loved the queen also above all other ladies all the days of his life, and for her he did many deeds of arms and saved her from the fire through his noble chivalry.

210. *Ibid.*, pp. 172, 173. "And by Jesus," said Sir Kay, "Sir Launcelot took my armor and left me his, and I rode in God's peace and no man would have anything to do with me."

And so at that time Sir Launcelot had the greatest name of any knight in the world, and he was honored most by high and low.

lytyll mencion, that whyle she lyved she was a trew lover, and therefor she had a good ende.[211]

Two things are striking. First, Malory reveals the high value of love: Guinevere had a good end because she was a true lover. Second, the love referred to is Guinevere's love for Lancelot, not for her husband, Arthur. As in the tale of Tristan, marriage was not the main issue. Instead, Malory champions true love between a knight and a lady regardless of society's explicit institutions.

Arthur's court, for Malory, was a golden age of chivalry and a place for love; all the tales in his *Works* except the Grail story serve to extol love in those days. In a melancholy critique, Malory contrasts the instability of modern love with the love that existed in the days of Arthur:

> But nowadayes men can nat love sevennyght but they must have all their desyres. That love may nat endure by reson, for where they bethe sone accorded and hasty, heete sone keelyth. And ryght so faryth the love nowadayes, sone hote sone colde. Thys ys no stabylyte. But the olde love was nat so. For men and women coulde love togydirs seven yerys, and no lycoures lustis was betwyxte them, and than was love trouthe and faythefulnes. And so in lyke wyse was used such love in kynge Arthurs dayes.[212]

Arthur's court is the fictive kingdom in which true love flourished. By the Arthurian tales, Malory argues for the relatively novel claim (for the time) that Romantic Love is a virtue. Each lover loves the other more than himself. As Malory turns the phrase, "worship in arms may never be foiled":

> Therefore, lyke as May moneth flowryth and floryshyth in every mannes gardyne, so in lyke wyse lat every man of worshyp florysh hys herte in thys worlde: firste unto God, and nexte unto the joy of them that he promysed hys feythe unto; for therre was never worshypfull man nor worshypfull woman but they loved one bettir than anothir; and worshyp in armys may never be foyled. But firste reserve the honoure to God, and secundely thy quarell must come of thy lady. And such love I calle vertuouse love.[213]

---

211. *Ibid.*, p. 649. And therefore, all you who are lovers, call to your memory the month of May, as did Queen Guinevere, for whom I make here a little mention that while she lived she was a true lover, and therefore she had a good end.

212. *Ibid.*, p. 649. But nowadays men can not love seven nights but they must have all their desires. That love may not endure by reason, for where they be soon and hastily reconciled heat soon cools. And just so love fairs today: soon hot, soon cold. This is no stability. But the old love was not so. For men and women could love together seven years, and no lecherous lusts were between them, and then was love true and faithful. And just so was love in King Arthur's days.

With the appearance of the Grail, the life of the Round Table radically changes. Upon Sir Gawain's pledge to enter the Grail quest, King Arthur senses that from this point on, his court will never be united as it had been:

> "Now," seyde the kynge, "I am sure at this quest of the Sankegreall [the Holy Grail] shall all ye of the Rownde Table departe, and nevyr shall I se you agayne hole togydirs. . . .[214]

Even as Arthur senses that the Grail Quest will dissolve his court, so in Malory's text the ideals of Chivalric Romance will be undone by the monastic ideals of the Grail Quest.

The Holy Grail is not a mere relic. It has supernatural powers. When the Grail first appears at a Pentecost feast, supernatural phenomena attend its presence: Loud thunder-claps herald its coming and a supernal light illuminates the court:

> Than anone they harde crakynge and cryynge of thundir, that hem thought the palyse sholde all to-dryve. So in the myddys of the blast entyrde a sonnebeame, more clerer by seven tymys than ever they saw day, and all they were alyghted of the grace of the holy Goste. Than began every knyght to beholde other, and eyther saw other, by their semyng, fayrer than ever they were before. Natforthan there was no knyght that myght speke one worde a grete whyle, and so they loked every man on other as they had bene doome.[215]

The Grail floats into the hall covered with white silk. A sweet smell fills the hall and the Grail provides each knight with the food that each likes best. Then

---

213. *Ibid.* Therefore, like as the month of May flowers and flourishes in every man's garden, so in like wise let every man of worship flourish in his heart in this world: first unto God, and next unto the joy of them that he promised his faith unto; for there was never worshipful man nor worshipful woman but they loved each other better than themselves; and worship in arms can never be foiled. But first reserve the honor to God, and secondly your interest must come in your lady. And such love I call virtuous love.

214. *Ibid.*, p. 520. "Now," said King Arthur, "I am sure at this quest of the Holy Grail shall all you of the Round Table depart, and never shall I see you again whole and together . . ."

215. *Ibid.*, p. 521. Then at once they heard clapping and crying of thunder and they thought the palace would burst to pieces. And in the middle of the thunder-clap a sun-beam entered more clear by a factor of seven times than they ever saw day, and they were all illuminated by the Holy Spirit. Then each knight began to look at each other, and to the appearance each knight looked more fair than they ever had before. Nevertheless there was no knight that might speak one word a great while, and each man looked at the other as if they had been dumb.

it vanishes. Clearly, this is no ordinary relic. In a later passage, the Grail is identified with Christ's flesh and blood, and in yet another passage it is referred to by the capitalized pronoun "He" i.e., God Himself.

The quest then begins. The goal is to find the Grail that caught Christ's blood when the spear pierced his side on the cross. After finding the Grail, the Grail Knight is to heal the maimed "Fisher King." But since this is a holy quest, only a holy knight can achieve it. Despite his great renown, Launcelot is severely lacking in holiness. Each encounter Launcelot has with the Grail ends with Launcelot's failure due to his sins. By denigrating Launcelot the very ideals of chivalry he represented are denegrated.

One by one, trial by trial, Launcelot lapses in honor. Before he actually sets out on the quest, a lady arrives in Arthur's court weeping, and fortelling the reversal of Launcelot's esteem:

> Than she sayde all with wepynge chere,
> "A, sir Launcelot! How youre grete doynge ys chonged sytthyn thys day in the morn!" . . .
> "Sir, I say you sothe," seyde the damsell, "for ye were thys day in the morne the best knyght of the worlde. But who sholde sey so now, he sholde be a lyer, for there ys now one bettir than ye be, . . . And that ys the change of youre name and levynge. Wherefore I make you a remembraunce that ye shall nat wene henseforthe that ye be the best knyght of the worlde.[216]

The conclusion of this dialogue states the spiritual contrast that will control the story line of the quest: the contrast between holy life and worldly life. Despite Launcelot's modesty, the portentous lady affirms Launcelot's greatness — of the sinful men of the world:

> "As towchyng unto that," seyde sir Launcelot, "I know well I was never none of the beste."
> "Yes," seyde the damesell, "that were ye, and ar yet, of ony synfull man of the worlde."[217]

---

216. *Ibid.*, p. 520. Then she said all with weeping chear, "A Sir Launcelot! How your great doing is changed since this day in the morn! Sir, I tell you truly," said the damsel, "for you were this day in the morn the best knight of the world. But whoever says so now, he would be a liar, for there is now one better than you are, . . . And that is the change of your name and life. Wherefore I remind you that you should not expect from henceforth that you are the best knight of the world.

217. *Ibid.* "As for that," said Sir Launcelot, "I know well I was never none of the best."
"Yes," said the damsel, "that you were, and are yet, of any sinful man of the world."

Malory draws a line between monastic life and the life in the world. The episodes that follow this prophesy further dramatize the distinction between monastic and worldly values.

One way holiness is defined in the Grail quest is by sexual abstinence. All the doctrines that we looked at in the last chapter come to play. Considering the lofty Romantic sentiments that Malory attaches to Arthur's court in the rest of his *Works*, it is ironic that the first act imposed on the Grail knights is to renounce their lovers. We need not assume that the lovers were all adulterers. Rather, as we saw in the Tristan story, sexual love itself was considered unholy from the perspective of monastic Christianity. Even though the knights are said to hold their ladies in "honoure and charite," their love was considered impure. Leaving their lovers is called being "clene of hys synnes" (clean of his sins), as if loving itself were a sin. The ladies of Arthur's court all raised up a cry of grief at the command that the knights leave them to pursue this quest. They were ready to accompany the knights, but a holy man said that this was not possible in "so hyghe a servyse":

> Whan the quene, ladyes, and jantillwomen knew of thys tydynges they had such sorrow and hevynes that there myght no tunge telle, for tho knyghtes had holde them in honoure and charite. But aboven all othir quene Gwenyver made grete sorow.
> "I mervayle," sayde she, "That my lorde woll suffir hem to departe fro hym."
> Thus was all the courte trowbled for the love of the departynge of these knyghtes, and many of tho ladeys that loved knyghtes wolde have gone with hir lovis. And so had they done, had nat an olde knyght com amonge them in relygious clothynge and spake on hyght and sayde,
> "Fayre lordis whych have sworne in the queste of the Sankgreall, thus sendith you Nacien the ermyte worde that none in thys queste lede lady nother jantillwoman with hym, for hit ys nat to do in so hyghe a servyse as they laboure in. For I warne you playne, he that ys nat clene of hys synnes he shall nat se the mysteries of oure Lorde Jesu Cryste."
> And for thys cause they leffte thes ladyes and jantilwomen.[218]

Lancelot's love for Guinevere motivated the knight to perform deeds of chivalry. When he confessed to a holy hermit, Lancelot's love and his quest for honor are considered sins. Launcelot does get a glimpse of the Holy Grail in his quest, but due to his sins, he is smitten with a holy fire, and falls down unconscious:

Ryght so entird he into the chambir and cam toward the table of silver, and whan he cam nyghe hit he felte a breeth that hym thought hit was entromedled with fyre, which smote hym so sore in the visayge that hym thought hit brente hys vysayge. And therewith he felle to the erthe and had no power to aryse.[219]

Launcelot lies unconscious for twenty-four days. During this time he apparently has a mystical vision of utmost sweetness. So delightful is the vision that Launcelot complains when he is awakened:

"Why have ye awaked me? For I was more at ease than I am now. A, Jesu Cryste, who myght be so blyssed that myght se opynly Thy grete mervayles of secretnesse there where no synner may be?"

"What have ye seen?" seyde [they aboute hym].

"I have sene," seyde he, "grete mervayles that no tunge may telle, and more than ony herte can thynke. And had nat my synne bene beforetyme, ellis I had sene muche more."[220]

Launcelot interprets his twenty-four day swoon as punishment for twenty-four years of sin. He laments his sins to a hermit, and claims that his shame was largely due to his loving a queen "unmesurabely and oute of mesure longe" (too deeply and too long). At no time does the word adultery enter into this confession. We are led to wonder if it is love alone that is Launcelot's sin, or the

218. *Ibid.*, p. 523. When the queen, ladies, and gentlewomen knew of these tidings they had such sorrow and heaviness that no tongue may tell, for those knights had held them in honor and charity. But above all queen Guinevere made great sorrow.

"I marvel," said she, "That my lord will allow them to depart from him."

Thus was all the court troubled for the love of the departing these knights, and many of those ladies that loved knights would have gone with their loves. And so they would have done, had not an old knight come among them in religious clothing and spoke on high and said,

Fair lords which have sworn in the quest of the Holy Grail, thus Nacien the hermit sends you word that none in this quest lead neither lady nor gentlewoman with him, for one must not do so in so high a service as they labor in. For I warn you plain, he that is not clean of his sins will not see the mysteries of our Lord Jesus Christ."

And for this cause they left these ladies and gentlewomen.

219. Right so he entered into the chamber and came toward the table of silver, and when he came near it he felt a breath that he thought was mingled with fire, which smote him so hard in the face that he thought it burnt his face. And therewith he fell to the Earth and had no power to arise.

220. *Ibid.*, p. 597. Why have you awakened me? For I was more at ease than I am now. A, Jesus Christ, who might be so blessed that might see openly Thy great marvels of secrecy there where no sinner may be?"

"What have you seen?" said those about him.

"I have seen," said he, "great marvels that no tongue may tell, and more than any heart can think. And if my sin hadn't been before this I would have seen much more."

fact that it is a queen that he has loved. But his love for Guinevere is mingled with a confession that Launcelot's great adventures were for the sake of worldly honor, or in other words the ideals of chivalry:

> "My synne and my wyckednes hath brought me unto grete dishonoure! For whan I sought worldly adventures for worldely desyres I ever encheved them and had the bettir in every place, and never was I discomfite in no quarell, were hit ryght were hit wronge. And now I take upon me the adventures to seke of holy thynges, now I se and undirstonde that mine olde synne hyndryth me and shamyth me, that I had no power to stirre nother speke whan the holy bloode appered before me."
> . . . And than he tolde there the good man all hys lyff, and how he had loved a quene unmesurabely and oute of mesure longe. . . .
> "And all my grete dedis of armys that I have done for the moste party was for the quenes sake, and for her sake wolde I do batayle were hit ryght other wronge. And never dud I batayle all only for Goddis sake, but for to wynn worship and to cause me the bettir to be beloved, and litill or nought I thanked never God of hit."[221]

The overall impact of the Grail quest on Lancelot is stated rather neatly within Malory's text — "he was overtaken with synne, that he had no power to ryse agayne the holy vessel. Wherefore aftir that many men seyde hym shame" (he was [so] overtaken with sin that he had no power to rise before the holy vessel. Therefore, after that, many men called him shameful).[222]

The knights who succeed in the Grail quest are examples of Bernard's Knights Templars. Three (that most holy number) knights achieve the quest together. All are ranked according to their sexual purity. Sir Galahad is the true Grail knight and he has maintained his virginity all his life. He is seconded by Sir Perceval, who also is a virgin, but thought about sex, once. Sir Bors comes in third, because although he "was never gretly correpte in fleysshly lustes" (was

---

221. *Ibid.*, pp. 538, 539. My sin and my wickedness have brought me into great dishonor! For when I sought worldly adventures for worldly desires I always achieved them and had the better in every place, and never was I discomfited in any quarrel, whether it was right or wrong. And now I take upon me the adventures to seek holy things, and now I see and understand that my old sin hinders me and shames me, so I had no power to stir nor speak when the holy blood [the Grail] appeared before me.

And then he told there the good man all his life, and how he had loved a queen too much and too long.

And all my great deeds of arms that I have done for the most part were for the queen's sake, and for her sake would I do battle whether it was right or wrong. And never did I do battle only for God's sake, but [rather] to win worship and to cause me the better to be beloved, and little or not at all did I thank God for it.

222. *Ibid.*, p. 537.

never greatly corrupt in fleshly lusts), he had sex once and begat a certain Elyan le Blanke. But he was under magic duress, so "all ys forgyffyn hym" (all is forgiven him). The latter two knights are tempted by demons who often appear as lovely ladies. They overcome these temptations and preserve their virginity, which seems to be the only temptation the Cistercian author cares about.

These stories of temptation parallel events traditionally recorded in the lives of saints. Perceval's temptation, for instance, parallels one of St. Benedict's. Perceval beholds a beautiful lady and proffers his love to her. They lie down naked in a bed, but Perceval sees his sword, which has a cross on it. This causes him to recall his pledge at the beginning of the Grail quest, and his own virginity. He makes the sign of the cross on his forehead and wondrous events explode in the castle. It turns upside down and it turns into a cloud of black smoke. Perceval realizes how close he was to losing his virginity and draws his sword, mortifying his flesh by wounding himself in the "thigh" — the euphemism for genitalia. The woman enters a ship and departs with the wind. As it departs, water appears to boil and burn after it — a metaphor Malory uses frequently for lust.

In parallel, St. Benedict is tempted by a lovely lady. He withstands the temptation, and afterward mortifies his flesh (though to a lesser degree):

> One day while he was alone, the Tempter was present. A small dark bird . . . began to flutter about his face . . . After it had left, however, a greater temptation of the flesh than he had ever experienced overtook the holy man. For the evil spirit brought back before his mind's eye a certain woman whom he had once seen. So intensely did the Tempter inflame his mind by the sight of that woman that he could hardly control his passion. He was overcome by sensuality, and almost considered abandoning his solitary retreat. Then God graciously looked upon and he returned to himself. Since he saw that thickets of nettles and thorn bushes were growing nearby, he stripped off his garments and flung himself naked upon those stinging thorns and the burning nettles . . . So through the wounds of the skin he drew out from his body the wound of the mind by changing his lust to pain.[223]

Sir Bors is tempted by a whole host of lovely ladies. Their leader is wealthy and promises all her wealth if Bors will take her as his lady. He demurs, whereupon all the ladies threaten to jump off the towers of the castle if he does not consent. Bors stands his ground. Then he hears a great sound as if all "the

---

223. Gregory the Great, "Saint Benedict," in *The Dialogues of Gregory the Great*, Book II, (Indianapolis: Bobbs-Merrill Educational Publishing, 1967), pp. 6-7.

fyndys of helle had bene about hym" (all the devils of hell had been around him). Everything vanishes and Bors finds out that the ladies were all devils.

But the greatest Grail Knight, Sir Galahad, never undergoes any of these temptations. However, to preserve the Chivalric flavor of this tale, Sir Galahad has a lady of his own — a unique one. She is identified only as Sir Perceval's sister. But she also is a virgin, and in order to make a belt for a special sword that the Grail knight must wear, she cuts her hair. Although she had been proud of her lovely locks, upon entering the service of the Grail she willingly shears it off. This means that she has essentially become a nun, as they also cut their hair when they undertake their vows. Galahad's sword carries an auspicious inscription on it: its belt must come from a pure virgin of high birth and the inscription carries a dire consequence for the lady, should she ever lose her virginity:

> HIT OUGHT NAT TO BE DONE AWAY BUT BY THE HONDIS OF A MAYDE, AND THAT SHE BE A KYNGS DOUGHTER AND A QUENYS. AND SHE MUST BE A MAYDE ALL THE DAYES OF HIR LYFF, BOTH IN WYLL AND IN WORKE; AND IF SHE BREKE HIR VIRGINITE SHE SHALL DY THE MOSTE VYLAYNES DETH THAT EVER DUD ONY WOMAN.[224]

Befitting such a knight as Galahad, his lady has taken perhaps the most perilous vow of chastity ever recorded.

While Launcelot's greatness as a lover was proclaimed by Isolde herself, so Perceval's sister receives her praise for purity by Galahad, who takes her as his lady: brother and sister in Christ:

> "Now recke I nat though I dye, for now I holde one of the beste blyssed maydns of the worlde, whych hath made the worthyest knyght of the worlde."
> "Damesell," seyde sir Galahad, "ye have done so muche that I shall be your knyght all the dayes of my lyff."[225]

---

224. Malory, *Works*, p. 582. IT OUGHT NOT BE DONE AWAY BUT BY THE HANDS OF A MAID, AND SHE MUST BE THE DAUGHTER OF A KING AND QUEEN. AND SHE MUST BE A MAID ALL THE DAYS OF HER LIFE, BOTH IN WILL AND IN WORK; AND IF SHE BREAK HER VIRGINITY SHE SHALL DIE THE MOST VILLAINEST DEATH THAT EVER DID ANY WOMAN.

225. *Ibid.*, p. 587. "Now I care not though I die, for now I hold one of the best blessed maidens in the world, who has made the worthiest knight in the world.

"Damsel," said Sir Galahad, "you have done so much that I shall be your knight all the days of my life."

The holy pair of Galahad and Perceval's sister recalls common stories of saints and saintesses whose lives are connected; one such tale tells of St. Boniface and St. Leoba, who united on their quest to evangelize Germany.

The trinity of Grail knights enter a ship called "Faythe" (Faith) and are brought to the Grail. The actual attainment of the quest by Sir Galahad assumes a minor role compared to the adventures of Lancelot, Bors, and Perceval. The Fisher King is quickly healed, and Galahad assumes possession of the Grail and spear. They take the Grail out of England to a far off land, since in England God "ys nat served nother worshipped to hys ryght by hem of thys londe, for they be turned to evyll lyvyng, and therefore I shall disherite them of the honoure whych I have done them"[226] (is not served nor worshipped right by those of this land, for they are turned to evil living, and therefore I will disinherit them of the honor which I have done them).

The Grail quest has undone the reputation of the greatest knight and greatest lover — Lancelot. It has also undone Arthur's kingdom's high reputation for chivalry, by taking the Grail from that land. The influence of the Grail quest is felt through to the end of Malory's Arthurian Romance.

Lancelot at first remains distant from Guinevere, recalling his failure in the Grail quest. Guinevere accuses Lancelot of unfaithfulness for this reason. But he attempts a defense:

> "A, Madame," seyde sir Launcelot, "in thys ye must holde me excused for dyvers causis: one ys, I was late in the quest of the Sankgreall, and I thank God of Hys grete mercy, and never of my deservynge, that I saw in that queste as much as ever saw ony synfull man lyvynge, and so was hit tolde me. And if that I had nat had my prevy thoughtis to returne to youre love agayne as I do, I had sene as Grete mysteryes as ever saw my sonne sir Galahad, Percivale, other sir Bors. And therefore, madam, I was but late in that queste, and wyte you well, madam, hit may nat be yet lyghtly forgotyn, the hyghe servyse in whom I dud my dyligente laboure."[227]

---

226. *Ibid.*, p. 604.

227. *Ibid.*, p. 612. "A, Madame," said Sir Launcelot, "in this you must hold me excused for diverse causes, one is, I was recently in the quest of the Holy Grail, and I thank God of His great mercy, and never of my deserving, that I saw in that quest as much as ever any sinful man living saw, and so it was told me. And if I had not in my private thoughts returned to your love again as I do, I would have seen as great mysteries as my son Galahad saw, or Perceval, or sir Bors. And therefore, madam, I was only recently in that quest, and know you well, madam, it may not be yet lightly forgotten, the high service in which I did my diligent labor.

The tensions between Chivalric Love and monastic perfection remain rather unresolved even up to the end of Malory's Romance. In a supremely ironic move, Lancelot's love and fidelity to Guinevere cause them to enter a monastery, and a convent, respectively, and never to see each other again:

> "Therefore, sir Launcelot, wyte thou well I am sette in suche a plyght to get my soule hele. And yet I truste, thorow Goddis grace and thorow Hys Passion of Hys woundis wyde, that aftir my deth I may have a syght of the blessed face of Cryste Jesu, and on Doomesday to sytte on Hys ryght syde; for as synfull as ever I was, now ar seyntes in hevyn. And therefore, sir Launcelot, I requyre the and beseche the hartily, for all the love that ever was betwyxt us, that thou never se me no more in the visayge. And I commaunde the, on Goddis behalff, that thou forsake my company."[228]
>
> "Now, my sweet madame," seyde sir Launcelot, "wolde ye that I shuld turne agayne unto my contrey and there to wedde a lady? Nay, madame, wyte you well that shall I never do, for I shall never be so false unto you of that I have promised. But the selff desteny that ye have takyn you to, I woll take me to, for the pleasure of Jesu, and ever for you I caste me specially to pray . . . for in the queste of the Sankgreall I had that tyme forsakyn the vanytees of the worlde, had nat youre love bene. And if I had done so at that tyme with my harte, wylle and thought, I had passed all the knyghts that ever were in the Sankgreall excepte syr Galahad, my sone. And therefore, lady, sythen ye have taken you to perfeccion, I must nedys take me to perfection, of ryght. For I take recorde of God, in you I have had myn erthly joye, and yf I had founden you now so dysposed, I had caste me to have had you in myn owne royame. But sythen I find you thus desposed, I ensure you faythfully, I wyl ever take me to penaunce and prayre whyle my lyf lasteth."[229]

Apparently Lancelot's prayers work — his death is attended by mystical phenomena. His bishop sees a vision of heavenly company bearing him up into paradise. As if he had attained some sort of mystical perfection, like the saints, Lancelot's body seems to have been purified by his penance and effuses a sweet odor upon the knight's demise (may the knight's bones be suggested as candidates for holy relics?):

---

228. *Ibid.*, p. 720. "Therefore, Sir Launcelot, know you well I am set in such a pledge to get my soul healed. And yet I trust, through God's grace and through his passion of his wide wounds, that after my death I may have sight of the blessed face of Christ Jesus, and on Doomsday to sit on his right side; for there are now in heaven saints who were as sinful as ever I was. And therefore, Sir Launcelot, I require you and beseech you heartily, for all the love that ever was between us, that you never see me any more face to face. And I command you, on God's behalf, that you forsake my company.

And so after mydnyght, ayaenst day, the Bysshop that was hermyte, as he laye in his bedde aslepe, he fyl upon grete laughter. And therewyth al the felyshyp awoke and came to the Byssop and asked hym what he eyled.

"A, Jesu mercy!" sayd the Bysshop, 'why dyd ye wake me? I was never in al my lyf so mery and so wel at ease."

"Wherefore?" sayd syr Bors.

"Truly," sayd the Bysshop, "here was syr Launcelot with me, with mo angellis than ever I sawe men in one day. And I sawe the angellys heve up syr Launcelot unto heven, and the yates of heven opened ayenst hym" . . .

So whan syr Bors and his felowes came to his bedde they founde hym starke dede; and he laye as he had smyled, and the swettest savor aboute hym that ever they felte.[230]

But the final eulogy given to Launcelot is a catalogue of chivalric virtues, not monastic ideals. And among the chivalric virtues that Launcelot is praised for is his loyalty to his beloved:

"A, Launcelot!" he sayd, "thou were hede of al Crysten knyghtes! And now I dare say," sayd syr Ector, "thou sir Launcelot, there thou lyest, that thou were never matched of erthly knyghtes hande. And thou were the curtest knyght that ever bare shelde! And thou were the truest frende to thy lovar that ever bestrade hors, and thou were the kyndest man that ever

---

229. *Ibid.*, pp. 720, 721. "Now, my sweet madam," said Sir Launcelot, "Do you wish that I should turn again to my country and there to wed a Lady? No, madam, know you well that I shall never do, for I shall never be so false unto you of that which I have promised. But the same destiny that you have taken you to, I will take me to, for the pleasure of Jesus, and ever for you I intend specially to pray . . . For in the quest of the Holy Grail I would have then forsaken the vanities of the world had not your love been. And if I had done so at that time with my heart, will, and thought, I would have passed all the knights that ever were in the Holy Grail except Sir Galahad, my son. And therefore, lady, since you have taken yourself to perfection, I must take myself to perfection, by all right. For by God, in you I have had my earthly joy, and if I had found you now so disposed, I had planned to have had you in my own kingdom. But since I find you thus disposed, I ensure you faithfully, I will take me to penance and pray while my life lasts."

230. *Ibid.*, p. 724. And so after midnight, before the day, the Bishop that was a hermit, as he lay in his bed asleep, fell into a great laughter. And with that all the fellowship awoke and came to the Bishop and asked him what was going on?

"A, Jesus mercy!" said the Bishop, "why did you wake me? I was never in all my life so merry and so well at ease."

"Why?" said Sir Bors.

"Truly," said the Bishop, "here was Sir Launcelot with me, with more angels than ever I saw men in one day. And I saw the angels heave up Sir Launcelot into heaven, and the gates of heaven opened before him . . ."

So when Sir Bors and his fellows came to his bed they found him stark dead; and he lay as if he were smiling, and the sweetest smell was about him that they ever smelled.

cam emonge prees of knyghtes, and thou was the meekest man and the jen-
tyllest that ever ete in halle emonge laydes, and thou were the sternest
knyght to thy mortal foo that ever put spere in the reeste."[231]

While it seems appropriate that Lancelot's eulogy is couched in chivalric
terms, and although we are glad that Lancelot has found mystical perfection as
well, the clash of ideals is hardly resolved. In order to obtain holy perfection,
Lancelot and Guinevere separate, never to rejoin in this life — or, no doubt, in
the next. That fact jars against the recollection that he was "the truest frende to
thy lovar."

Perhaps Malory thought he could have it both ways. While it is clear that
one can't be a lover in the chivalric sense while practicing the path to monastic
perfection, certain passages in Malory suggest an attempt at reconciling the
polarities between the monastery and the court. Adultery aside (an issue the text
doesn't seem much to care about), perhaps Malory is saying that the tragic flaw
in the love between Lancelot and Guinevere is in its one-sidedness, not its
nature. Lancelot's error, then, is not the act of loving itself, but the failure to
include a consideration for God in his love. This, at least, is what Lancelot seems
to mean by his confession during the Grail quest. He did battle for the queen's
love and to win worldly honor. He didn't care about whether he fought on the
side of right or wrong, and didn't battle for God's kingdom as the Knights
Templars of Bernard did:

> And all my grete dedis of armys that I have done for the most party was
> for the quenes sake, and for her sake wolde I do batayle were hit ryght
> other wronge. And never dud I batayle all only for Goddis sake, but for to
> wynn worship and to cause me the bettir to be beloved, and litill or nought
> I thanked never God of hit.[232]

Malory's "vertuouse love" is a properly subordinated dynamic: love God
first, your lady second. While he may not have been aware of the details of the

---

231. *Ibid.*, p. 725. "A, Launcelot!" he said, "you were the head of all Christian knights! And now I
dare say," said Sir Hector, "you Sir Launcelot, there you lie, that was never matched by any earthly
knight's hand. And you were the most courteous knight that ever bore shield! And you were the
truest friend to your lover that ever sat on horse, and you were the kindest man that ever came in the
press of knights, and you were the meekest man and the gentlest that ever ate in a hall among ladies,
and you were the sternest knight to your mortal foe that ever put spear in rest.
232. Malory, *Works*, p. 539. And all my great deeds of arms that I have done for the most part
were for the queen's sake, and for her sake would I do battle whether it was right or wrong. And
never did I battle all only for God's sake, but rather to win worship and to cause me the better to be
loved, and little or not at all did I ever thank God for it.

theological cross-currents that were inundating his text, Malory nonetheless argues for a synthesis of chivalry and holiness:

> Lat every man of worshyp florysh hys herte in thys worlde: firste unto God, and nexte unto the joy of them that he promysed hys feyth unto; . . . But firste reserve the honoure to God, and secondly thy quarell must come of thy lady. And such love I calle vertuouse love.[233]

Then, is holiness attainable without renouncing those personal attachments that chivalry so valued? The inclusion of the Grail quest in Malory's collection of Chivalric Romance tales illustrates the conflicts between monastic life and courtly life that were going on in his culture. Malory's definition of "vertuous love" seems to argue for a synthesis.

Malory hoped his work would have a redemptive effect on his readers, in love, if not theology. To hear and reflect on the tales of King Arthur's fellowship of the Round Table would temper and bring stability to the lovers who read his story, and bring to mind "olde jantylnes and olde servyse, and many kinde dedes that was forgotyn by neclygence." Malory treats love as if it were a divine blessing, written into the purposes of the seasons themselves. I leave this chapter with perhaps the most tender and poignant passage ever written about love, in Malory's own words:

> And thus hit passed on frome Candylmas untyl Easter, that the moneth of May was com, whan every lusty harte begynnyth to blossom and burgyne. For, lyke as trees and erbys burgenyth and florysshyth in May, in lyke wyse every lusty harte that is ony maner of lover spryngith, burgenyth, buddyth, and florysshyth in lusty dedis. For his gyvyth unto all lovers, that lusty moneth of May, in somthynge to constrayne hym to som maner of thynge more in that moneth than in ony other moneth, for dyverce causys: for than all erbys and treys renewyth a man and woman, and in lyke wyse lovers callyth to their mynde olde jantylnes and olde servyse, and many kynde dedes that was forgotyn by neclygence.
>
> For, lyke as wynter rasure dothe allway arace and deface grene summer, so faryth hit by unstable love in man and woman, for in many persones there ys no stabylite: for we may se all day, for a lytyll blaste of wyntres rasure, anone we shall deface and lay aparte trew love, for lytyll or nowght,

---

233. *Ibid.*, p. 648. Let every honorable man flourish his heart in this world: first unto God, and next the joy of them that he promised his faith unto; . . . But first reserve the honor to God, and secondly your concern must come of your lady. And such love I call virtuous love.

that coste muche thynge. Thys ys no wysdome nother no stabylite, but hit ys fyeblenes of nature and grete disworshyp, whosomever usyth thys. . . .

But nowadays men can nat love sevennyght but they muste have all their desyres. That love may nat endure by reson, for where they bethe sone accorded and hasty, heete sone keelyth. And ryght so faryth the love nowadayes, sone hote sone colde. Thys ys no stabylyte. But the olde love was nat so. For men and women coulde love togydirs seven yerys, and no lycoures lustis was betwyxte them, and than was love trouthe and faythefulnes. And so in lyke wyse was used such love in Kynge Arthurs dayes.

. . . And therefore all ye that be lovers, calle unto youre remembraunce the moneth of May, lyke as ded quene Gwenyver, for whom I make here a lytyll mencion, that while she lyved she was a trew lover, and therefor she had a good ende.[234]

---

234. *Ibid.*, pp. 648-649. And thus it passed from Candlemass until Easter, when the month of May had come, when every lusty heart begins to blossom and to burgeon. For, just as trees and herbs burgeon and flourish in May, in like wise every lusty heart that is any manner of lover springs, burgeons, buds, and flourishes in lusty deeds. For that lusty month of May gives to all lovers a prompting to something more than any other month for diverse causes: for then all herbs and trees renew a man and woman, and in like wise lovers call to their minds old gentleness and old service, and many kind deeds that were forgotten by negligence.

For, like as winter's devastation always erases and defaces green summer, so fairs it by unstable love in man and woman, for in many persons there is no stability: for we may see every day, for a little blast of winter's devestation, at once we shall deface and lay apart true love, for little or nothing, which costs dearly. This is no wisdom nor stability, but it is feebleness of nature and great dishonor whoever does this . . .

But nowadays men can not love seven nights but they must have all their desires. That love cannot endure by reason, for where they are soon and hastily satisfied, heat soon cools. And just so fairs love nowadays, soon hot, soon cold. This is no stability. But the old love was not so. For men and women could love each other seven years, and no lecherous lusts were between them, and then love was truth and faithfulness. And so in like wise was love exercised in King Arthur's days.

. . . And therefore all you who are lovers, call unto your mind the month of May, like as did Queen Guinevere, for whom I make here a little mention, that while she lived she was a true lover, and therefore she had a good end.

Chapter VI. A Crippled Attempt to Salvage Marriage and A Popular Movement Against It: Thomas Aquinas and *The Cloud of Unknowing*

Thomas Aquinas

In the thirteenth century, a giant arose from the ranks of the Dominican orders. His encyclopedia-length *Summa Theologica* laid the foundations for modern Catholicism — foundations which still hold today. He is Thomas Aquinas. Having spent most of his adult life in the Dominican monastery, Thomas was highly influenced by the Church Fathers. A thorough-going rationalist, Thomas is also the first Christian theologian to introduce Aristotle's ideas and methodologies into Christian thought. His *Summa Theologica* is a ponderous compendium of nearly all the philosophical and theological materials known in thirteenth-century Europe. In an age in which the monastery was touted as the only sure way of salvation, Thomas's theology attempts to provide a way of salvation for the man still involved in the affairs of the world. His *Supplement* to the *Summa Theologica* describes the way the grace of the Church operates through its system of sacraments: by receiving baptism, confirmation, holy Eucharist, and attending mass, an ordinary person still living outside of the monastery walls could obtain salvation. In his discussion of these sacraments, Thomas also includes the sacrament of marriage, the subject of our interest.

Thomas was progressive, for his era, in the way he treats marriage. For Thomas, one could marry and still achieve salvation — a considerably novel perspective in the Middle Ages. Holiness was considered incompatible with sexual love. In Thomas's system, though, marriage is allowed, and in this Thomas was ahead of his time.

But his heavy reliance on the theologians that preceded him make Thomas's attempts somewhat stilted. For one thing, love isn't an issue for him. As with the earlier theologians — and the genealogy can be traced all the way back to Plato — Thomas is primarily worried about the passion attending sexual intercourse. This concern leads to difficult conclusions for a modern reader.

Thomas opens his marriage text with a discussion of sex. Even before he defines marriage — definitions being necessary sooner or later in any good philosophical or theological discussion — Thomas enters into a discussion about the "marriage act," or sex; and all the passages we considered in Chapters 3 and 4 are brought into the discussion. We find St. Paul's 1 Corinthians 7 passage, Jerome's *Contra Jovinianus*, and Augustine's teaching that sex is always accompanied by shame.

Thomas considers a given question, such as, "Is sex always sinful?" He then lists a set of arguments to the positive, and another set of arguments to the contrary; then, he states his imperious, "I answer that. . . . " The passage concludes with rebuttals to the arguments opposing his conclusion. In his discussion of the "marriage act," Thomas begins with a citation from Paul: "They . . . who have wives, be as if they had none."[235] His second citation is the Old Testament passage in which the Israelites were about to see God on Mount Sinai. They were told to abstain from sex with their wives. In this passage, Thomas includes a reference to Jerome that says that the sex act separates man from God (recall Chapter 4). In his third proposition, he alludes to Augustine by stating that sex is always attended by a sense of shame. His fourth proposition is where he claims that the marriage act needs to be excused by the blessing of the ceremony — sex requires an excuse. We will look at this doctrine in greater detail below, when we consider the "marriage goods." Skipping his fifth proposition, Thomas's sixth proposition is the typical Platonic complaint that in sex the pleasure is so intense that it drives out reason, and whatever drives out reason can't be good; in fact, it must be sinful.

Thomas's response to this onslaught of complaints against the marriage act is remarkable. It is one of the very few times that we can sense a tone of passion in this extremely even-tempered theologian. He argues that nothing created by a

---

235. 1 Corinthians 7:29.

good God can be bad. Since sex is the means of reproducing the species, it cannot be always sinful:

> *I answer that,* If we suppose the corporeal nature to be created by the good God, we cannot hold that those things which pertain to the preserva-tion of the corporeal nature and to which nature inclines, are altogether evil; wherefore, since the inclination to beget an offspring . . . is from nature, it is impossible to maintain that the act of begetting children is altogether unlawful, . . . unless we suppose, as some are mad enough to assert, that corruptible things were created by an evil god, . . . wherefore this is a most wicked heresy.[236]

Thomas is well spoken in this rounding support for sex. But when he responds to the arguments that precede this statement, he is becomes a little problematic. Thomas begins well when he interprets Paul — "By these words the Apostle did not forbid the marriage act. . . . " So far, so good. But then Thomas adds that "he [Paul] forbade enjoyment" — Paul did not forbid sex, only enjoying sex. Thomas proceeds, haltingly, in his defense of the marriage act, considering whether it severs one from God. Grace, Thomas says, unites one with God and one receives grace with the marriage ceremony. Thus, married people are not cut off from God. But then he adds that those who deal with holy things have to be celibate — at least when they handle divine things or contemplate divinity. This is because the intensity of sexual pleasure distracts the mind from God:

> . . . a lawful occupation about lower things distracts the mind so that it is not fit for actual union with God; and this is especially the case in carnal intercourse wherein the mind is withheld by the intensity of pleasure. For this reason those who have to contemplate Divine things or handle sacred things are enjoined not to have to do with their wives for that particular time. . . .[237]

We can see the influence of Plato, transmitted through Augustine, in this passage. It is based on the idea that extreme pleasure is not Godly. Clearly, this is another manifestation of Plato's idea that reason is the only way to approach the imperishable world of Ideal Forms, now Christianized into God's kingdom. Of course, this Platonic idea is buttressed by the Old Testament passage stating

---

236. Thomas Aquinas, *Summa Theologica Supplement*, Volume III, *Summa Theologica*, trans. Fathers of the English Dominican Province (New York: Benziger Brothers, Inc., 1948), Question 41, article 3.
237. Thomas Aquinas, *Summa Theologica Suppliment*, Q. 41, Reply, Objection 2.

that the Israelites abstained from intercourse before God appeared on Mount Sinai; but a Christian differently disposed than a mystical Platonist would be able to respond differently. One could claim (as Paul and many other Christians do) that the Sinai event occurred under the Old Law. Christ's incarnation broke the Old Law and Christians are now under the New Law of Christ; Old Testament rules are no longer binding. But Thomas holds onto the teachings of Jerome, and states that those who administer divine things, i.e., priests and monks, must abstain from sex.

This medieval doctrine holds today in Modern Catholicism. Monks and nuns who are occupied with contemplation of God are celibate, as are priests, who administer the holy things of worship. Thomas follows Augustine verbatim when he talks about the shame attending all sexual acts. This shame is punishment for disobedience in the Garden of Eden.

> The shamefulness of concupiscence that always accompanies the marriage act is a shamefulness not of guilt, but of punishment inflicted for the first sin, inasmuch as the lower powers and the members do not obey reason.[238]

Once again, we see Plato's emphasis on reason, mediated as it is through the Church Fathers and Aristotle, on Thomas's doctrine of marriage.

Thomas is really concerned about sexual desire. We saw above his fear of losing reason in the sex act. But what about pleasure, itself? For Thomas, to intend to have sex for the sake of pleasure is always wrong. This is a given. His only worry is whether it is a "mortal sin" or a "venial sin." In discussing this point, Thomas makes an interesting distinction. He ponders how a man treats his wife. Does the man treat her like any other woman? Unfortunately, Thomas does not give us much to go on when he distinguishes an ordinary woman from a wife. But he does give us an inkling of the difference. It is a mortal sin to desire too much — as if one's wife were just another woman; it is only a venial sin to desire pleasure in one's wife, as a wife:

> Consequently the right answer to this question is that if pleasure be sought in such a way as to exclude the honesty of marriage, so that, to wit, it is not as a wife but as a woman that a man treats his wife, and that he is ready to use her in the same way if she were not his wife, it is a mortal sin; wherefore such a man is said to be too ardent a lover of his wife, because his

---

238. Aquinas, *Summa Theologica Suppliment*, Q. 41, Reply, Objection 3.

ardor carries him away from the goods of marriage. If, however, he seek pleasure within the bounds of marriage, so that it would not be sought in another than his wife, it is a venial sin.[239]

This passage is clear by reference to certain specific terms used by Thomas. If the lover's desire leads him beyond "the goods of marriage," then the lover wants pleasure only. This is a mortal (the worst) sin. One of the goods of marriage is the desire for children. For Thomas, this is the very purpose of marriage. To seek pleasure without the intention of procreation is a mortal sin; but to have sex with the intention of pleasure, even if it includes children as a side effect, is always at least a venial sin. And this is exactly what is behind modern Catholicism's refusal to accept birth control devices. Taking the possibility of procreation out of the sex act leaves only pleasure as the motive for engaging in sex.

As complex and mystifying as so much of Thomas's theology is, his definition of marriage is quite simple. Marriage is a joining of husband and wife for the purpose of begetting and raising children — just as business partners or soldiers unite to achieve their common goals:

> Now things directed to one purpose are said to be united in their direc-
> tion thereto, thus many men are united in one military calling or in pursu-
> ing one business, in relation to which they are called fellow-soldiers or
> business partners. Hence, since by marriage certain persons are directed to
> one begetting and upbringing of children, and again to one family life, it is
> clear that in matrimony there is a joining in respect of which we speak of
> husband and wife; and this joining, through being directed to some one
> thing, is matrimony; while the joining together of bodies and minds is a
> result of matrimony.[240]

Thus the intent to give birth to and raise children is matrimony, and the union of bodies and minds in marriage is a side issue.

In fact, women are created only as helpers to men in the creation of children. In Genesis 2:18, God creates a woman for Adam as "a helper fit for him." Thomas explains that women are not created to help man in areas other than childbirth, because another man would be more helpful, there. No, women were created to help man propagate the species:

---

239. *Ibid.*, Q. 49, Article 6.
240. *Ibid.*, Q. 44, Article 1.

I answer that, It was necessary for woman to be made, as the scripture says, as a helper to man; not, indeed as a helpmate in other works, as some say, since a man can be more efficiently helped by another man in other works; but as a helper in the work of generation.[241]

Hence women are defined chiefly as mothers:

... as Augustine says (Contra Faust. xix. 26), because a woman's sole purpose in marrying should be motherhood.
... Although the father ranks above the mother, the mother has more to do with the offspring than the father has. Or we may say that woman was made chiefly in order to be man's helpmate in relation to the offspring, whereas the man was not made for this purpose. Wherefore the mother has a closer relation to the nature of marriage than the father has.[242]

In this doctrine of Thomas, we can see the origin of the strong Catholic emphasis on the madonna image that so dominates Renaissance art and Catholic iconography. We can also see the influence of Genesis 3:16 and Ephesians 5, which state that the husband rules over his wife.

In Thomas's discussion of female subservience, he emphasizes the rational mind as the cause for man's superiority over women. Men are more rational than women, and therefore should predominate:

There is another kind of subjection ... whereby the superior makes use of his subjects for their own benefit and good . . . For the good of order would have been wanting in the human family if some were not governed by others wiser than themselves. So by such a kind of subjection woman is naturally subject to man, because in man the discernment of reason predominates.[243]

In our own time, this idea has had an interesting history. In the feminist movement of the 1960s, women were claiming to be equal in all areas to men. This was asserted to equalize power relations between the sexes. Today, however, feminist literature asserts a basic psychological difference between the sexes; today, the idea that women are more motivated by relationships and emotion more so than men are is accepted by some feminists. In this way, an

---

241. Thomas Aquinas, *Summa Theologica*, Q. 92, Article 1, in *Basic Writings of St. Thomas Aquinas*, edited by Anton C. Pegis, Vol. I, (New York: Random House, 1945), p. 879.

242. Aquinas, *Summa Theologica Supplement*, Q. 44, Article 2; Reply, Objection 1

243. Aquinas, *Summa Theologica*, Q. 92, Article 1, Reply, Objection 2, in *Basic Writings of St. Thomas Aquinas*, edited by Anton C. Pegis, Vol. I, p. 879.

agreement exists between Thomas's analysis of human nature and feminist literature. However, some feminists would disagree with Thomas's assertion that reason should predominate. Because the sexes approach life from differing perspectives and values, men and women should be equal in order to assure that a full humanity — rational and emotional — becomes socially instituted.

But besides producing children, another reason to have sex is discussed in the Summa Theologica Supplement. It is a fairly strange doctrine, called the "marriage debt"; it means that partners must "pay" the "debt" of sex to each other on demand as a part of their marriage contract. In becoming married, one loses the power over one's own body and yields that power up to one's partner. Thus, you have sex because you owe it to one another. In another progressive move, Thomas argues that paying the debt is more important than marital fidelity!

> Just as the marriage promise means that neither party is to have inter-course with a third party, so does it require that they should mutually pay the marriage debt. The latter is indeed the chief of the two, since it follows from the power which each receives over the other.[244]

This passage echoes 1 Corinthians 7:4, "For the wife does not rule over her own body, but the husband does; likewise the husband does not rule over his own body, but the wife does" (RSV).

Thus, there are actually two allowable ways to have sex: 1) with the intent to have children, and 2) with the intent of paying the debt:

> Consequently there are only two ways in which married persons can come together without any sin at all, namely in order to have offspring, and in order to pay the debt; otherwise it is always at least a venial sin.[245]

This gets a little confusing. You can pay your wife the debt, if it will help her from straying from her marital vows. But you can't make her pay you the debt to prevent you from straying:

> If a man intends by the marriage act to prevent fornication in his wife, it is no sin, because this is a kind of payment of the debt that comes under the good of *faith*. But if he intends to avoid fornication in himself, then there is a certain superfluity, and accordingly there is a venial sin.[246]

---

244. Aquinas, *Summa Theologica Supplement*, Q. 49, Article 2.
245. *Ibid.*, Q. 49, Article 5.
246. *Ibid.*, Q. 49, Article 5, Reply, Objection 2.

Only in marriage is the begetting of children proper. But Thomas is a rigorous enough theologian to ponder the nature of sex in and of itself. He asserts that the sex act is apparently the same between married and unmarried people, when considered as a biological act. But from a theological point of view, only married sex is allowable; sex outside of marriage is fornication and wrong.

> . . . the intercourse of fornication and that of marriage are of the same species as regards the species of nature. But the intercourse of fornication is wrong in itself.[247]

The difference is that one act has a mystical grace given to it by the marriage blessing in the Church. This grace permits the couple to perform the same actual sex act as the fornicator, but in such a way that it isn't sinful:

> Therefore, since in matrimony man receives by Divine institution the faculty to use his wife for the begetting of children, he also receives the grace without which he cannot becomingly do so.[248]

Thomas never gets over the problem of passion. He wants to argue for the validity of marriage, but in doing so he comes up against the wall of passion that Plato and the Church Fathers have condemned. To justify marriage in the face of passion, Thomas teaches that the married pair gets certain "goods" as compensation for the passion of sex. His overriding concern is the damage done to reason by passion, echoing Plato. In discussing this problem, we see yet another reference to 1 Corinthians 7, and to Thomas's beloved Aristotle.

> No wise man should allow himself to lose a thing except for some compensation in the shape of an equal or better good. Wherefore for a thing that has a loss attached to it to be eligible, it needs to have some good connected with it, which by compensating for that loss makes that thing ordinate and right. Now there is a loss of reason incidental to the union of man and woman, both because the reason is carried away entirely on account of the vehemence of the pleasure, so that it is unable to understand anything at the same time, as the Philosopher says (*Ethic.* Vii. 11); and again because of the tribulation of the flesh which such persons have to suffer from solicitude for temporal things (1 Cor. vii. 28). Consequently the choice of this union cannot be made ordinate except by certain compensations whereby

---

247. *Ibid.*, Q. 49, Article 1.
248. *Ibid.*, Q. 42, Article 3.

that same union is righted; and these are the goods which excuse marriage and make it right.[249]

Notice that Thomas thinks that sex needs to be excused. The marriage goods excuse sex. There are three goods: faith, offspring, and sacrament. Faith means that you remain faithful to your spouse. Offspring means that you have children. Sacrament is a somewhat complex doctrine. As we saw back in Chapter 3, in several Bible passages God's relationship with the people of Israel and with the Christian Church is compared to a marriage. In Thomas's doctrine, Christ's union with the Church is the source of the sacrament that comes with the marriage blessing. Marriage is a visible sign of the mystical connection of Christ and the Church. And since Christ is permanently united with the Church, so married couples must remain permanently married: "By sacrament we are to understand not only indivisibility, but all those things that result from marriage being a sign of Christ's union with the Church."[250]

Marriage is permanent, however, for earthly life only. The only excuse for marriage at all is to have children. Grace allows the couple to do this in a holy way. In the next life, one doesn't beget children; so there the marriage tie dissolves. Thomas supports this claim by citing Augustine and the familiar trick question in Matthew 22:30:

> According to Augustine (*De Bono Conj. ix*), marriage is a good of mortals, whereby in the resurrection *they shall neither marry nor be married* (Matth. xxii 30). Hence the marriage bond does not last after the life wherein it is contracted.[251]

In Thomas Aquinas' detailed and complex treatment of marriage, his preoccupation with sexual passion seems to preclude a discussion of love. Perhaps this is why King Arthur's knights were required to leave their ladies in the Grail Quest. The knights were united to their ladies primarily by love, not by the intent to have children. (At least, love is the leading plot motivation in Chivalric Romance literature.) Therefore, the knights were considered sinful by theologians like Thomas and by his predecessor, Bernard of Clairvaux. Is this what the hermit in the Romance of *Tristan* has in mind when he castigates Tristan and Yseut for their love for one another?

---

249. *Ibid.*, Q. 49, Article 1.
250. *Ibid.*, Q. 49, Article 2.
251. *Ibid.*, Q. 49, Article 3, Reply, Objection 3.

Exiles, what great suffering love forces on you! How long will this madness last? You have been leading this life for too long, and I beg of you to
repent.[252]

But in a society still dominated by the cloister, a society in which the
teachings of Bernard of Clairvaux were still fresh, a society suspicious of life
outside the walls of the monastery, Thomas Aquinas was progressive. He
justified the life of those who lived in the secular world. His doctrines are still
normative for modern Catholicism. His insistence on childbirth as the primary
definition for marriage is the reason why modern Catholics are not allowed birth
control. And present-day priests, monks and nuns must remain celibate due to
the Old Testament account of the Mount Sinai appearance of God, coupled with
the Platonic notion that passion disrupts the rationality necessary to unite the
mind with God. Still, although highly restricted and austere from a modern point
of view, Thomas does argue for married life. He states that one can live in the
world, married, and still receive the grace necessary for salvation. Although he
might appear restrictive to a modern reader, he was probably a breath of fresh air
to those living in the Middle Ages.

The Cloud of Unknowing

The generation that followed Thomas Aquinas and his fellow scholastics
saw a reaction against their rigorous scholarship. A drive arose that emphasized
the heart over the head. Simple devotion to God through love was taught by an
influential Parisian theologian named Jean Gerson.[253] He emphasized the works
of the ancient Church Fathers, as well as Augustine's *Confessions* and *City of God*,
Bernard of Clairvaux's *Commentary on Song of Songs*, as well as the meditational
work of a mystic named Richard of St. Victor. From this assortment of texts one
can see the monastic emphasis of Gerson's curriculum. Although he taught from
books drawn from the Christian tradition, Gerson's emphasis was anti-
scholastic. He favored turning within one's self to find God in one's own heart.

He taught in an age that had grown thirsty for monastic ideals. Even among
ordinary people who hadn't taken monastic vows, a desire for monastic life
arose. A certain Gerard Groote founded quasi-monastic a lay-movement called

252. Beroul, *The Romance of Tristan*, (New York: Penguin Books, 1970), p. 99.
253. Steven Ozment, *The Age of Reform, 1250-1550* (New Haven: Yale UP, 1980), pp.73-78.

the Modern Devotion.[254] Groote himself was not ordained. He reportedly refused ordination out of humility. Large numbers of laymen joined this movement which taught poverty, celibacy, and obedience. Thus among the clergy and the laity, a return to the monastery and the desire for a personal relationship with God was in the air.

It was in this climate that a highly popular text on spirituality was written — *The Cloud of Unknowing*. It is significant that this text is written in Middle English and not Latin; this indicates that it was intended for common laymen and women who couldn't read Latin. Indeed, the text itself says that it is intended for someone who has been engaged in a practical occupation before attempting the contemplative life.

> I have in mind a person who, over and above the good works of the active life, has resolved to follow Christ (as far as is humanly possible with God's grace) into the inmost depths of contemplation. Do your best to determine if he is one who has first been faithful for some time to the demands of the active life, for otherwise he will not be prepared to fathom the contents of this book.[255]

The *Cloud of Unknowing* is based on a Platonic form of contemplation which was mediated to Christianity by a mystic named Dionysius the Areopagite and by Gregory of Nyssa (whom we have already looked at in Chapter 3). As in Plato and in Gregory, in the *Cloud of Unknowing* God utterly transcends everything in the created world:

> And so I say again to anyone who wants to become a real contemplative like Mary [Magdalene, see below], let the wonderful transcendence and goodness of God teach you humility. . . . Attend more to the wholly other-ness of God rather than to your own misery. . . . Whoever possesses God, as this book attests, needs nothing else in this life.[256]

Like Plato's philosophy, the primary driving force that propels one to union with the divine is love. Love drives one upward over the rungs of the ladder of love to union with God himself. As in Plato, to rise up this ladder one must

---

254. *Ibid.* p.96.

255. *The Cloud of Unknowing* trans. William Johnston (Garden City, New York: Image Books, 1973) p. 43.

256. *The Cloud of Unknowing*, p. 79.

relinquish all attachments to created beings and devote one's love to God alone. All created things, all creatures, are to be covered behind a "cloud of forgetting":

> You are to concern yourself with no creature whether material or spiritual nor with their situation and doings whether good or ill. To put it briefly, during this work you must abandon them all beneath the *cloud of forgetting.*[257]

Friend or foe, family or stranger — all go in order to fix the mind on God alone.

> . . . during the time of this work a real contemplative does not dwell on the thought of any person in particular, neither friend, enemy, stranger, nor kin. For he who desires to become perfect in this work must forget about everything except God.[258]

In this contemplative work, cognitive thought is also to be abandoned. This is a counter-attack on the generation of rigorous theological scholarship preceding this book. The follower of *The Cloud of Unknowing* approaches God with a non-rational, naked love alone. "A naked intent toward God, the desire for him alone, is enough."[259] Suspicious of academic approaches to theology, this text also discourages reason. Mary Magdalene forgets everything "material and spiritual" except love alone:

> Therefore, she [Mary Magdalene] fastened her love and longing on to that *cloud of unknowing* and learned to love him without seeing him in the clear light of reason or feeling his presence in the sensible light of devotion. So absorbed did she become in love that often she forgot whether she had been sinner or innocent. Yes, and I think that she became so enamored of the Lord's divinity that she scarcely noticed the beauty of his human presence as he sat there before her, speaking and teaching. From the Gospel account it would seem that she became oblivious of everything both material and spiritual.[260]

The Bible reference that the writer alludes to is in Luke 10:38-42. Two sisters receive Jesus into their home. One, Martha, scurries around busily serving

---

257. *Ibid.*, p. 53.
258. *Ibid.*, p. 81.
259. *Ibid.*, p. 56.
260. *Ibid.*, p. 70.

their guest. Mary simply sits at Christ's feet listening to him talk. When Martha complains that she is doing all the work, Jesus responds that "Mary has chosen the good part" (RSV). In the history of Christianity, Martha is often compared to those outside the monastery who are busily engaged in worldly things. Mary is compared to the monastic who contemplates God full-time.

In another place, the text teaches its followers to avoid intellectualizing and academic argument:

> If you want to gather all your desire into one simple word that the mind can easily retain, choose a short word rather than a long one. A one-syllable word such as "God" or "love" is best. But choose one that is meaningful to you. . . . If your mind begins to intellectualize over the meaning and connotations of this little word, remind yourself that its value lies in its simplicity. Do this and I assure you these thoughts will vanish. Why? Because you have refused to develop them with arguing.[261]

This method of meditation is analogous to certain Eastern practices in which a single word, such as "Om," or a short phrase called a "koan," is repeated by the devotee. While a direct influence is not likely, this practice may point to a commonality in mysticism that developed in widely different cultures.

Sometimes, *The Cloud of Unknowing* seems to use erotic language. Cupid's arrows of love are employed in one passage. "Yes, beat upon that thick *cloud of unknowing* with the dart of your loving desire and do not cease come what may" (55). In another, what is called a "sweet love" between Mary Magdalene and Jesus recalls the Chivalric Romances:

> Sweet was the love between Mary and Jesus. How she loved him! How much more he loved her! Do not take the Gospel account lightly as if it were some superficial tale. It depicts their relationship in utter truth. Reading it, who could fail to see that she loved him intensely, withholding nothing of her love and refusing the comfort of anything less than his in return.[262]

Despite its erotic language all particular relationships, such as that between lover and beloved are to be left behind in the work of radical contemplation of God. As with Plato, God is utterly transcendent in *The Cloud of Unknowing*. The whole material world — and the whole spiritual world, for that matter — is below God and needs to be covered in the cloud of unknowing. But

---

261. *Ibid.*, p. 56.
262. *Ibid.*, p. 77.

unlike Plato, all cognitive thought is also to be relinquished. The mystic who wrote *The Cloud of Unknowing* had to overcome the heavy scholarship that developed during the time of Thomas Aquinas. He did so by denouncing reason and academic argument. But the writer retains the Platonic use of love. Human love is transformed into a purely contemplative force impelling the devotee upward from Earth and heaven to God alone. Covering friend, family and every other created thing beneath the cloud of unknowing, the mystic abandons those personal attachments that the Romance writers so valued.

We are back to the original problem of Chapter One: Daphnis and Chloe versus Plato. In his own stilted way Thomas Aquinas attempted to reconcile spiritual salvation with the bonds of matrimony. The author of *The Cloud of Unknowing* wants to undo the work of schoolmen like Thomas, and return devotees to the world-renouncing way of life taught by Bernard of Clairvaux. And like Bernard, the author of *The Cloud of Unknowing* wants all people to devote themselves to the monastic life.

Against the millennia of opposition to Romance, the Reformers of the sixteenth century came out swinging. Given the entrenched ideas they had to overcome, the language of the Reformers is particularly strong. The Reformation is an exciting chapter in the evolution of love.

CHAPTER VII. THE ROMANCERS STRIKE BACK: MARTIN LUTHER, SIR EDMUND SPENSER, AND THE PURITANS

By the time the Renaissance dawned, certain portions of Christendom had had it with the doctrines of Platonic Christianity. The Protestant Reformers fought against the notion that only in celibacy could one reach God. But even as the Reformers sought to revise doctrines about celibacy, in literature the unbridled wildness of Ovid and the Chivalric tradition was nervously revised. Spenser's *Faerie Queene* draws on both Ovid and the Chivalric traditions, but revises them by mixing in Aristotle and Cicero's doctrines of philosophical friendship. In the seventeenth century, the Puritan movement in England softened much of the rhetoric of the early Reformers. In the Puritans, love and tenderness find a place in the theology of Romantic Love.

What's Love Got To Do with It — Martin Luther

When he's wound up, Luther can be fun. He gets particularly riled when he is arguing against monastic institutions that insist on celibacy:

> But our monastics, who neither pray nor learn God's Word but torture themselves with the regulations of men and murmur and howl in the choir, they would do better to tend pigs as married people.[263]

In another place, Luther calls those who argue against marriage "smart alecks and sophisticates, that is, the principal fools and blind men in the sight of God."[264] Their writings amount to nothing more than "foolish scribbling and screeching."[265] These writers should "shut their blasphemous mouths."[266]

Luther is not afraid to name names: "Of this kind is that arch-fool, Johann Schmid of Constance, that renowned whoremonger. . . ."[267] Luther finds their writings shameful:

> If I were chastity herself, I could think of no greater and more unbearable shame and disgrace than to be praised by such rascals, whoremongers, and enemies of chastity.[268]

Luther thinks that Schmid has nothing substantial to teach — "as if this ass must first teach us what every village peasant knows."[269] In the face of God's Word, writers like Schmid,

> . . . would like to teach us according to their own famed sagacity and contrary to God that all women should be strangled or banished [!]. This would make a fine fool of God: what He does is no good; what we do is well done.[270]

As the earliest of the Reformers, Luther had to wrestle with his own feelings as well as with Church doctrine. Luther was the first of the Protestant reformers to argue against the institution of monasticism, which had become a dominant force in the high Middle Ages (see Chapter Five and Six). In this respect Luther makes a fascinating study of attempts to moderate the harsh Church doctrines we looked at in Chapter Four. Luther seeks a way to appropriately channel the sexual desire that seems innate in humanity.

Luther's writings on sexuality are sometimes contradictory, reflecting Luther's own personal growth and development. Also, much of what Luther has to say on sexuality is in response to specific occasions and specific questioners.

263. Martin Luther, 'Commentary on 1 Corinthians 7' in *Luther's Works*, Vol. I, Hilton C. Oswald, ed. (Saint Louis: Concordia Publishing House, 1973), p. 53.
264. Martin Luther, "Commentary on 1 Corinthians 7," p. 5.
265. *Ibid.*
266. *Ibid.*, p. 6.
267. *Ibid.*, pp. 5-6.
268. *Ibid.*, p. 6.
269. *Ibid.*
270. *Ibid.*

Luther's statements about sexuality have an unsystematic quality; they generally fall under two categories: sexuality as a religious institution; and sexuality as a biological drive. Love is also addressed, when specific questions involving love are asked. But one comes away from Luther with the feeling that love is not his central concern. Instead, what we frequently find in Luther is an observation from human nature concerning the sex drive. For most of us, there is little choice — "women must be used either for marriage or for fornication."[271]

Luther began his career as a monk. It must have taken considerable courage for the friar to evolve out of his early vocation and come to oppose the values he was taught. This evolution can especially be seen in Luther's developing ideas about sexuality. He tells us that when he was younger, "marriage was considered so infamous on account of impious and impure celibacy that I thought I could not think about married life without sin."[272] It is easy to understand this sexual guilt, given Luther's early life in the monastery. He comments on a very strange practice that the Franciscans observed bordering on a fear or perhaps even disgust for women:

> Nay, if ever some honest matron or virgin passed through the cemetery of the Franciscans, the friars quickly swept the holy place with brooms and purged it with fire. A most disgraceful performance, implying contempt of our Creator! After all, women are our mothers. And the flame of evil lust, derived from original sin, cannot be put out with brooms or fire. By this method it is only stirred up and irritated the more.[273]

Luther was strongly interested in revising people's understanding of marriage and celibacy. Since he was the first to attempt a modification of the Church's strong stance on monasticism, much of his writing compares those two institutions. One of his principal concerns is that those who are supposed to practice celibacy do not:

> They rail against us, charging that we are enemies of chastity and pro-moters of marriage who prefer to see men married; and we are to consider them extremely wise, though they cannot but devote themselves to inces-sant fornication and though they praise chastity with their pens only and defame the married state.[274]

---

271. *Ibid.*

272. Martin Luther, *What Luther Says*, Compiled by Ewald M. Plass, Vol. II (Saint Louis: Concordia Publishing House), #2771.

273. Luther *What Luther Says*, #2775.

Priestly fornication was so common that in Mansfeld, Germany, a law was passed in 1512 requiring distinctive clothing "for all the women of priests and other public and common prostitutes."[275] Hence, it became clear to Luther that the sex drive could not be suppressed by most humans. And as he puts it, "whoever does not feel that he has that precious quality [of celibacy] but rather is inclined to fornication, he is commanded to marry."[276]

Human nature drives one to sexual fulfillment, and this is holy only in marriage. There are many reasons for marriage, including, as we will see, the desire for children, but Luther's primary teaching is that need demands it: "But St. Paul gives but this one reason . . . namely, need. Need commands it."[277] The need to procreate is natural, so Luther speaks of the origins of marriage in Nature:

> Nature will express itself, fructify, and multiply, and God does not want this outside marriage, and so everyone because of this need must enter into marriage if he wants to live with a good conscience and in favor with God.[278]

Recognizing the strength of the sex drive leads Luther to compare sexual relations to other bodily functions.

> The spirit permits the body its ways and natural functions, so that it eats, drinks, sleeps, and eliminates like any other human body.
> Therefore mankind is not deprived of its male or female form, members, seed, and fruit, so that the body of a Christian must fructify and multiply just like that of other human beings, birds, and all the animals, as it was created by God to do according to Gen. 1:28.[279]

Luther makes a particularly humorous comparison to bodily functions when championing the sex drive. For Luther, it is impossible to stop up the natural sex drive by simply commanding it from the pulpit. To show how futile such a command is, Luther describes a man who tried to stop urinating. He made

---

274. Luther, "Commentary on 1 Corinthians 7," in *Works*, Vol. I, p. 6.
275. Luther, *What Luther Says*, #2778, n. 8.
276. Luther *Works*, p. 9.
277. *Ibid.*, p. 27.
278. *Ibid.*
279. *Ibid.*, p. 26.

it four days before he became quite ill and wished for death. Ultimately, he was talked out of his senseless mortification of the flesh. So it is for teachers who tell people to refrain from marriage. Luther makes his point again, by a similarly earthy metaphor:

> Still there is none so miserable who, if he were ordered to hold his urine or excrement, would not rather choose the state he was in rather than accept such an impossible order; but since nobody is bound by such an order, nobody pays attention to the benefits and delight of elimination.[280]

The burning of passion is quenched for those who marry and they give no thought to the pain of unexpressed passion. But the poor celibate who has not the special gift for celibacy is like the miserable man mentioned above! "The former must hold what cannot be held, and do it all for nothing and waste all the bitter effort — that is indeed a terrible pity!"[281] No, for Luther the sex drive is like any other bodily function:

> If a girl is not sustained by great and exceptional grace, she can live without a man as little as she can without eating, drinking, sleeping, and other natural necessities. Nor, on the other hand, can a man dispense without a wife. The reason for this is that procreating children is an urge planted as deeply in human nature as eating and drinking. That is why God has given and put into the body the organs, arteries, fluxes, and everything that serves it. Therefore what is he doing who would check this process and keep nature from running its desired and intended course? He is attempting to keep nature from being nature, fire from burning, water from wetting, and a man from eating, drinking, and sleeping.[282]

Thus, Luther holds that the sex drive is implanted in our bodies like other natural functions. This doctrine introduces a theological point: marriage is a remedy for sin. Humans are driven to sexual gratification. The only proper outlet for this drive is marriage. But one wants gratification alone, not necessarily only in marriage. Any other way than marriage is the sin of fornication or adultery. Since marriage prevents these unholy expressions of sexuality, marriage is considered a remedy for sin. In discussing marriage as a remedy for sin, Luther's

---

280. *Ibid.*, p. 30.
281. *Ibid.*
282. Luther, *What Luther Says*, #2777.

medieval background surfaces. He describes a seething caldron of evil desire. Our flesh is diseased and marriage is the medicine for that disease.

> According to the spirit he has no need of marriage. But because his flesh is the common flesh, corrupted in Adam and Eve and filled with evil desires, therefore because of this very disease, marriage is a necessity for him and it is not in his power to get along without it. For his flesh rages, burns, and fructifies just like that of any other man, unless he helps and controls it with the proper medicine, which is marriage.[283]

Luther's medieval background surfaces in another way. He appears to hold on to the dogma that we saw earlier in St. Augustine. The sexual passion we feel is a result of Adam's original sin. In the Garden of Eden, one would not have felt the passions we now experience. For Luther, it would have been more delightful to live without sexual passion:

> In Paradise marriage would have been most delightful. The heat and fury of sexual desire would not have been so intense there; flesh and blood would have been different. . . . Our original sin, which has defiled and ruined our entire human nature, is to blame for this.[284]

While Luther in several places states that procreation is the best reason for entering the married state, he also allows it as a remedy, as mentioned above.

> But if you cannot without sin abstain from uniting with a woman, then make use of the remedy which God points out to you. And if you do not seek to become a father, seek at least a remedy against sin that you may avoid fornication and adultery, pollutions, and irregular satisfaction of evil desires.[285]

Thus, marriage is a medicine for the fornications, adulteries, and other perverse desires of those who cannot restrain themselves from sexual activity. Our society has recently witnessed appalling consequences of attempts to stop up the sex drive by priests who don't possess the rare capacity of celibacy. In the Boston Archdiocese, at least 24 priests have been accused of no fewer than 250

---

283. Luther, *Works*, p. 26.
284. Luther, *What Luther Says*, #2799.
285. *Ibid.*, #2803.

cases of pedophilia, sexual abuse on a minor, sexual assault, rape, and adultery.[286] In response to the Boston Archdiocese scandal, at least 325 priests across the country have been dismissed or have resigned.[287] Are these not examples of Luther's "pollutions and irregular satisfaction of evil desires" that he so feared from those attempting to repress the natural sex drive without the grace of celibacy?

Writing in a time period in which monastic institutions held a strong influence on popular thought, Luther affirms the value of monastic practices. Luther says that celibacy is a noble institution — if you can restrain yourself from sex without any difficulty. "The man who has the gift to live chastely without a wife is an angel on Earth and enjoys a quiet life." [288]

It becomes extremely difficult to try to pin Luther down on the issue of celibacy as compared with marriage. In some places, he speaks so highly of the life of contemplation — the life of the monks and nuns — that he seems to prefer it over marriage. In other places, Luther plainly prefers marriage. It would appear that Luther is trying to hold on to both vocations, and that his preference runs with whatever vocation he is writing about at the time. A sample of a few statements will show Luther's ambiguity.

At one point he says that marriage is better than celibacy:

> Still one must not deny that before God a married woman is better than a virgin, although a married woman has much labor and trouble here on Earth, and the virgin much happiness, ease, and comfort.[289]

Then, in the same essay, he says that virginity and marriage are equal in the eyes of God. But this claim is made after stating that virginity is nobler than marriage:

---

286. "Predator Priests." Boston Globe Online 9 May, 2003 http://www.boston.com/globe/spotlight/abuse/predators; "Records on 10 clergy released." Boston Globe Online 9 May, 2003 http://www.boston.com/globe/spotlight/abuse/stories4/013103_records.htm; Michael Rezendes and Matt Carroll, "More abuse records released." Boston Globe Online 11 February, 2003. 9 May, 2003. http://www.boston.com/globe/spotlight/abuse/stories4/021103_records.htm.

287. Margaret Stafford, "Priests struggle with fallout from sex abuse crisis," *Naples Daily News* 10 May, 2003, 11A

288. Luther, *What Luther Says*, #2769.

289. Luther, *Works*, p. 11.

For when one compares marriage and virginity, then of course chastity is a nobler gift than marriage. Nevertheless, marriage is just as much a gift of God . . . as chastity is. . . . Therefore marriage and virginity are equal before Him, for both are a divine gift, even though, when compared, one is better than the other.[290]

Finally, in the same essay, again, Luther suggests that the contemplative life of prayer is "more pleasing to God" than a life filled with the cares of the world. In this part of the essay, Luther's monastic experience seems to stay with him. He admits that a life given up to continual prayer and meditation on God's Word — i.e., the life of monks and nuns — is a better life than one immersed in the affairs of the world.

Here we see another fruit and use of chastity on Earth: that one may better please the Lord. . . [O]ne should, in a blameless way, attend to the Word of God, read daily, pray, act, and preach as Paul advises Timothy. For a married man cannot give himself up entirely to reading and praying but is, as St. Paul says, "divided"; that is, he must devote much of his time to making life agreeable for his wife, and like Martha,[291] he is bound up in the multitude of concerns demanded by married life. An unmarried person is undivided by such concerns and can give himself entirely to God.[292]

Here, it appears that Luther still thinks that the contemplative life is superior to the life of worldly business. Missing here is the idea we saw in Daphnis and Chloe, in which married life fulfils God's design. Luther does not seem to grant divine status to the actual love between married partners. Here, he seems to think that the life of contemplation — praying and attending to the Word of God — is more noble:

But the apostle does not want to condemn the married estate on this account. For he does not say that the married man is anxious only about the affairs of this world, or is separated from God. He says only that he is divided and is anxious about many affairs and cannot constantly pray or attend to the Word of God; although his work and care is good, still it is much better to be free to pray and attend to God's Word. In so doing the

---

290. *Ibid.*, p. 16.

291. The reference here is to the New Testament story from Luke 10:38-42 that we looked at in the previous chapter. Martha was busy serving Jesus, and the Christian tradition compares her to life in the world. Mary sat at Jesus' feet and listened and the tradition compares her to the contemplative life of monks and nuns.

292. Luther, *Works*, p. 53.

unmarried person is of much use and comfort to many people, yes, to all of Christendom, and this reason is great and noble enough to keep everyone from marrying who has the grace to remain single.[293]

It is difficult indeed to argue for the value of marriage, if contemplation is nobler. But Luther does just that. After all this praise of contemplation, does Luther view marriage as a religious institution? His answer depends on the context in which the question is asked.

Luther's inconsistency stems from the fact that much of his discussion about marriage is in response to the institution of celibacy. And when Luther compares marriage to the "religious orders" — that is, monks, nuns, and priests — marriage comes out looking very good. Compared with those so-called "religious orders," marriage is "heavenly, spiritual, and godly."[294] Before Luther, marriage was called "secular" and the other orders "religious." But Luther reverses these designations:

> . . . let us look a bit further and show that matrimony is the most reli-
> gious state of all, and that it is unjust and wrong to refer to others as "reli-
> gious orders" while calling marriage a "secular order." It should be just the
> reverse, that marriage should be called the real religious order, as in truth it
> is, and these other orders should be called the real secular orders, which in
> truth they are.[295]

Contrary to the statements on the contemplative life that we saw above, Luther claims that marriage brings one into a state of faith, the highest religious condition in his theology:

> . . . marriage is of such a kind that it drives, impels, and forces men to the
> most inward, highest spiritual state, to faith. And there is no higher or more
> inward state than faith, for it depends solely on God's Word and is naked
> and divested of all that is not God's Word.[296]

If one could hold just that one statement, all would be well. But there are problems with it: 1) at another point he reverses himself; and 2) his reasoning is unconvincing. What got him to this conclusion was the consideration that in this world one has many problems. It requires faith to trust that all will be well

---

293. *Ibid.*
294. *Ibid.*, p. 20.
295. *Ibid.*, p. 17.
296. *Ibid.*, p. 19.

in the end. Hence, his conclusion is based on the problems of living on Earth, and not a consideration of any spiritual qualities that are bound up in the institution of marriage itself. The consideration of problems on Earth associated with marriage is what leads Luther at another point to deny its spiritual nature:

> Surely, no one can deny that marriage is an external, a secular, affair, subject to secular government, as are clothing, food, house and home. . . . Nor do I find any instance in the New Testament in which Christ or the apostles interested themselves in such matters.[297]

A number of citations could be produced on both sides of this issue, but these two define well enough Luther's ambiguity on this issue.

There is one point on which Luther does seem consistent. That is his claim that the essential purpose of marriage is to bring children into the world. In this, Luther agrees with Thomas Aquinas, with children as one of the marriage "goods" that justify the institution (see Chapter Five).

> The first class of married people is made up of those who are looking for children and enter upon this way of life in order to become parents; . . . These people are actually angels in comparison with others. . . . The second class is made up of those who take wives in order to avoid fornication. They are not averse to children, nor do they hate them. But their principal purpose for getting married is to live a chaste and decent life. These, too, are good people; but they are not the equals of those in the first class. . . .
> The third class is made up of those who desire wives for the sake of pleasure only . . . and want to have a pretty girl with whom they may amuse themselves.[298]

We may be fairly safe to conclude that Luther's overall position is that marriage is a holy institution for the sake of childbirth:

> This is a true definition of marriage: Marriage is the God-appointed and legitimate union of man and woman in the hope of having children or at least for the purpose of avoiding fornication. . . .[299]

Luther even applied this measuring stick to himself — "For it is a great gift of God to expect and desire only children from my wife."[300]

297. Luther, *What Luther Says*, #2764.
298. *Ibid.*, #2800.
299. *Ibid.*, #2761.

But this somewhat narrow definition of marriage does not stop Luther from giving marriage his highest blessing, calling it a "matter of divine seriousness":

> Therefore God has also most richly blessed this estate above all others and, in addition, has made everything in the world serve it and depend on it that this estate might without fail be well and amply provided for. Hence married life is . . . a splendid institution and a matter of divine seriousness.[301]

Luther even calls the marital estate the most precious institution on Earth, since its purpose is to bring new children into Christian faith:

> The best thing in married life . . . is the fact that God gives children and commands us to bring them up to serve Him. To do this is the noblest and most precious work on Earth, because nothing may be done which pleases God more than saving souls.[302]

Neither does Luther leave love out of the picture, although it does not dominate his discussion. At times, Luther sounds like a Romance writer. He describes the plaintive love of a young girl who has been compelled to live in a convent:

> And of what help is it to a girl to shut her up so that she neither sees nor hears a man, when her heart sighs day and night, without ceasing, for a young man?[303]

Luther is quite a Romantic when he praises married love. He is capable of lavish descriptions:

> Conjugal love excels all other love. The love toward one's spouse burns like a fire and seeks nothing but the person of the spouse. It says: I do not desire what is yours; I desire neither silver nor gold, neither this nor that; I desire you yourself; I want you entirely or not at all. All other love seeks something else than the person of the loved one. Conjugal love alone wants the entire person of the loved one himself.[304]

---

300. *Ibid.*, #2800.
301. *Ibid.*, #2767.
302. *Ibid.*, #2836.
303. Luther, *Works*, p. 10.
304. Luther, *What Luther Says*, #2818.

Luther, then, represents one of the attempts to harmonize the two categories of love we have been looking at. But can he? The presuppositions involved in each category argue against one another. This may be one reason for Luther's ambiguity on the issues of marriage, celibacy, and love. If constant prayer and contemplation of the Word of God is the highest life, then marriage certainly drags one down from the Platonic Christian heights. He doesn't seem to say, as Longus does, that the acts of interpersonal love are divine in and of themselves. But Luther does go on to say that the love of marriage excels all other love, and God has "richly blessed this estate above all others." If marriage is blessed above all others, wouldn't this cast a pall on celibate contemplation? Luther thinks he can have it both ways. Each is a gift. Much of this ambiguity must be the result of Luther's own personal evolution as he moves from monk to Protestant Reformer. Perhaps if Luther had lived in another time, and had fewer salient theological issues to combat, he would have been one of the great romancers like Longus. Perhaps he is, after all.

Sir Edmund Spenser's Faerie Queene

In the days of Queen Elizabeth, Sir Edmund Spenser wrote a massive epic Romance poem about knights, ladies, magicians, beasts, and castles: the Faerie Queene. Even as Luther attempted to reform Romance doctrines in the Church, Spenser attempted to rework literary Romance themes. There are seven books in his epic and all but one allegorically treat a virtue. The knights, ladies, magicians, beasts, and castles are all symbolic of six virtues: holiness, temperance, chastity, friendship, justice, and courtesy. In this epic poem, love and chastity are frequent themes, and Spenser's treatment is extremely complex. Characters abound, and their many stories interweave with each other as the epic unfolds.

Stylistically, *The Faerie Queene* is like a Chivalric Romance (with jousts, battles, giants, sorcerers, and, of course, ladies and their knights) but the epic was written after the age of chivalry, so the knightly trappings of Spenser's epic are primarily stylistic. Spenser is at great pains to adapt and rework the love stories that precede him. He borrows extensively from Ovid for imagery and characters. Each book of *The Faerie Queene* is based on a story from Ovid's Metamorphosis. And being a Romance epic, Venus and Cupid appear as actual characters in the poem. Spenser also borrows themes from the Chivalric Romance period that preceded him.

But Spenser is uncomfortable with the wild passion of both Ovid and Chivalric Romance. By means of his characters, stories, and allegories Spenser seeks to rework the way love has been treated. He does this specifically through the characters of two books: "Book III: The Legend of Britomartis, or of Chastitie," and "Book IV: The Legend of Cambel and Telamond, or of Friendship."

In Book III, love is distinguished from lust through a number of ways. One way is by a literary replacement of Ovid's imagery with Spenser's own Elizabethan imagery. This can be seen in the creation of the primary character, Amoret. Her name is derived from the Latin word for love, Amor. Amoret is conceived and born by a miraculous process. Her mother, Chrysogone, falls asleep in the forest. The sun beats down on her and the sunbeams conceive Amoret miraculously in Chrysogone's womb. Significantly, when Spenser mentions the sun-god whose rays penetrate the womb, he doesn't use the lustful god Apollo (who pursued nymphs and mortals in his lustful heat). The sun is called by the name of the older god, Titan. In another miracle, Chrysogone falls asleep again and gives birth without pain. We can see a Platonic avoidance of passion in this birth account. Amoret was conceived without sexual pleasure:

> Unawares she them conceiv'd, unawares she bore:
> She bore withouten pain, that she conceived
> Withouten pleasure. . . .[305]

To retain the mythical image of love, but to distinguish his own character from Ovid's, Spenser has Amoret raised by Venus. The connection with Ovidian love is retained by including his goddess of love, but is broken through the use of his own literary creation in Amoret.

In the course of the narrative, Amoret is captured by a sorcerer named Busyrane who tries by magic to obtain her love. The sorcerer's castle is filled with Ovidian imagery. The symbolism is clear — Ovid's type of love is a form of sorcery. The castle is surrounded by flames, a symbol of lust. The connection with Ovid is made in two major ways: by means of an embroidered tapestry, and by means of a pageant (actually an old dance called a masque). The walls of Busyrane's castle are covered by a tapestry that illustrates all the amorous escapades of Ovid's gods and men. This tapestry relies on Ovid's book The

---

305. Spenser, *Poetical Works*, (Oxford: Oxford UP, 1983), Book III, C. vi, 27.

Metamorphosis. All the acts of love depicted on the tapestry are considered Cupid's work; he made war on the gods to enlarge his empire.

> And in those Tapets [tapestries] weren fashioned
> Many faire pourtraicts, and many a faire feate,
> And all of love, and all of lusty-hed,
> As seemed by their semblaunt did entreat;
> And eke all Cupids warres they did repeate,
> And cruell battles, which he whilome fought
> Gainst all the Gods, to make his empire great;
> Besides the huge massacres, which he wrought
> On mighty kings and kesars [caesars], into thralldom brought.[306]

The list of characters on the tapestry is impressive and shows Spenser's knowledge of Ovid, even as it shows how gigantic Cupid's empire is. It begins with Jove (Jupiter) and the various animals he assumed to rape Helle, Europa, Danae, Leda, Semelee, Alcmena, Asterie, and others. The tapestry then proceeds to list Apollo's conquests: Daphne, Hyacynth, Coronis, Climene, and Isse. Then Neptune's exploits are listed; then Saturn's. Finally, in a comment to illustrate just how cruel Cupid is, Spenser says that the god didn't even spare his own mother: "Ne did he spare (so cruell was the Elfe)/His owne deare mother."[307]

In addition to the Ovidian tapestry, a dance occurs that illustrates all the negative aspects of Ovidian love. The first characters in the dance are Fancy, Desire, Doubt, Danger, Fear, Hope, Dissemblance, Suspect, Grief, Fury, and finally Cruelty. Then Cupid himself arrives, riding on a ravenous lion. He has more disparaging characters in his entourage. He is attended by Reproach, Repentance, Shame, Strife, Anger, Unthriftihood, Loss of Time, Sorrow, Change, Disloyalty, Riotous, Dread, Infirmity, Poverty, and lastly, "Death with infamie.[308]

Spenser really wants to drive home his thesis that Cupid, and Ovidian love, is terrible and cruel. This point is particularly illustrated in a passage where Venus has lost her son, and seeks Cupid in court, city, and country. Everywhere everyone complains about Cupid, having been visited by him. The terms used to castigate Cupid are "wicked," poisonous, "crueltie," "mischievous," "the disturber of all civill life," venomous, and other terms — all of which Venus smiles at.

---

306. Book III, C.xi, 29.
307. III, C.xi, 45.
308. III, C. xii, 7-52.

First she sought him in Court, where most he used
Whylome to haunt, but there she found him not;
But many there she found, which sore accused
His falsehood, and with infamous blot
His cruell deedes and wicked wyles did spot:
Ladies and Lords she every where mote [might] heare
Complayning, how with empoysned [poison] shot
Their wofull harts he wounded had whyleare [lately],
And so had left them languishing twixt hope and feare.

She then the Cities sought from gate to gate,
And every one did aske, did he him see;
And every one her answered, that too late
He had him seene, and felte the crueltie
Of his sharpe darts and whot artillerie;
And every one threw forth reproaches rife
Of his mischievous deedes, and said, That hee
Was the disturber of all civill life,
The enimy of peace, and author of all strife.

Then in the countrey she abroad him sought,
And in the rurall cottages inquired,
Where also many plaints to her were brought,
How he their heedless harts with love had fyred,
And his false venim through their veines inspyred;
And eke the gentle shepheard swanyes, which sat
Keeping their fleecie flockes, as they were hyred,
She sweetly heard complaine, both how and what
Her sonne had to them doen; yet she did smile thereat.[309]

Several other stanzas in book III call Cupid "merciless" and monstrous. In another room of Busyrane's castle monstrous images of love are displayed. The intent of these images is to show the inhumanity of false love:

A thousand monstrous formes therein were made,
Such as false love doth oft upon him [self] weare,
For love in thousand monstrous formes doth oft appeare.[310]

---

309. III, C. vi, 13, 14, 15.
310. III, C. xi, 51.

The entrance to this room contains another reference to Ovid. Over the doorway the words "Be bold" are inscribed, an allusion to Ovid's injunction "First, be a confident soul, and spread your nets with assurance./Women can always be caught."[311] Or in another place, "Venus favors the bold!"[312] Within the room are votive spoils to Cupid, who is referred to as a merciless and insolent victor:

> And all about, the glistring walles were hong
> With warlike spoiles, and with victorious prayes [booty],
> Of mighty Conquerours and Captaines strong,
> Which were whilome captived in their dayes
> To cruell love, and wrought their owne decayes:
> Their swerds and speres were broke, and hauberques [chain mail]
>   rent;
> And their proud girlonds of tryumphant bayes [laurels]
> Troden in dust with fury insolent,
> To shew the victors might and merciless intent.[313]

As an image of the nature of Ovidian love, Amoret is literally enthralled — she is held prisoner, chained to a column with a dart lodged in her heart (another reference to Cupid's arrows which penetrate the heart). The sorcerer writes magical spells with Amoret's blood in an attempt to obtain her love by magic. She is rescued by a Chivalric heroine named Britomart. The lady knight, after releasing Amoret from her Ovidian bondage, forces the sorcerer to read his magic charms backwards. As he does so, the fire surrounding the castle disappears, and the whole castle shakes apart. Britomart then binds the sorcerer in his own chain. The rescue of Amoret from the Ovidian castle ends Spenser's book on love, and sets the stage for the next book on friendship wherein Spenser reshapes Chivalric love traditions by including Aristotle's doctrines on friendship, which we looked at in Chapter Two, and also Aristiotle's teachings about virtue.

Spenser uses several images in Book IV to illustrate his revision of love themes. Having denounced Ovidian tenets of love, Spenser draws on the friendship philosophers and infuses love stories with ideas drawn from them. His intent is to add the concept of virtue to love stories. Virtue will then steady the wildness of unbridled passion.

---

311. Ovid, *The Art of Love*, trans. Rolfe Humphries (Bloomington, Indiana: Indiana UP, 1957), p. 113.
312. *Ibid.*, p. 124.
313. III, C. xi, 52.

He states that in the ancient age of humankind, love was chaste and virtuous. But as the world grew older, the beauty of God was debased into lawless lust:

> But antique age yet in the infancie
> Of time, did live then like an innocent,
> In simple truth and blameless chastitie,
> Ne then of guile had made experiment,
> But voide of vile and treacherous intent,
> Held vertue for itselfe in souveraine awe:
> Then loyall love had royall regiment,
> And each unto his lust did make a lawe,
> From all forbidden things his liking to withdraw.
>
> ... But when the world woxe old, it woxe warre old,
> (Whereof it hight) and having shortly tride
> The traines of wit, in wickednesse woxe bold,
> And dared of all sinnes the secrets to unfold.
>
> Then beauty, which was made to represent
> The great Creatours owne resemblance bright,
> Unto abuse of lawlesse lust was lent,
> And made the baite of bestiall delight:
> Then faire grew foule, and foule grew faire in sight, ... [314]

Spenser finds friendship higher than love of kindred or Romance. Friendship contains virtue and discipline which comes from the soul. Family affection and Cupid's passion come from the heart and both cease over time:

> Hard is the doubt, and difficult to deeme,
> When all three kinds of love together meet,
> And doe dispart the hart with powre extreme,
> Whether shall weigh the balance downe; to weet
> The deare affection unto kindred sweet,
> Or raging fire of love to woman kind,
> Or zeale of friends combyned with vertues meet.
> But of them all the band of vertuous mind
> Me seemes the gentle hart should most assured bind.
>
> For naturall affection soone doth cease,
> And quenched is with Cupids greater flame:

---

314. IIII, C. viii, 30, 31, 32.

But faithfull friendship doth them both suppresse,
And them maystring discipline doth tame,
Through thoughts aspyring to eternall fame,
For as the soule doth rule the earthly masse,
And all the service of the bodie frame,
So love of soule doth love of bodie passe,
No lesse then perfect gold surmounts the meanest brasse.[315]

But Spenser is still a Romantic, and tells stories of virtuous love between men and women. In these stories, Spenser differentiates love from lust, and love becomes purified by friendship. One particularly graphic story again concerns Amoret, Spenser's exemplar of virtuous love. A hideous beast that exemplifies lust has captured Amoret. He is described as a hairy man-like creature, with teeth like a boar's tusks, a large, purple nose engorged with the blood of his victims, and with big ears that hang down to his waist. He intends to rape Amoret and then devour her. A knight appears, and is about to release her; but the task is an extremely delicate one: the lust monster is holding Amoret as a shield. The knight can hardly strike the beast without injuring Amoret. Here, Spenser is narrating in allegorical form the difficulty of separating lust from love while preserving the integrity of virtuous love. In this story, another reference is made to Ovid. As Amoret is running from the lust-monster, before being captured, she is compared to Daphne running from Apollo's lust: "more swift then Myrr' or Daphne in her race."[316] She is rescued, but not without receiving numerous wounds. Spenser's emblem of love is detached from Ovid's lustful legacy.

Another story with a similar meaning is in canto ix. A giant's daughter named Poeana is described by Spenser as outwardly beautiful, but inwardly "defaste" with "lewd loves and lust intemerate." She is married to a squire and then amends her ways so that "all men much admyrde her change, and spoke her praise."[317]

An important and highly delightful episode illustrates Spenser's efforts to purify lust into virtuous love. A battle takes place between two knights, one a lady and the other a man. In a move rather unique in the corpus of Chivalric Literature, Spenser has created a powerful lady knight named Britomart. She is any man's equal in force of arms. This is proven in numerous battles, and

315. IIII, C. ix, 1,2.
316. IIII, C. vii, 22.
317. IIII, C. ix, 160.

particularly in her battle with Artegall. In the Chivalric tradition, often a knight's true worth is shown in a battle to the draw with a knight of already established worth. (So in Chretien de Troyes' Yvain story, Yvain battles with the seasoned knight Gawain. But this story contains an ironic turn. Yvain and Gawain are best friends, but since they are fully armed, they don't recognize one another. The battle is mortal, and the narrator tells how each knight wishes to utterly destroy the other, who is his best friend. The tension between love and hate is thus wonderfully united in this battle to the draw.) Spenser adapts this tradition in the battle between Britomart and Artegall. Britomart has seen Artegall and fallen in love with him six cantos earlier in the storyline. But since the two knights are fully armed, they do not recognize each other. It is the battle to the draw between two dear friends all over again, but this time friendship is raised a notch into love. And the narrative of the battle is charged with words that suggest sexual passion. Britomart is said to fight in "hastie heat" and with "panting breath."[318] When her visor is cut off, Britomart's face appears more flushed than seems right:

> With that her angels face, unseen afore,
> Like to the ruddie morne appeard in sight,
> Deawed with silver drops, through sweating sore,
> But somewhat redder, then beseem'd aright,
> Through toylesome heate and labour of her weary fight.[319]

Artegall's armor is cut apart showing "all his bodie bare."[320] The rising strength of Artegall suggests mistreating one's loved one through lustful abuse: "Ah cruell hand, and thrise more cruell hart,/That workst such wrecke on her, to whom thou dearest art."[321] Spenser suggests that the "madness" of lustful passion can wreck the early first love that couples feel toward one another:

> What yron courage ever could endure,
> To worke such outrage on so faire a creature?
> And in his madness thinke with hands impure
> To spoyle so goodly workmanship of nature,
> The maker selfe resembling in her feature?
> Certes some hellish furie, or some feend

---

318. IIII, C. vi, 16.
319. IIII, C. vi, 19.
320. IIII, C. vi, 16.
321. IIII, C. vi, 16.

> This mischiefe framed, for their first loves defeature,
> To bath their hands in bloud of dearest freend,
> Thereby to make their loves beginning, their lives end.[322]

By suggesting "hastie heat," "hands impure," "panting breath," a bare body, "madness," "outrage," and faces that appear redder than "beseem'd aright," this battle clearly suggests sexual passion.

The conclusion of the battle mediates the excesses of the battle's passion into reverence and love. Spenser weaves Cicero's friendship philosophy, which is derived from Aristotle, into his Chivalric Romance. In Cicero, friendship is the "handmaid of virtue" and a means whereby passion is subdued. Cicero's description of friendship is so intimate that it reminds the modern reader of Romantic love. Cicero even uses the Latin word *amor*, which means love, for the feelings of friendship. "For it is love from which the word 'friend' is derived" (Amor enim, ex quo amicitia nomina est).[323]

> Now if the force of integrity is so great that we love it . . . what wonder that men's souls are stirred when they think they see clearly the virtue and goodness of those with whom a close intimacy is possible? And yet love (*amor*) is further strengthened by the receiving of a kindly service, by the evidence of another's care for us, and by a closer familiarity, and from all these, when joined to the soul's first impulse to love, there springs up, if I may say so, a marvelous glow and greatness of goodwill.[324]

Instead of panting with passion for the object of one's impure desire, one reverences one's friend. So virtue and reverence subdue passion and grant love to friends:

> But the fair thing is, first of all to be a good man yourself and then to seek another like yourself. It is among such men that this stability of friendship . . . may be made secure; and when united by ties of goodwill, they will first of all subdue those passions to which other men are slaves . . . and they will not only cherish and love, but they will also revere each other. For he who takes reverence from friendship, takes away its brightest jewel. . . . Friendship was given to us by nature as the handmade of virtue . . . because virtue cannot attain her highest aims unattended, but only in union and fellowship with another.[325]

---

322. IIII, C. vi, 17.
323. Cicero, "De Amicitia" in *Loeb Classical Library* (Cambridge: Harvard UP, 1953), p. 139.
324. *Ibid.* p.141.

Spenser clearly has this citation from Cicero in mind when he narrates the outcome of the passionate battle between Artegall and Britomart. Artegall eventually strikes off the visor of Britomart's helmet and sees her face for the first time. He is struck with reverence for her, kneeling down, feeling that he is seeing a heavenly vision:

> And he himself long gazing thereupon,
> At last humbly downe upon his knee,
> And of his wonder made religion,
> Weening some heavenly goddess he did see,
> Or else unweeting, what else it might bee;
> And pardon he besought his errour frayle,
> That he had done outrage in so high degree.[326]

In the depth of his overwhelming reverence for the heavenly beauty of Britomart, Artegall curbs his passion into "lawfull bounds":

> Yet durst he not make love so suddenly,
> Ne thinke th' affection of her hart to draw
> From one to other so quite contrary:
> Besides her modest countenance he saw
> So goodly grave, and full of princely aw,
> That it his ranging fancie did refraine,
> And looser thoughts to lawfull bounds withdraw;
> Whereby the passion grew more fierce and faine,
> Like to a stubborne steede whom strong hand would restraine.[327]

In this passage we also see Plato's imagery from the Phaedrus. There, the charioteer subdues his unruly horse into submission as in Spenser — "Like to a stubborne steede whom strong hand would restraine." Artegall is counselled by a wise character named Glauce to yield to love that is knit with virtue. As in the earlier Chivalric tales, love is here taught to be the "crowne of knighthood":

> Ne henceforth be rebellious unto love,
> That is the crowne of knighthood, and the band
> Of noble minds derived from above,
> Which being knit with virtue, never will remove.[328]

---

325. *Ibid.* p.191.
326. Spenser, *Faerie Queene*, IIII, C. vi, 22.
327. IIII, C. vi, 33.

In this passage, Spenser paraphrases Cicero's doctrine of friendship: "Virtue, . . . both creates the bond of friendship and preserves it. For in virtue is complete harmony, in her is permanence, in her is fidelity."[329] Drawing on Cicero's friendship doctrines, then, Spenser purifies the passionate lust of the wild Chivalric accounts of love that preceded him into something more stable and virtuous.

A final image concludes Spenser's love imagery. Book IV contains yet another poetic distancing from Ovid in favor of the virtuous love that Spenser wants to teach. The knight Scudamor, whose name contains the Latin word for love (Amor) enters the temple of Venus, the goddess of love. Recalling the philosopher Empedokles, whom we looked at in Chapter 1, Venus is said to be the creatress of the universe and of all joy:

> So all the world by thee at first was made,
> And dayly yet thou doest the same repayre:
> Ne ought on Earth that merry is and glad,
> Ne ought on Earth that lovely is and fayre,
> But thou art the root of all that joyous is,
> Great God of men and women, queene of th'ayre,
> Mother of laughter, and welspring of blisse.[330]

Scudamor sees Amoret in the temple of Venus and thinks to remove her. But he hesitates, fearing that to do so would be a sacrilege. Here, again, we can detect Spenser's trepidation at removing love from Ovid's context and bringing it into his Elizabethan world of virtue.

> Whom soone as I beheld, my heart gan throb,
> And wade in doubt, what best were to be donne:
> For sacrilege me seem'd the Church to rob,
> And folly seem'd to leave the thing undonne,
> Which with so strong attempt I had begonne.
> Tho shaking off all doubt and shamefast feare,
> Which ladies love I heard had never wonne
> Mongst men of worth, I to her stepped neare,
> And by the lilly hand her labour'd up to reare.[331]

---

328. IIII, C. vi, 31.
329. Cicero, "De Amicitia," p. 207.
330. IIII, C. x, 47.
331. IIII, C. x, 53.

Yet Spenser makes his peace with Ovid, and has Venus smiling at his literary project. So with the approval of Venus, Scudamor leads Amoret from the temple of Venus in front of all the devotees:

> And evermore upon the Goddesse face
> Mine eye was fixt, for feare of her offence,
> Whom when I saw with amiable grace
> To laugh at me, and fauour my pretence,
> I was emboldned with more confidence,
> And nought for nicenesse nor for envy sparing,
> In presence of them all forth led her thence,
> All looking on, and like astonisht staring,
> Yet to lay hand on her, not one of them daring.
>
> . . . Thus safely with my love I thence did wend.[332]

Thus Spenser makes his peace with Ovid. Although much of his *Faerie Queene* is indebted to Ovid's imagery, Spenser's poetic mission was to reshape Ovid's style of love. Spenser mixes Cicero and Aristotle's friendship doctrines into love traditions to make Romantic Love more stable and above all virtuous. Spenser wants to delicately separate lust from love. He adds reverence to the passion of sexuality. He removes the kind of deceit that Ovid seemed to emphasize in the Art of Love. With the kind of refinements that Spenser argues for in the Faerie Queene, Romantic Love can be added to the other Renaissance virtues of Holiness, Temperaunce, Iustice, and Courtesie.

The Puritans

Although in modern culture Puritans connote prudery, from our perspective the Puritans were progressives in the history of Romantic Love. In their theology they have much to say about love and friendship in marriages. In Thomas Aquinas and Luther, the primary emphasis was on the sex drive and sexual passion. Luther's strident, ground-breaking attacks on celibacy were already one hundred years old. The initial Protestant arguments for marriage had already been made by him, by Calvin, and by the Church of England. Thus the Puritans were liberated to add an element of Romance into Church dogma.

---

332. IIII, C. x, 56, 58.

In reading through the Puritan theologians on marriage, we find familiar Bible passages: 1 Corinthians 7 and Ephesians 5. 1 Corinthians comes up to argue for the equality between marriage and celibacy. Whereas the Church Fathers we looked at in Chapter 4 use 1 Corinthians to argue that celibacy is the preferred condition, denying the body of Christ to those who engage in sex, the Puritans use the same passage to argue, as Luther did, for the equality between celibacy and marriage:

> If they are simply and by themselves considered, there is neither virtue nor vice, nor any worke morally good or bad included in either, because they are naturall formes of living, neither of which is either enioiyned or forbidden, I Cor 7. 25. Seeing then, that neither state is morally good but indifferent, it cannot bee properly said of either, that it is better then the other.[333]

Although Ames has just stated that marriage and celibacy are equal, he adds that "the state of Wedlocke seemeth more excellent." It is ordained by God in Eden, and it promotes virtue by discouraging fornication.

The Puritans define marriage in a novel way. Whereas Thomas Aquinas saw marriage as a sacramental institution, emphasizing the religious ceremony itself, the Puritans emphasize the act of living together in a relationship extended over time. Their emphasis is on the social aspect of marriage. In a much more tender way of describing marriage than we have seen in any of the theologians so far, Cleaver speaks of marriage in terms of friendship, honesty, help, and comfort:

> Wedlocke or Matrimonie, is a lawfull knot, and unto God an acceptable yoking and ioyning together of one man, and one woman. . . to the end that they may dwell together in friendship and honestie, one helping and comforting the other, eshewing whoredome, and . . . bringing up their children in the feare of God.[334]

The new model for marriage that the Puritans create is the family as a small commonwealth. A large commonwealth is composed of these small components.

---

333. William Ames, *Conscience with the Power and Cases Thereof* (London: Printed by E. G., 1643), pp. 196-197.

334. Robert Cleaver, *A Godlie Forme of Householde Government*, 1603, p. 98.

A household is as it were a little Common-wealth, by the good Government whereof, Gods glorie may be advanced, the Common-wealth which standeth of several families, benefitted, and all that live in that familiy receive much comfort and commoditie.[335]

As a little commonwealth, the husband is seen as a benevolent governor. This reflects the Ephesians 5 teaching that the husband is the head of the wife as Jesus is the head of the Church. As the head of the little commonwealth, the husband has the obligation to:

Excell in knowledge and prudence, that so hee may rightly give example, governe and direct the wife depending upon him . . . Hee ought to provide for her all things necessary, according as his estate and condition give leave . . . Hee ought to governe her in those things, which belong to good manners, and householde affaires.[336]

Although the Puritans draw on Ephesians 5 in their teachings about the little commonwealth, they soften the power dynamic considerably. The conjunction between husband and wife is as close as that between soul and body. And the woman is the husband's constant companion in all he does:

. . . he doth think himselfe to bee the head and soul, and the woman (as it were) the flesh and the body . . . She is the fellowe and companion of his goods and labours.[337]

Recall that for Thomas, the wife was the husband's partner only in begetting children and raising them. In Cleaver, the wife is called "fellowe and companion of his goods and labours" — expanding her role into the whole life of her husband.

And the unique contribution of the Puritans to the history of Romance is their inclusion of love in their discussions of marriage. In Thomas Aquinas and in Martin Luther, the primary concern is sexual passion. The Puritans say little about that, and much about the quality of love between married partners. To Ames, "there ought to be a most sociable and intimate affection between Man

---

335. *Ibid.*, p. 157.
336. William Ames, pp. 154-157.
337. Robert Cleaver, p. 172.

and Wife," unique to those who are married, and has a special name. It is "a speciall love, and such a one as is proper to Man and Wife, which therefore may bee termed conjugall, *Ephes. 5. 28. 29. Genes. 2. 24.*"[338] Cleaver adds a beautiful description of married love that sounds like Aristotle's discussion of philosophical friendship. The minds and bodies of married partners are one:

> By yoking, ioning, or coupling, is meant, not only outward dwelling together of the married folks . . . but also an uniforme agreement of minde, and a common participation of body and goods.[339]

One may have noticed the significant inclusion of the body in the couple's union. Here Cleaver affirms sexuality.

Again, although the unequal subordination between man and woman in Ephesians 5 is retained, the Puritans soften it. The husband loves and cherishes his wife as Christ does the Church. He cares for her as he would his own body. Cleaver clearly spells out the husband's duties:

> 1. That he live with his wife discreetly, according to knowledge. 2. That hee bee not bitter, fierce, and cruell unto her. 3. That hee love, cherish, and nourish his wife, even as his owne body, and as Christ loveth the Church.[340]

In Cleaver, as in Spenser, an effort is made to distinguish this special married love from lust. Love should be enjoyed within the virtues of temperance and moderation — "neither are husbands to turn their wives into whores, or wives to turn their husbands into whoremaisters, by immoderate, intemperate, or excessive lust."[341] Neither are the world's seductions to be a cause for entering into marriage. "For there be some marriages made, whom God coupleth not together, but carnall lust, beautie, riches, goods, and lands, flattery, and friendship."[342]

Although the Puritans do not define marriages by sacrament, as Thomas Aquinas did, they do suggest that the faith in God will make the experience of

---

338. Ames, p. 205.
339. Cleaver, p. 98.
340. *Ibid.*, p. 97.
341. *Ibid.*, p. 158.
342. *Ibid.*, p. 98.

marriage blessed. The couple will communicate to each other their spiritual life. Thus religious grace does enter into the marriage doctrine of the Puritans.

> Now Christ communicateth that life and grace which is in him to those that are members of his body: If I then being a member of that mysticall body, be linked by that neare and inviolable bond of marriage to one of the members of that body, what hope is there of mutuall communicating to one another of those gifts and graces which either of us receive from Christ our head?[343]

But marriage being a form of social contract, the contract is void when one of its components is removed by death. As with Thomas Aquinas, for the Puritans marriage is an institution for this life only. "Are they who have buried their husband or wife so free, as they may marie again? Yea, as free as they who were never before married..."[344]

Emerging from the austere teachings of the Church Fathers, the Puritans championed married love. They brought into religion tender sentiments of love previously the stuff of poetry and literature alone. John Milton, that great poet of the Puritans, distinguishes between holy married love and lust, and also, like Spenser, rescues love from the courtly expressions of the Chivalric romancers in his own Paradise Lost. He also attacks the teachings of celibacy, finding their source in the "foe to God and man" or the devil. In Milton, sexual love, "the rites/ mysterious of connubial love," "God declares/Pure" and "leaves free to all." In his narration of Paradise, Milton includes a hymn to married love between Adam and Eve. There, married love was first given to humans in bliss and even today retains its holy estate. It is fitting to give him the closing words on this chapter of love:

> ... into their inmost bower
> Handed they went; and, eased the putting-off
> These troublesome disguises which we wear,
> Straight side by side were laid; not turned, I ween,
> Adam from his fair spouse, nor Eve the rites
> Mysterious of connubial love refused:
> Whatever hypocrites austerely talk
> Of purity, and place, and innocence,
> Defaming as impure what God declares

---

343. William Gouge, *Domesticall Duties* (London: John Haviland for William Blader, 1622), p. 191.
344. Gouge, p. 187.

Pure, and commands to some, leaves free to all
Our Maker bids increase; who bids abstain
But our destroyer, foe to God and Man?
Hail, wedded Love, mysterious law, true source
Of human offspring, sole propriety
In Paradise of all things common else!
By thee adulterous lust was driven from men
Among the bestial herds to range; by thee,
Founded in reason, loyal, just, and pure,
Relations dear, and all charities
Of Father, son, and brother, first were known.
Far be it that I should write thee sin or blame,
Or think thee unbefitting holiest place,
Perpetual fountain of domestic sweets,
Whose bed is undefiled and chaste pronounced,
Present, or past, as saints and patriarchs used.
Here Love his golden shafts employs, here lights
His constant lamp, and waves his purple wings,
Reigns here and revels; not in the bought smile
Of harlots, loveless, joyless, unendeared,
Casual fruition; nor in court amours,
Mixed dance, or wanton mask, or midnight ball,
Or serenade, which the starved lover sings
To his proud fair, best quitted with distain.
These, lulled by nightingales, embracing slept,
And on their naked limbs the flowery roof
Showered roses, which the morn repaired. Sleep on,
Blest pair! And, O! yet happiest, if ye seek
No happier state, and know to know no more![345]

---

345. John Milton, *Paradise Lost* (Norwalk, Connecticut: The Easton Press, 1976), pp. 99-100.

CHAPTER VIII. RADICAL THEOLOGIAN OF TRUE LOVE: EMANUEL SWEDENBORG

What if Plato was wrong? That would certainly change things. What if Empedokles was closer to the truth (see Chapter 1)? He thought that the universe was created and held together by Aphrodite, the Greek goddess of love? What if the underlying force behind the whole created order was the same love that man feels for woman and she for him? Then Plato's eternal world of sterile, rational contemplation wouldn't be real nor would life on Earth be characterized by those norms. Instead, the eternal world would be a place of joyous passion presided over by Aphrodite, and life here would anticipate the next with romance and joyous sexual love.

These are some of the assumptions that Emanuel Swedenborg entertains as he writes his compendious book on sexual love, *De Amore Congugiali*. The Latin title is best translated as *Marital Love*. In it, Swedenborg grounds the special love between husband and wife in the order of creation, the foundations of the universe. It is a remarkable work in content and style. Swedenborg, an Enlightenment Swedish nobleman, writes in an orderly, rational style. He outlines each chapter by topic and sub-topic, reasoning his way through his subject matter. But as a figure with one foot in the Enlightenment and the other in the nascent Romantic age, Swedenborg interlaces his reasoning with beautiful visionary stories, such as the following:

> Looking up to heaven one morning I saw one expanse after another above me.

. . . Thereon there appeared, descending from the highest or third heaven, a chariot in which one angel was seen; but as it approached two were visible in it. At a distance the chariot glittered like a diamond before my eyes. Young horses, white as snow, were harnessed to it; and the occupants held two turtledoves in their hands. . . .

They came, and lo! They were a husband and his wife.

"We are married partners," they said. "We have lived blessed in heaven since the first age, called by you the Golden Age; and always in the same flower of youth in which you behold us today."

I observed them attentively, perceiving that they represented marital love, both in its life and in its adornment; in its life in their faces, and in its adornment in their apparel. . . . The husband looked to be of an age between youth and early manhood. From his eyes beamed a light sparkling with the wisdom of love. His face seemed inmostly radiant from this light, and in the irradiation from it the very skin seemed refulgent. His whole face was one shining comeliness. He was dressed in a robe which reached to the ankles, and wore under this a blue garment, girded with a golden girdle with three precious stones on it, two sapphires at the sides and in the middle a carbuncle. His stockings were of shining linen interwoven with threads of silver; and his shoes were wholly of silk. This was the representative form of marital love with the husband.

But with the wife it was this: I saw her face and did not see it. I saw it as beauty itself, and did not see it because this was inexpressible. For in her face was the flame-like light which is found with angels of the third heaven, and it dazzled my sight. I was simply dumbfounded. Observing this she spoke to me, saying,

"What do you see?"

I answered, "I see only marital love and the form of it. I see and do not see."

At this she turned herself obliquely from her husband, whereupon I was able to regard her more intently. Her eyes sparkled with the light of heaven, which, as was said, is flame-like and derived from the love of wisdom. . . . Hence her beauty was a beauty no painter could emulate and portray in its form; for there is no such coruscation in his color, nor is there any such symmetry expressible by his art. Her hair was gracefully arranged to suit her beauty, with diadems of flowers in it. She wore a necklace of carbuncles, and pendent from it a rosary of chrysolites; and she had bracelets of large pearls. She was dressed in a flowing red robe, and under this had a bodice of purple clasped in front with rubies. But, what astonished me, the colors varied according to her address to her husband, and according to it they were also now more, now less brilliant, more when the two turned toward each other, and less when they were partly turned away from each other. . . .

At length they said, "We are recalled. We must go."

Once again they seemed to be conveyed in a chariot, and were borne along a paved way between flower-gardens around which stood olive trees and well-laden orange trees. As they approached their heaven young women came out to meet them, and received them and conducted them in.[346]

How is Swedenborg able to arrive at this doctrine of spiritual married love? He begins with different assumptions than theologians before him; interprets traditions differently than his predecessors, and bases his ideas on Bible passages that others have ignored. (How he is able to see heavenly visions, I cannot explain, other than to cite what he himself says — that God gave them to him. But Christian mystics have a history of visionary experiences, from the Apostle John, through Saint Anthony, Joan of Arc, Julian of Norwich, and our Emanuel Swedenborg. I do not worry about his visions. Rather, I revel in them and let the seer transport me to his wondrous place of beauty and wisdom.)

Swedenborg's writing style is somewhat difficult. Even the American philosopher Ralph Waldo Emerson, who was deeply affected by Swedenborg, observed that he was "The most imaginative of men, yet writing with the precision of a mathematician, he endeavored to engraft a purely philosophical Ethics on the popular Christianity of his time."[347] It is in this "purely philosophical Ethics" that one confronts difficulties. Every topic Swedenborg writes about is imbedded in a philosophical consideration and it is extremely difficult to find a succinct statement outside of the philsosophical context in which it appears. The path to Swedenborg's theology may be technical but the rewards are there.

Swedenborg sees the whole structure of the created world differently than Plato. The universe was created by a God of love, out of love, by love, and for love. And this is not an abstract God, nor an abstract love. It is all very human. Swedenborg takes to heart the Apostle John who speaks of Jesus as the true gate for the sheepfold:

I tell you the truth, the man who does not enter the sheep pen by the gate, but climbs in by some other way, is a thief and a robber. . . . I am the

346. Emanuel Swedenborg, *Marital Love*, trans. By William Frederic Wunsch (New York: Swedenborg Publishing Association, 1938), n. 42. Swedenborg's books are written with paragraph numbers, and cited by them rather than by page number.

347. Ralph Waldo Emerson, 'The American Scholar,' in *Five Essays on Man and Nature*, Crofts Classics (Arlington Heights, Illinois: AHM Publishing Corporation, 1954) p. 57.

gate; whoever enters through me will be saved. He will come in and go out, and find pasture.[348]

Jesus is the form of God that Swedenborg accepts. Thus, as Swedenborg says in another work "God is very human."[349] In this he follows Saint Paul, "For in Christ all the fullness of the Deity lives in bodily form, and you have been given fullness in Christ, who is the head over every power and authority."[350] Due to his emphasis on God's human qualities, spiritual love is akin to human love. God is a divine human, and human love is divine. Thus with these assumptions, Swedenborg does not see the need to transcend the human world as Plato did.

And the human God that Swedenborg envisions is a God of love. God created the universe in order to have someone to love and give joy to and be loved by in turn. The best way to give us joy was the creation of the special love between man and woman. Each could love and give joy to the other, even as God gives joy to humans. In this way, the blessing of Genesis was fulfilled, "So God created man in his own image, in the image of God he created him; male and female he created them. God blessed them and said to them, 'Be fruitful and increase in number.'"[351]

Swedenborg also takes to heart the language of Genesis 1. Man and woman were both created in God's image, so God must possess some kind of duality. This leads to a fundamental doctrine that fills all of Swedenborg's writings. Probably influenced by John Locke, Swedenborg views a human being as the union of understanding and will, or thinking and feeling. Locke said:

> The two great principal Actions of the Mind, which are most frequently considered, and which are so frequent, that every one that pleases, may take notice of 'em in himself, are these two:
> - Perception, or Thinking, and
> - Volition, or Willing.
> The Power of Thinking is called the Understanding, and the Power of Volition is called the Will, and these two Powers or Abilities in the Mind are denominated Faculties.[352]

348. John 10:1, 9 (NIV).

349. Emanuel Swedenborg, *Divine Love and Wisdom*, Standard Edition (New York: Swedenborg Foundation, 1928), n. 11.

350. Colossians 2:9.

351. Genesis 1:27, 28.

352. John Locke, *An Essay Concerning Human Understanding* (Oxford: Oxford UP, 1975), p. 128.

Swedenborg follows Locke as he describes the essential human psychic structure:

> [M]an is man by virtue of will and understanding. For not only do all things which take place in the mind come from these two faculties, but also all things which take place in the body. Who does not know that the body does not act of itself, but the will by the body? Likewise that the mouth says nothing by itself, but the thought by the mouth? If, therefore, the will were taken away, activity would cease instantly, and if thought were taken away, the speech of the mouth would cease instantly.[353]

Swedenborg generalizes these two faculties to the created universe and its Creator; the entire universe is a creation of love and wisdom of which human will and understanding are reflections. And Jesus, or God-Man, is the perfect union of love and wisdom. The married pair reflects this duality. In general, the male reflects divine wisdom, while the female reflects divine love. Thus, the married pair is a reflection of God's divine love and wisdom. This is not entirely a unique doctrine. Swedenborg acknowledges that persons in his time know that will and understanding, or good and truth, are components of the created order:

> *The origin of this love is in the marriage of good and truth.* The intelligent Man acknowledges that all things in the universe are referable to good and truth; . . . All things in the universe are referable to good and truth, and good is united with truth and truth with good, because the two proceed from the Lord and do so as one. . . . Let the heat and light proceeding from the sun serve for illustration; these pervade all vegetation, for it germinates as they are present and they are present together. Natural heat, moreover, corresponds to spiritual heat, which is love; and natural light to spiritual light, which is wisdom.
>
> . . . Love for the sex and marital love come by an influx of the marriage of good and truth from the Lord. Good and truth, we have said, are the universals of creation and so are in all created things, in each according to its form. . . . Now, because this universal sphere, which is the sphere of the marriage of good and truth, flows into subjects according to the form of each (n. 86), it follows that the male receives it according to his form, thus in the understanding, because he is an intellectual form; and that the female receives it according to her form, thus in the will, because she is a volitional form. . . . Inasmuch as the same sphere is also one of prolification, it follows that sexual love is thence.[354]

---

353. Swedenborg, *Marital Love*, n. 494.
354. *Ibid.*, nos. 60, 92.

This idea anticipates what some modern gender studies argue. We read in certain studies about the essential differences between the two genders. Whether males are castigated for it or simply observed to function by it, we are approaching a consensus that most males tend to be more reason-oriented and linear in their thinking. Most women are considered to be more driven by relationships and nurturing roles, and dominated by right-brain structures.

Swedenborg was a serious student of human anatomy before turning to theology, and his discussion of married love is filled with metaphors from anatomy. Love and wisdom are compared to the two hemispheres of the brain, and the union of man and wife is as intimate as the functioning of the heart and lungs. (The man is compared to the lungs and the wife to the heart.) In this comparison, Swedenborg breaks with the tradition that precedes him. The heart and lungs are co-equal in their joint functioning; just so, man and woman are complete equals. As we have seen, the Ephesians 5 passage compares the husband and wife relation to that between Jesus and the Church. Swedenborg rejects this model, and claims that both husband and wife together are the Church. To assert that the husband represents God and the wife the Church is to take the metaphor too literally:

> It is commonly said in the Church that as the Lord is the head of the Church, so the husband is the head of the wife, which would imply that the husband represents the Lord, and the wife the Church. But while the Lord is the head of the Church, man and woman together, and still more husband and wife together, make the Church . . .
>
> There is therefore no correspondence of the husband with the Lord or of the wife with the Church in the marriages either of the angels in heaven or of men on Earth.[355]

In fact, Swedenborg asserts that any hint of inequality or striving for superiority hurts the loving relationship. Any hint of superiority or inferiority, of dominance or submission destroys the mutual giving of lovers.

> *The third of the external causes [of emotional cold between partners] is striving for the upper hand between partners.* For marital love looks foremostly to a union of wills and to freedom of decision. Any striving for the upper hand or for dominion casts both of these out of marriage, dividing and cleaving asunder

---

355. *Ibid.*, nos. 125, 126.

the wills, and changing freedom of decision into servitude. When the striving persists, the spirit of one contemplates violence against the other. Were their minds laid open then and regarded with spiritual vision, the partners would appear like people fighting with daggers, and looking at each other with alternate hatred and favor — with hatred while in the vehemence of striving, and with favor while in the hope of dominating or in lust.[356]

Swedenborg does agree with the great body of literature preceding him that regards God's union with the Church as the spiritual source for the love between married partners. We saw in Chapter 6 that for Thomas Aquinas, the perpetual love of God for the Church is the source of the sacrament of marriage. And in Chapter 3, we looked at the many Bible passages that compare God's relationship with His people to marriage. Swedenborg supplies these Bible passages in n. 117. His primary reason for including this chapter in his work is to emphasize, as Thomas Aquinas did, that marriages are completely holy and proceed from God:

> In view of its origin and correspondence, this love is celestial, spiritual, holy, pure and clean above every love which the angels of heaven or men of the Church have from the Lord. It was briefly confirmed above, but only by way of anticipation, that marital love is of this character due to its origin, which is the marriage of good and truth; also to its correspondence with the marriage of the Lord and the Church. These two marriages, out of which marital love springs like an offshoot, are very sanctities. If then marital love is received from its Author, who is the Lord, holiness follows from Him, which constantly refines and purifies it. Given a desire and effort after it in the will, this love becomes clean and pure daily to eternity. . . . Regarded in its essence and origin, it is holy and pure above every love with angels and men, because it is the head, as it were, of all other loves.[357]

In fact, since God's union with the Church is the source for married love, couples feel deeper and more profound love for each other, the more they grow spiritually:

> . . . Marital love is inevitably bound up with a wisdom which shuns the evil of adultery as a bane to soul, state and body. This wisdom springs from things spiritual, moreover, which are of the Church, and it follows that marital love is according to the state of the Church with a man, with which

---

356. *Ibid.*, n. 248.
357. *Ibid.*, n. 64.

his state of wisdom accords. By this is meant, too, as has been said frequently in what precedes, that as far as a man is spiritual, so far he is in true marital love; for man is made spiritual through the spiritual things of the Church.[358]

Swedenborg's use of the term "Church" in the passage above is a technical term. He doesn't mean the Church buildings, or even regular Church attendance. The Church for Swedenborg is a personal connection with God. Since Churches teach ways to approach God, Swedenborg uses that term to mean the personal appropriation of spiritual doctrines.

Although Swedenborg's treatment of the origin of marital love follows Thomas Aquinas' sacramental description, Swedenborg follows Lutheran doctrine in regard to the sacraments: for Swedenborg marriage is not, strictly speaking, a sacrament. The only sacraments in his theological system are baptism and holy communion.

One might have noticed a few remarks that have been made in passing about marital love and angels. Swedenborg is unique in his understanding of the spiritual nature of marriage, and also in his understanding of angels. All good humans who die and come into the spiritual world become angels. Angels, then, are not a different class of beings than humans. They are all from the human race and every good human who dies becomes an angel. Thus life in the next world is not radically different than life here; it is rather a continuation of the choices that an individual makes on Earth. In fact, Swedenborg refers to good humans on Earth as angels in the flesh. But Swedenborg makes an even more radical claim about marriage that opposes all the theologians before him. He claims that marriages and sex continue in the spiritual world. Since people are not radically different in the next life, neither is sexuality. For Swedenborg, spirit moves the body; therefore the body's actions are physical derivations of spirit. Sex, then, is spiritual in its origin. In fact, sex is more delightful in the next life than here because the true inner nature of an individual is revealed there, and the desires of one's heart and spirit are more perceptible. So if one loves another, that love becomes more clear, present, perceptible, and thus more delightful.

> *Partners enjoy an intercourse like that in the world, but pleasanter and more blessed* ... Partners enjoy an intercourse like that in the world for the reason that male is male after death, and female female, and an inclination to union is

---

358. *Ibid.*, n. 130.

implanted in each from creation. This inclination in the human being is of the spirit and thence of the body, wherefore after death, when man becomes a spirit, the same mutual inclination persists. This is not possible without intercourse. For the human being is a human being as before, nor is anything lacking in either male or female; they are like themselves in form as well as in affections and thoughts. What else can follow except that there is similar intercourse? And because marital love is chaste, pure and holy, that the intercourse is full? . . . The intercourse becomes pleasanter and more blessed because that love, on becoming of the spirit, becomes interior and purer, and so more perceptible. All pleasure increases according to perception, and grows until the blessedness is felt in the pleasure.[359]

To make this point, Swedenborg needed to address the passage from Mark 12:18-27 that we looked at in Chapter 3. Recall that in the Mark passage the Sadducees thought that they had an argument against the idea of life after death. They posed a question about a woman who, according to Jewish law, married the brothers of her husband after he died, one by one as each brother died childless. If there is a life after death, she would be married to seven men. Jesus' response is that there is indeed a life after death, but then one is not given in marriage, as on Earth. Many theologians take that phrase to mean that there is no marriage in heaven. Swedenborg asserts that the passage contains two lessons. The first lesson is what we have already stated, that there is a life after death. But the second lesson concerns Biblical language. As theologians before him have done, including Origen, Gregory of Nyssa, Saint Augustine, and even certain Lutheran theologians, Swedenborg puts a spiritual interpretation on the passage. He claims that marriage, in the Bible, refers to the union of God with the Church. Swedenborg's interpretation is that if one has not entered into a union with God here on Earth ("spiritual marriage"), one would not be joined with God in the hereafter (or "marry" or "be given in marriage").

Aside from his radical doctrines on life hereafter, what makes Swedenborg noteworthy is his enthusiastic praise for marital love as the highest form of human experience. It is the actual experience of love that Swedenborg continually emphasizes in his book. He claims that all the delights that a human can feel are gathered into this one special love and the whole human being is thereby exalted.

Into marital love all joys and delights are gathered from first to last. All the joys we feel imply a love. The love shows itself in them, in fact exists and lives in

---

359. *Ibid.*, n. 51.

them. . . . But marital love is fundamental among all good loves, and (as was shown above) is inscribed on the least things in man. Therefore its joys exceed those of all other loves. It also gladdens these other loves to the extent that it is present and united with them. For it expends the inmost things both of the mind and of the body, as its delicious current sweeps through them and opens them. All joys from first to last are gathered into marital love . . . all the beatitude, satisfaction, joy, gladness and pleasure that can ever be conferred on man by the Lord the Creator, are gathered into this human love.[360]

Notice that, due to his initial assumptions, namely that the universe was created by a God of love and that that God is very human, Swedenborg champions the experience of human love. One's happiest condition is in the sacred estate of matrimony. The origin of this love is God himself, who is love.

The states of this love are innocence, peace, tranquility, inmost friendship, full trust, a desire in mind and heart to do the other every good; and from all these blessedness, satisfaction, joy, pleasure, and in eternal fruition of these, heavenly happiness. These states are all in marital love and issue from it, because marital love has its origin in the marriage of good and truth, and this marriage is from the Lord. Love wishes to share its gladness with another whom it loves from the heart, indeed to bestow them on him, and in turn to find its own. Infinitely more does the Divine Love of the Lord bear itself so toward the human being. The Lord created man a receptacle of both the love and the wisdom proceeding from Him, and having created him so (the man to receive wisdom, and the woman to receive love for man's wisdom), He has infused in them from the inmosts a marital love, on which He can bestow all things blessed, happy, joyous and pleasant, . . . for these [persons] alone are receptive of them. Innocence, peace, tranquility, inmost friendship, full trust, and the mutual desire in mind and heart to do each other every good are severally named, because innocence and peace are of the soul, tranquility is of the mind, inmost friendship of the bosom, full trust of the heart, and the mutual desire in mind and heart to do each other every good is of the body from them.[361]

What Swedenborg is talking about in his effusive style is an experience that lovers recognize. When one is in love, all of life becomes more pleasant. Being in love fills the soul with happiness that one carries around wherever one is.

---

360. *Ibid.*, n. 68.
361. *Ibid.*, n. 180.

With Swedenborg's primary interest in love as it is perceived by humans, he devotes much material to the mental and spiritual relationship between partners. He is the first, and perhaps only, theologian who describes the experience of what we might call soul-mates within a Christian context. Two married partners grow closer mentally and as they do so, as in Spenser, friendship is added to their initial passion, which adds stability to their initial love:

> *With those in true marital love conjunction of minds increases, and friendship with it*
> . . . we have already shown that conjunction of minds increases with those in true marital love. The conjunction increases as friendship is joined to love, because friendship is as it were the face of the love, and also its garment, and conjoining itself to the love as a garment, and conjoining itself to it as a face. The love preceding friendship resembles love for the [whole] sex, and wanes after the marriage vow, whereas love with friendship adjoined, remains and is steadfast. For it enters deeply into the breast, where friendship introduces it, making it truly marital, and then the love in turn makes this friendship marital, differing markedly from the friendship of any other love, so full is it.[362]

Following the Puritans, Swedenborg asserts that married partners wish to form a common life.

> *Those in true marital love continually wish to be one human being, while those not in marital love wish to be two.* Marital love in its essence is nothing else than the wish to be one; that is, the partners desire their two lives to be made one life. This desire is the perpetual endeavor of this love, from which all its effects flow. . . . . It follows that those in true marital love continually endeavor, that is, will to be one human being.[363]

Married partners actually feel themselves to be so completely united spiritually that they feel themselves to be "in" the other. Raised on Enlightenment philosophy, Swedenborg describes this feeling of union philosophically. In Swedenborg's system, the structure of an individual is described as soul, mind and body. Soul flows into mind, and mind flows into body. Following Aristotle, Swedenborg claims that the body is activated by the soul and mind. So Soul and mind are intimately present in all the parts of the body. The souls and minds of lovers are deeply united. Since the body is

---

362. *Ibid.*, n. 214.
363. *Ibid.*, n. 215.

activated by the soul and mind, and the soul and mind of lovers are united, so the experience of lovers is that they are "in" one another body and soul. This experience is what friendship philosophers such as Michel de Montaigne before Swedenborg have called "one soul in two bodies."[364] Swedenborg applies this idea to married lovers.

> *Those in true marital love feel they are a united human being and, as it were, one flesh.* . . . I have heard some who have lived for ages with their partners in heaven, testify that they feel themselves so united, husband with wife and wife with husband, and each in the other mutually, seemingly in the flesh, even when separated. They said the reason for this . . . is that the unition of their souls and minds is felt in their flesh, for the soul makes the inmosts not only of the head, but of the body, too. Likewise, the mind, mediate between soul and body, though it appears to be in the head, is actually in the whole body, too. They said that this is the reason why acts which soul and mind intend, issue instantly from the body. Thence, too, it is, they said, that after the discarding of the body in the former world they themselves are still complete human beings. Now as soul and mind are so closely adjoined to the flesh of the body in order to operate and bring about their effects, it follows that the unition of partners in soul and mind is felt in the very body as if they were one flesh.[365]

Swedenborg considers marriage to be holy, chaste, and pure. Swedenborg devotes a whole chapter of his book to a consideration of the notion of chaste and unchaste ways of life. And we have seen that Swedenborg considers the marital state to be the highest and most delightful condition of mortals. He states his case in the strong form. All chastity is measured by marriage. One's marital relations are the measure of one's chastity. The striking conclusion is that all other states of life that are not married are to that extent less chaste — including celibacy. Some of his statements are obvious. For instance, adulterers are not chaste. Other statements are curious. Eunuchs are not chaste because they are not capable of experiencing the full physical expression of marital love. As Swedenborg puts it, "Anything of inclination thereto is rendered neuter in them and is neither chaste nor unchaste; what is neuter cannot be called one or the other."[366] Interestingly, chastity cannot be credited to children before they reach sexual maturity because they are not capable of marital love. This accords

---

364. Michel de Montaigne, 'Of Friendship' in *The Complete Essays of Montaigne*, trans. Donald M. Frame (Stanford, California: Stanford UP, 1965), p. 141.

365. *Ibid.*, n. 178.

366. *Ibid.*, n. 151.

with Swedenborg's general theology that good or evil are possible only by adults with full rational faculties. Those who think that marriages are unchaste, such as the Fathers we looked at in Chapter 4, are themselves not chaste. Finally, there is the hot issue of celibacy. Here, Swedenborg breaks with the vast Christian tradition before him. He claims that those who have undertaken a vow of celibacy are not chaste. Marriages are the measure of chastity. In fact, as with Luther, Swedenborg states that it can be dangerous to repress the sex drive that God has implanted in the created order. A repressed sex drive can fester within the psyche and infest the soul.

> Chastity cannot be predicated of those who have renounced marriages, vowing perpetual celibacy, unless they have and retain a love for a true marital life. Of these there can be no predication of chastity for the reason that after a vow of perpetual celibacy, marital love is thrust out, of which alone, however, is there any predication of chastity. Moreover, from creation and thus by birth, inclination toward sex is still present, and when this is restrained and repressed, it turns inevitably to heat and with some into a burning, which, though it is bodily, rises into the spirit, infesting and in some befouling it.[367]

Thus for Swedenborg, the condition of marriage is not equal to celibacy, as it was for Luther, but preferred.

> *The state of marriage is to be preferred to the state of celibacy.* This is plain from what has been said so far of marriage and of celibacy. The state of marriage is preferable, being intended by creation. Its origin is the marriage of good and truth; its correspondence is with the marriage of the Lord and the Church . . . its use excels all other uses in creation, for by marriage is the orderly propagation of the human race and also of the angelic heaven, which is from the human race. Add to these reasons that marriage is the fullness of the human being — by it one becomes a full human being . . . None of these things is true of celibacy.[368]

As the passage above suggests, love for children is a part of marital love. As stated in Genesis 1, marital love cooperates with God's creative plan to establish the whole race of humans. And since for Swedenborg all angels come from the human race, the propagation of the species cooperates with God's intention to form a heaven of angels from the human race. Recalling some of the assumptions

---

367. *Ibid.*, n. 155.
368. *Ibid.*, n. 156.

we spoke of in the early section of this chapter, God is love and wants someone he can love and who can love God in return. Marital love participates in this grand intention by cooperating with creation. For this reason, marital love contains the greatest blessings that humans can find. We become co-creators with God.

> All joys from first to last are gathered into marital love on account of the excellence of its use above that of any other love. Its service is the propagation of the human race and of the angelic heaven therefrom. Because this use is the end of ends in creation, all the beatitude, satisfaction, joy, gladness and pleasure that can ever be conferred on man by the Lord the Creator, are gathered into this human love.[369]

Many of Swedenborg's claims are radical. Some will be hard for those conditioned by traditional Christian theology to accept. (It was his book on married love that got Swedenborg thrown out of his homeland in Sweden by the national Lutheran Church.) Swedenborg continued his theological career in the more tolerant atmosphere of England. But for lovers who have felt a spiritual force behind their love, who have felt that their love joins each other together in an ecstatic universe, Swedenborg provides a systematic treatment of married love within a Christian context. Neither before Swedenborg, nor after him, can one find a more thorough and idealistic treatment of married love.

Swedenborg's great contribution is to include Romantic Love in Christian theology. Now, Romantic Love is a topic that theology can discuss instead of relegating it to poetry and literature alone. All the tenderness and passion of the Chivalric writers now has a home in Christian theology. Swedenborg is able to do this by proceeding from different assumptions than the Christian theologians who follow Plato. For Swedenborg, God is a God of love who wants his people to feel and express love for one another as deeply and as delightfully as the Deity does for them. This love is most profoundly felt in the marriage of husband and wife.

---

369. *Ibid.*, n. 68.

CHAPTER IX. THE ETERNAL FEMININE: SHELLEY AND INTELLECTUAL BEAUTY

Considering how we have been treating Platonism so far, the way Percy Bysshe Shelley approaches it may be surprising. His use of Platonism in his rhapsodic poem "Epipsychidion" is based on an idealized love for a woman. Since the ancient Greek philosophical schools were exclusively for males and shunned passion and sexuality, it might seem strange to idealize the feminine figure in the pursuit of philosophical truth. But even in ancient Greek philosophy, a tradition had grown up that idealized the feminine form. The wisdom that philosophers sought came to be represented as a human, and the human form representing philosophy was feminine. Wisdom was a woman. Her name was "Sophia," the Greek word for "wisdom." Lady Wisdom shined on the philosophers as a source of inspiration. Perhaps the drive to see wisdom personified as a beautiful woman reflects a sublimation of ordinary sexuality. Philosophy, after all, was a celibate male occupation practiced in the academies far removed from the tender influences of womankind. But whatever the reason, Lady Sophia became the human form of philosophical wisdom.

Under Greek influence, Hebrew writers borrowed this image and created an apocryphal Biblical book now found in the Catholic Bible called *Wisdom*, or *The Wisdom of Solomon*. *Wisdom* is a collection of sayings, or proverbs, much like the book of *Proverbs*. In this Biblical book *Wisdom*, we find that Greek image of Lady Wisdom, or Sophia. Sophia shines in divine brilliance, reflecting God, her source. She is the embodied form of God's creative Wisdom, the source of illumination for devout Jews, the structure of the universe.

> For she is a breath of the power of God,
> And a pure emanation of the glory of the Almighty;
> Therefore nothing defiled gains entrance into her.
> For she is a reflection of eternal light,
> A spotless mirror of the working of God,
> And an image of his goodness. . . .
> She is more beautiful than the sun,
> And excels every constellation of the stars.
> Compared with the light she is found to be superior,
> For it is succeeded by the night,
> But against wisdom evil does not prevail.[370]

The author of Wisdom employs romantic imagery in treating Lady Wisdom. His relationship with her is personal. He talks about her beauty, about companionship with her, and even friendship with Sophia. His use of metaphor even goes so far as to narrate falling in love with Wisdom, and desiring to "marry" her:

> I loved her and sought her from my youth;
> I desired to take her for my bride,
> And became enamored of her beauty. . . .
> Therefore I determined to take her to live with me, . . .
> For companionship with her has no bitterness,
> And life with her has no pain, but gladness and joy. . . .
> And in friendship with her, pure delight.[371]

Having entered the Jewish tradition through this Biblical book, the feminine representation of Wisdom is carried into Christianity both through this book and through Christianity's adoption of Greek philosophical traditions. One early image can be found in Boethius, the Christian philosopher of the sixth century. Having been condemned to death by the Barbarian King Theodoric, Boethius wrote a treatise on philosophy to console himself. In his book, *The Consolation of Philosophy*, Lady Wisdom (philosophy) first comes to him while he is wallowing in misery — he is writing poetry bewailing his fate. She is a supernatural being who reaches as high as the heavens:

---

370. *Wisdom of Solomon*, in *The Holy Bible containing the Old and New Testaments with the Apocryphal/ Deuterocanonical Books*, New Revised Standard Version (Oxford: Oxford UP, 1977), 7: 25-30.
371. *Wisdom* 8.2, 9, 16, 18.

While I was quietly thinking these thoughts over to myself and giving vent to my sorrow with the help of my pen, I became aware of a woman standing over me. She was of awe-inspiring appearance, her eyes burning and keen beyond the usual power of men. She was so full of years that I could hardly think of her as of my own generation, and yet she possessed a vivid colour and undiminished vigour. It was difficult to be sure of her height, for sometimes she was of average human size, while at other times she seemed to touch the very sky with the top of her head, and when she lifted herself even higher, she pierced it and was lost to human sight. Her clothes were made of imperishable material, of the finest thread woven with the most delicate skill. (Later she told me that she had made them with her own hands.). . . . There were some books in her right hand, and in her left hand she held a scepter.[372]

In typical Platonic fashion, Lady Wisdom chides Boethius for wallowing in sorrow and immersing himself in poetry. Platonism, after all, saw poetry as a damaging threat to the even temper a philosopher is supposed to maintain. (While philosophy calms the passions, poetry feeds and nurtures them.) Lady Wisdom feared that her careful work of teaching Boethius philosophy would be ruined by the Muses of poetry:

At the sight of the Muses of Poetry at my bedside dictating words to accompany my tears, she became angry.

"Who," she demanded, her piercing eyes alight with fire, "has allowed these hysterical sluts to approach this sick man's bedside? They have no medicine to ease his pains, only sweetened poisons to make them worse. These are the very women who kill the rich and fruitful harvest of Reason with the barren thorns of Passion. They habituate men to their sickness of mind instead of curing them. If as usual it was only some ordinary man you were carrying off a victim of your blandishments, it would matter little to me — there would be no harm done to my work. But this man has been nourished on the philosophies of Zeno and Plato. Sirens is a better name for you and your deadly enticements: be gone, and leave him for my own Muses to heal and cure."[373]

The style of Boethius' *The Consolation of Philosophy* is a Platonic dialogue between Boethius and Lady Wisdom. She teaches Boethius how to accept his fate through philosophical argument and reason. In book two of this work, a beautiful hymn teaches Boethius that the whole universe is held together by

---

372. Boethius, *The Consolation of Philosophy* (New York: Penguin Books, 1978), pp. 35-36.
373. Boethius, *The Consolation of Philosophy*, p. 36.

Love, the same love that holds married couples and friends together, reflecting the philosophy of Empedokles:

> The world in constant change
> Maintains a harmony,
> And elements keep peace
> Whose nature is to clash.
> The sun in car of gold
> Draws forth the rosy day,
> And evening brings the night
> When Luna holds her sway.
> The tides in limits fixed
> Confine the greedy sea;
> No waves shall overflow
> The rolling field and lea.
> And all this chain of things
> In Earth and sea and sky
> One ruler holds in hand:
> If Love relaxed the reins
> All things that now keep peace
> Would wage continual war
> The fabric to destroy
> Which unity has formed
> With motions beautiful.
> Love, too, holds peoples joined
> By sacred bond of treaty,
> And weaves the holy knot
>
> Of marriage's pure love.
> Love promulgates the laws
> For friendship's faithful bond.
> O happy race of men
> If Love who rules the sky
> Could rule your hearts as well![374]

Through his dialogue with Sophia, Boethius comes to accept his fate and reconciles himself to the human condition, made immortal by philosophy.

Lady Wisdom becomes thoroughly Christianized in the work of the great Italian poet Dante. As one of the first great literary works written in the author's native language (instead of the ancient language of Latin), Dante's *Divine Comedy*

---

374. *Ibid.*, p. 77.

made a lasting impression on all poets who followed him, including Shelley. Shelley is inspired when he praises Dante's poetry:

> Dante was the first awakener of entranced Europe; he created a language, in itself music and persuasion, out of a chaos of inharmonious barbarisms. He was the congregator of those great spirits who presided over the resurrection of learning;. . . . His very words are instinct with spirit; each is as a burning spark, a burning atom of inextinguishable thought.[375]

In his body of work, Dante repeatedly draws on the image of an actual lady named Beatrice who acts as Lady Wisdom. Choosing her for such a constant and pivotal role in his works was remarkable. From what Dante tells us, the poet scarcely knew her at all. According to his book, *Vita Nuova*, he saw Beatrice once and saluted her. Shortly thereafter, she died. That was all Dante knew of Beatrice. But her image remains in Dante's imagination and she appears in all his subsequent works. In the *Convivio*, or *The Banquet*, she appears as philosophy. In this work, Dante writes a series of love poems, which he then "decodes" into philosophical treatises, taking them completely out of their Romantic context into the realm of Platonic reasoning. It is as if Dante felt that he could only justify love poems by turning them into philosophy. Thus, while Dante draws on the language of the troubadours when he writes the love lyrics in *Convivio*, he remains in the philosophical Platonic world of "Eros" when he interprets them.

Nowhere is the tension between human love and Platonic Christianity more evident than in Dante's magnificent *Divine Comedy*. The *Divine Comedy* is a massive literary display of the whole civilized world as Dante knew it. It is written in three sections, reflecting the Catholic Christianity of his day: *Infirno*, *Purgatorio*, and *Paradiso* or *Hell*, *Purgatory*, and *Paradise*. In *The Inferno*, the great Roman poet Virgil leads Dante on a tour of Hell. Hell is peopled with actual personages from European history and from Dante's own Italy whom the poet thinks deserve eternal damnation. But since Virgil was a pagan poet who didn't know Jesus, Virgil must stop at the borders of Hell, where Purgatory begins. He then yields to another tour guide through Purgatory and Paradise. Here, Beatrice appears to complete the journey.

---

375. Percy Bysshe Shelley, "A Defense of Poetry," in *The Selected Poetry and Prose of Shelley*, Harold Bloom, ed. (New York: New American Library, 1978), p. 438.

In describing Hell, Purgatory, and Paradise, Dante reveals his Platonic form of Christianity. Dante places the first writers of European love poetry, the troubadours, and the lovers who followed their precepts, at the very beginning of Hell and at the very end of Purgatory. For Dante, lovers are not fit for heaven. When Dante gets to Paradise, he finds the place peopled entirely with celibate monks and nuns.

But what of Dante's relationship with Beatrice? It is indeed a form of idealized love; but it is not what we would think of as a relationship. After that one salute, she remains an idealized figure in his mind, a figure of imaginary beauty. Beatrice and Dante don't experience any of the strains that actual lovers do in day to day life. Dante has a perfect, trouble-free beloved in his imagination. Shelley, however, was very much taken by Dante's imaginary love.

> His apotheosis of Beatrice in Paradise, and the gradations of his own love and her loveliness, by which as by steps he feigns himself to have ascended to the throne of the Supreme Cause, is the most glorious imagination of modern poetry.[376]

Beatrice is indeed a personification of Christian Wisdom. She teaches Dante about all the people he sees in Purgatory and Paradise. Her role is strictly one of education. And (in a passage that disappointed me to no end), when Dante finally makes it up to the highest place in heaven, the couple splits up. No parting is described. Instead, Dante says that he has totally merged with the "Prime Mover," and Beatrice no longer is mentioned. No "happily ever after," in Dante's heaven. Rather, his destination is a Christianized form of Aristotle's "First Cause" — the unmoved force moving the entire created world. In other words, as in Plato and Augustine, Dante totally merges his consciousness with God, leaving behind all that is less than the Absolute, all that is merely human. The relationship between Beatrice and Dante is inconsummate. She is an image of Divine Wisdom, and as Wisdom she shows the way to ultimate union with God, not herself.

The Romantic Movement in European Literature of the nineteenth century idealized womankind in a more intimate way. They drew on the legacy of the

---

376. Shelley, "A Defense of Poetry," p. 435. Shelley is right in referring to Dante's final end as the Supreme Mover of Aristotle. Dante was more directly affected by Aristotle than by Plato. I call him a Platonist because of his stance in regard to passion and erotic love. Also, as we saw in Chapter Two, Aristotle follows Plato in regard to his understanding of the passions.

Chivalric Romances of the Middle Ages, which idealized the personal relationships between knight and lady such as Lancelot and Guenivere or Tristan and Yseut. According to Shelley:

> Love became a religion, the idols of whose worship were ever present. It was as if the statues of Apollo and the Muses had been endowed with life and motion, and had walked forth among their worshippers; so that Earth became peopled by the inhabitants of a diviner world. The familiar appearance and proceedings of life became wonderful and heavenly, and a paradise was created out of the wrecks of Eden.[377]

This religion of love bequeathed a special honor to the relationships between men and women. Wordsworth's "Lucy" poems honor Romantic love, and many of Coleridge's poems in *Sibylline Leaves* aim at a refined statement of Romantic love. As a philosopher-poet, Coleridge explains what he and his colleagues were after. In his *Notebooks*, he states his intention to:

> . . . write a series of Love Poems — truly Sapphic, save that they shall have a large Interfusion of moral Sentiment & calm Imagery on Love in all the moods of the mind — Philosophic, fantastic, in moods of high enthusiasm, of simple Feeling, of mysticism, of Religion — /comprise all the practice, & all the philosophy of Love.[378]

All these literary influences — The Greek Sophia, the Bible's Wisdom, Boethius's Lady Wisdom, Dante's Beatrice, the Romance religion of the Chivalric period, and the refined sentiments of the first generation of Romantic Poets of the nineteenth century — all these images and motifs play into Shelley's "Epipsychidion." But before we can look at that, we need to consider Shelley's own conception of the immortal Power he chose to symbolize by the feminine figure.

Shelley seems to have believed in a sort of Platonic idealism — or, at least, he thinks he did. Smarting from the wound that Plato inflicts on poetry in his *Republic*, Shelley responds with a lengthy "Defense of Poetry." Shelley calls Plato himself a poet of love. "Love, which found a worthy poet in Plato alone of all the ancients, has been celebrated by a chorus of the greatest writers of the renovated

---

377. *Ibid.*, p. 435.
378. Kathleen Coburn, ed. *The Notebooks of Samuel Taylor Coleridge*, 3 Vols. (New York: Pantheon Books, 1957), 1:1064.

world."[379] Shelley thinks of himself as a follower of Plato's belief in two worlds: one world is unseen and stands above the created, sensual world, and the other world is this dismal visible place of common experience. Shelley's poems often speak of an unseen power of Beauty that stands apart from the dark, mundane world. In one particular poem, Shelley calls this power "Intellectual Beauty," which closely echoes Plato's philosophy of Ideal Beauty. Shelley called this poem the "Hymn to Intellectual Beauty."[380]

Calling this poem a hymn brings up an important issue. In the Romantic Period, art was beginning to be considered a form of religion. Put strongly, one could even say that in the late Romantic Age, art took the place of religion. This is a highly significant move, and it paves the way for the Modern movement in literature. The transcendental world of Plato becomes translated into the human imagination. Religious revelation came through the artistic imagination less than holy writ. Thus Shelley's poem devoted to Intellectual Beauty is an artistic expression and also a religious "hymn." But since Shelley writes at the very beginning of this new ideology, it is difficult to locate exactly where his Spirit of Beauty is to be found. At times it seems to be an Ideal Power standing outside the created universe, as in Plato. But at other times it seems to be located within the human imagination as in the case with the later Romantic poets. So in his "Hymn" Shelley can speak of forms "containing thee," like Plato's Ideal Forms which the world reflects.[381] In later poets, such as Rimbaud and Mallarme, there is less ambiguity. They clearly identify the human imagination as the source of the divine power of art. But for our discussion of Shelley, we can consider the poet's adoration of Ideal Beauty to be an unclear mixture of Platonic Idealism, and the religion of art that sees Ideal Beauty within the human imagination.

While in "Epipsychidion" Shelley uses a feminine form to represent ideal Beauty, in the "Hymn to Intellectual Beauty" this transcendental force is treated abstractly. The power of Beauty lies, as in Plato, unseen throughout the created universe. But poetry can help to bring humans into contact with it. In his "Hymn to Intellectual Beauty," Shelley is quite clear that the poet can translate this beautiful power that underlies all creation into immortal verses. And he does just that in the poem.

379. Shelley, "A Defense of Poetry," p. 436.
380. Shelley, "Hymn to Intellectual Beauty," *In The Selected Poetry and Prose of Shelley*, pp. 80-83.
381. *Ibid.*, ll. 82, 84.

In expounding the nature of Intellectual Beauty, Shelley uses various images from nature as metaphors. He is not claiming, as other Romantic writers such as Wordsworth or Coleridge do, that nature is the finite symbol organically connected to and imaging forth some greater universal power. Rather, Shelley uses these natural images strictly as metaphors to describe the way this unseen power of Beauty visits the mortal world. And through his nature metaphors, and the music of meter and rhyme, Shelley creates delicate and delightful poetry:

> The awful shadow of some unseen Power
>   Floats though unseen among us — visiting
>   This various world with as inconstant wing
> As summer winds that creep from flower to flower —
> Like moonbeams that behind some piny mountain shower,
>   It visits with inconstant glance
>   Each human heart and countenance;
> Like hues and harmonies of evening —
>   Like clouds in starlight widely spread —
>   Like the memory of music fled —
>   Like aught that for its grace may be
> Dear, and yet dearer for its mystery.[382]

Shelley's metaphors do give us some understanding as to what the nature of this Ideal Beauty is like. It is a holy power that brings divinity to human action: it is a "Spirit of BEAUTY, that dost consecrate/With thine own hues all thou dost shine upon/Of human thought or form."[383] Its presence or absence brings "love and hate, despondency and hope."[384] This "power," this "spirit of beauty" is the source of love that passes between lovers' eyes: "Thou messenger of sympathies,/ That wax and wane in lovers' eyes."[385] Humans would become godlike if they could but keep this Ideal Beauty in their hearts:

> Love, Hope, and Self-esteem, like clouds depart
>   And come, for some uncertain moments lent,
>   Man were immortal, and omnipotent,
> Didst thou, unknown and awful as thou art,
> Keep with thy glorious train firm state within his heart.[386]

---

382. *Ibid.*, ll. 1-12.
383. *Ibid.*, ll. 13-15.
384. *Ibid.*, l. 24.
385. *Ibid.*, ll. 42-43.
386. *Ibid.*, ll. 37-41.

In keeping with the broad Romantic ideals of political liberation, this "awful LOVELINESS" is a power that can free the whole world:

> They know that never joy illumed my brow
>> Unlinked with hope that thou wouldst free
>> This world from its dark slavery,
>> That thou — O awful LOVELINESS,
> Wouldst give whate're these words cannot express.[387]

Including Plato in his Romanticism, Shelley's spirit of Beauty also nourishes the human intellect: "Thou — that to human thought art nourishment."[388] Although he phrased it in a plea, Shelley seems to assert that this power can give eternal life. The poet contrasts the shadow of this power against the grave's apparent "dark reality":

> Depart not as thy shadow came,
>> Depart not — lest the grave should be,
> Like life and fear, a dark reality.[389]

Shelley's delicate metaphors suggest that this power activates the world. In his imagery for Ideal Beauty, Shelley describes it in active contexts, as a driving and energizing force acting on passive objects from nature — mists that are driven by the winds, music caused by the wind on standing strings, or the light of the moon reflected on water. This active power gives grace and truth to our world. It is ultimate reality; the mundane world of common experience is merely a dream:

> Thy light alone — like mist o'er mountains driven,
>> Or music by the night wind sent
>> Through strings of some still instrument,
>> Or moonlight on a midnight stream,
> Gives grace and truth to life's unquiet dream.[390]

---

387. *Ibid.*, ll. 68-72.
388. *Ibid.*, l. 44.
389. *Ibid.*, ll. 46-48.
390. *Ibid.*, ll. 32-36.

As a poet, Shelley's imagination turns to the limits of language. He considers the names that past writers have vainly attempted to give to this unseen power of Beauty:

> No voice from some sublimer world hath ever
>> To sage or poet these responses given —
>> Therefore the names of Demon, Ghost, and Heaven,
> Remain the records of their vain endeavor.[391]

In the "Hymn to Intellectual Beauty" Shelley narrates his own encounter with this immortal power. Fittingly, during his youth, in the season of springtime when all natural beauty erupts, he first comes into contact with this source of Divine Beauty. It sends him into fits of ecstasy:

> While yet a boy I sought for ghosts, and sped
>> Through many a listening chamber, cave and ruin,
>> And starlit wood, . . .
> . . . at that sweet time when winds are wooing
>> All vital things that wake to bring
>> News of birds and blossoming —
>> Sudden, thy shadow fell on me;
> I shrieked, and clasped my hands in ecstasy![392]

Shelley's response is as a religious devotee. He vows to dedicate his life to the pursuit of this Power: "I vowed that I would dedicate my powers/To thee and thine — have I not kept the vow?"[393] But Shelley states that the vision of Beauty bringing him such ecstasy in boyhood has deserted the mature poet:

> Spirit of BEAUTY, that dost consecrate
>> With thine own hues all thou dost shine upon
>> Of human thought or form — where art thou gone?
> Why dost thou pass away and leave our state,
> This dim vale of tears, vacant and desolate?[394]

In keeping with the Romantic religion of art, Shelley's devotion to Beauty is even called worship. The poem concludes with a prayer to Intellectual Beauty,

---

391. *Ibid.*, ll. 25-28.
392. *Ibid.*, ll. 49-51, 56-60.
393. *Ibid.*, ll. 61-62.
394. *Ibid.*, ll. 13-17.

beseeching its return. And not wholly disengaged with religious norms of his day, Shelley claims that this Spirit of Intellectual Beauty moves the poet to a Christian love for all human kind:

> Thus let thy power, which like the truth
> Of nature on my passive youth
> Descended, to my outward life supply
> Its calm — to one who worships thee,
> And every form containing thee,
> Whom, SPIRIT fair, thy spells did bind
> To fear himself, and love all human kind.[395]

Shelley's encounter with Intellectual Beauty is again recounted in "Epipsychidion",[396] but this treatment of Ideal Beauty is dramatically different. The structure of "Epipsychidion" is that of a long, extended love poem addressed to a certain Emilia Viviani. It is a complex reverie involving philosophy as much as rapture. The title means something like Ralph Waldo Emerson's "Oversoul." It can be translated, as Shelley does in several places in the poem, as "soul out of my soul," or "soul within the soul." Thus, it clearly refers to some Platonic ideal soul somehow set apart from the body.

In this work, Shelley plainly draws on those antecedent literary Wisdom traditions that we looked at in the beginning of this chapter, and describes a new encounter with his "Intellectual Spirit of Beauty" brought on by a beautiful feminine form. At the beginning of "Epipsychidion," he signals his appropriation of the Wisdom tradition by citing Dante's *Vita Nuova*, translating Dante into rhyming English:

> My Song, I fear that thou wilt find but few
> Who fitly shall conceive thy reasoning,
> Of such hard matter dost thou entertain;
> Whence, if by misadventure, chance should bring
> Thee to base company (as chance may do),
> Quite unaware of what thou dost contain,
> I prithee, comfort thy sweet self again,
> My last delight! Tell them that they are dull,
> And bid them own that thou art beautiful.[397]

---

395. *Ibid.*, ll. 78-84.
396. Shelley, "Epipsychidion" in *The Selected Poetry and Prose of Shelley*, pp. 306-322.

"Epipsychidion" is Shelley's *Vita Nuova*, and Shelley introduces his own Beatrice. While traveling in Italy, Shelley met a certain Emilia Viviani who was "imprisoned" in a convent until her father could find a spouse for her. Emilia is a curious figure; most of the literary criticism on Shelley's "Epipsychidion" has little to say about her, if it mentions her at all. Yet, she is the person to whom the whole poem is addressed; she is the inspiration for the poem; and she reawakens in Shelley the very vision of Ideal Beauty that he saw as a youth. Perhaps Emilia's biography doesn't really matter all that much. As with Dante and Beatrice, Shelley had little direct contact with her. It is the verse that she generated and the vision of Ideal Beauty that she inspired that are important. As with Dante's Beatrice, Shelley's Emilia matters little as a person.

In the opening verses to Dante's *Vita Nuova* — the verses that Shelley use to open his own "Epipsychidion" — Dante says that there are only a "few/Who fitly shall conceive thy reasoning."[398] Shelley uses these opening words because his romance epic is about Ideal Intellectual Beauty, symbolized by the mortal form of Emilia Viviandi. He thinks that few will understand it because many readers will stop short at the love Shelley appears to have for Emilia and not see the deeper philosophical vision of Ideal Beauty.

Shelley begins his poem with strongly romantic language, as if he were about to write a conventional love poem:

> . . . Emily,
> I love thee; . . .
> How beyond refuge I am thine. Ah me!
> I am not thine: I am a part of *thee.*[399]

Her words, in good Platonic fashion, still Shelley's senses. But in an extremely un-Platonic way it is passion, not reason, that transports the poet,

> And from her lips, as from a hyacinth full
> Of honey-dew, a liquid murmer drops,
> Killing the sense with passion; sweet as stops
> Of planetary music heard in trance.[400]

---

397. Shelley, "*Epipsychidion*," ll. 1-9.
398. *Ibid*, ll. 1-2.
399. *Ibid.*, ll. 42-43, 51-52.
400. *Ibid.*, ll. 83-86.

As in the Wisdom tradition, Shelley perceives Emilia's beauty with his soul, not his body. But in a paradoxical statement, it is not reason that carries Shelley out of his senses, but sensation itself. Shelley "feels" a sweet, "wild odor" in his soul,

> Warm fragrance seems to fall from her light dress
> And her loose hair; and where some heavy tress
> The air of her own speed has disentwined,
> The sweetness seems to satiate the faint wind;
> And in the soul a wild odor is felt,
> Beyond the sense, like fiery dews that melt
> Into the bosom of a frozen bud.[401]

But despite the opening passion of the poem, Shelley doesn't see Emilia as a mortal woman with whom ordinary Romantic love could be experienced. She is much like Lady Sophia of *Wisdom* or *The Consolation of Philosophy*. His metaphors for Emilia take her out of the mortal realm, making of Emilia more than pure spirit; she is divine. She is a "High, spirit-winged Heart" (l. 13), "Seraph of Heaven! Too gentle to be human" (l. 21), "divinest presence" (l. 78), "one serene Omnipresence" (l. 95), she is "Scarce visible from extreme loveliness" (l. 104), she is immaterial, "A shadow of some golden dream" (l. 116), a literary device "A Metaphor of Spring and Youth and Morning;/A Vision like incarnate April" (ll. 120-121), even the goddess Venus: "a Splendor/Leaving the third sphere pilotless" (l. 116-117). These ideal metaphors for Emilia are finally gathered together into one vision of Eternity:

> See where she stands! A mortal shape indued
> With love and life and light and deity,
> And motion which may change but cannot die;
> An image of some bright Eternity.[402]

Shelley identifies his experience of Emilia with the youthful vision of Intellectual Beauty that he had spoken about in the "Hymn to Intellectual Beauty." As in the "Hymn," in "Epipsychidion" Shelley reiterates how he communed with Intellectual Beauty as a youth. This Intellectual Beauty is

---

401. *Ibid.*, ll. 105-111.
402. *Ibid.*, ll. 112-115.

identified with Platonic philosophy and truth, and is given the feminine pronoun:

> There was a Being whom my spirit oft
> Met on its visioned wanderings, far aloft,
> In the clear golden prime of my youth's dawn, . . .
> She met me, robed in such exceeding glory,
> That I beheld her not. . . .
> . . . in that best philosophy, whose taste
> Makes this cold common hell, our life, a doom
> As glorious as a fiery martyrdom;
> Her Spirit was the harmony of truth.[403]

This glorious Being is called by the title of Shelley's poem: the "soul out of my soul."[404] And as in the "Hymn to Intellectual Beauty," in "Epipsychidion" Shelley narrates how this youthful vision of Beauty deserted him in mature adulthood:

> But She, whom prayers or tears then could not tame,
> Passed, like a God throned on a winged planet, . . .
> Into the dreary cone of our life's shade;
> And as a man with mighty loss dismayed,
> I would have followed, though the grave between
> Yawned like a gulf whose specters are unseen: . . .
> And in that silence, and in my despair,
> I questioned every tongueless wind that flew
> Over my tower of mourning, if it knew
> Whither 'twas fled, this soul out of my soul; . . .
> But neither prayer nor verse could dissipate
> The night which closed on her. . . .[405]

But while the "Hymn to Intellectual Beauty" ends with a prayer that the divine Intelligence of his youth return to the mature poet, "Epipsychidion" celebrates the return of that Eternal Beauty through the vision of Emilia. She awakens the spirit of the poet, lifts up his body ("dreaming clay"), and fills him with living light:

---

403. *Ibid.*, ll. 190-193, 199-200, 213-216.
404. *Ibid.*, l. 238.
405. *Ibid.*, ll. 225-226, 227-231, 235-238, 241-242.

At length, into the obscure Forest came
The Vision I had sought through grief and shame. . . .
Soft as an Incarnation of the Sun,
When light is changed to love, this glorious One
Floated into the cavern where I lay,
And called my Spirit, and the dreaming clay
Was lifted by the thing that dreamed below
As smoke by fire, and in her beauty's glow
I stood, and felt the dawn of my long night
Was penetrating me with living light:
I knew it was the Vision veiled from me
So many years — that it was Emily.[406]

"Epipsychidion" exhibits a tension that wasn't present in Dante — Dante doesn't write about Beatrice until after she has died. At that point, she becomes a pure intellectual vision. Neither is Dante nor Beatrice married. But with Shelley, everything is different. Emilia is still alive when Shelley writes his poem to her; and further complicating the tension between Ideality and the real mortal world is the fact that Shelley is married to Mary Shelley while he pours out passionate words of love to Emilia. When he isn't thinking of Emilia as a finite instance of Intellectual Beauty, Shelley is in love with her. His verses play with several strange scenarios in which the two could be bound together. One scene is as two twins — "Would we had been twins of the same mother."[407] Another wishes that Emilia and Mary Shelley were sisters and both married to Percy Shelley! "Or, that the name my heart lent to another/Could be a sister's bond for her and thee,/ Blending two beams of one eternity!"[408] Finally, Shelley comes clean and declares his famous doctrine of "free love." He refuses to be bound by marriage to only one person.

I never was attached to that great sect,
Whose doctrine is, that each should select
Out of the crowd a mistress or a friend,
And all the rest, though fair and wise, commend
To cold oblivion, though it is the code
Of modern morals, and the beaten road . . .
With one chained friend, perhaps a jealous for,
The dreariest and the longest journey go.

---

406. *Ibid.*, ll. 321-322, 335-344.
407. *Ibid.*, l. 45.
408. *Ibid.*, ll. 46-48.

> ... Narrow
> The heart that loves, the brain that contemplates,
> The life that wears, the spirit that creates
> One object, and one form, and builds thereby
> A sepulcher for its eternity.[409]

The poem concludes with a unique Platonic marriage proposal. Shelley wants to unite with Emilia, but even in his desire he recognizes that they will remain bound only through their intellects. Therefore, in the last section, Shelley calls Emilia a "vestal sister." And in his proposal, Shelley recognizes that she will become united only *as* a bride, not one in fact.

> The day is come, and thou wilt fly with me.
> To whatsoe'er of dull mortality
> Is mine, remain a vestal sister still;
> To the intense, the deep, the imperishable,
> Not mine but me, henceforth be thou united
> Even as a bride. . . .[410]

Shelley recognizes the necessary division between himself and Emilia. But the ideal love he expresses in "Epipsychidion" unites them Platonically even in separation,

> The walls are high, the gates are strong, thick set
> The sentinels — but true Love never yet
> Was thus constrained: it overleaps all fence: . . .
> For it can burst his charnel, and make free
> The limbs in chains, the heart in agony,
> The soul in dust and chaos.[411]

The final section of "Epipsychidion" is a passionate invitation to fly with the poet into an imaginary world that the two can mentally inhabit. This section is a description of a fantasy island filled with images that the Romantic Period treasured. Here, Shelley builds a transition to the Modern Period in literature. For all his Platonic pretensions, Shelley seems to locate the Ideal World in the poet's imagination, rather than in a superior spiritual plane that stands above the mortal world. He invites Emilia not to use her reasoning intelligence to conceive

---

409. *Ibid.*, ll. 149-154, 158-159, 169-173.
410. *Ibid.*, ll. 388-393.
411. *Ibid.*, ll. 396-398, 405-407.

Ideal, Eternal Beauty, as Plato would, but rather to use her imagination to travel with Shelley to a pristine island filled with sensual images from the catalogue of picturesque Romantic nature imagery. As a poet, Shelley prefers pictures that feed the senses over reasonings that feed the intellect. The two will fly on "an albatross, whose nest/Is a far Eden of the purple East; . . . Beautiful as a wreck of Paradise."[412] Recalling the tradition of Daphnis and Chloe, the island is peopled by "pastoral people" who "Draw the last spirit of the age of gold,/Simple and spirited; innocent and bold."[413] Shelley devotes much of his description of the island to nature images such as forests, rivulets, ivy, flowers, mountains, and caves. These natural forms, grasped in Shelley's imagination, all resonate like music with the "soul within the soul." While claiming to be a Platonist, Shelley writes of sensual odors, not reasonings, that penetrate the brain:

> And from the moss violets and jonquils peep,
> And dart their arrowy odor through the brain
> Till you might faint with that delicious pain.
> And every motion, odor, beam, and tone,
> With that deep music is in unison:
> Which is a soul within the soul.[414]

Drawing on Samuel Taylor Coleridge's "Kubla Khan," Shelley describes an ancient Pleasure-Dome, now in typical Romantic ruins, on his imaginary island. As a Romantic poet, writing a poem about love, he conceives this ancient building is made for the purpose of sexual pleasure (something Plato would have abhorred):

> But the chief marvel of the wilderness
> Is a lone dwelling, built by whom or how
> None of the rustic island-people know:
> 'Tis not a tower of strength, though with its height
> It overtops the woods; but, for delight,
> Some wise and tender Ocean-King, ere crime
> Had been invented, in the world's young prime,
> Reared it, a wonder of that simple time,
> An envy of the isles, a pleasure house
> Made sacred to his sister and his spouse.
> It seems now a wreck of human art.[415]

412. *Ibid.*, ll. 416-417, 423.
413. *Ibid.*, ll. 426, 428-429.
414. *Ibid.*, ll. 450-455.

The poem reaches its end with breathtaking erotic language. But like the island, all this eroticism is locked up inside Shelley's mind. But what passion this island holds for reader and writer, despite the fact that it is entirely an experience of fantasy!

> We two will rise, and sit, and walk together, . . .
> And by each other, till to love and live
> Be one: . . .
> The rain
> Whose drops quench kisses till they burn again.
> And we will talk, until thought's melody
> Become too sweet for utterance, and it die
> In words, to live again in looks, which dart
> With thrilling tone into voiceless heart,
> Harmonizing silence without a sound.
> Our breath shall intermix, our bosoms bound,
> And our veins beat together; and our lips
> With other eloquence than words, eclipse
> The soul that burns between them, and the wells
> Which boil under our being's inmost cells,
> The fountains of our deepest life, shall be
> Confused in Passion's golden purity.[416]

From these highly passionate images, Shelley moves up Plato's ladder of love to consider the lovers' minds:

> Two overshadowing minds, one life, one death,
> One Heaven, one Hell, one immortality,
> And one annihilation.[417]

This romantic sequence finally erupts in a passionate climax: "I pant, I sink, I tremble, I expire!"[418]

Shelley's epic poem of ideal love reshapes the world derived from Plato and the ancient Wisdom traditions of the Eternal Feminine. As with Dante, Shelley's Emilia is a woman with whom the poet sustains no real romantic communion.

---

415. *Ibid.*, ll. 483-493.
416. *Ibid.*, ll. 541, 551-552, 558-571.
417. *Ibid.*, ll. 585-587.
418. *Ibid.*, l. 591.

She has been endowed with attributes that far surpass her own mortal character. Shelley has merged his quest for Ideal Beauty with a woman's mortal form. Although "Epipsychidion" is written as a long love poem, it is also a treatise on the Ideal world. Although Shelley may have thought that he has answered Plato's attack on love and poetry, Plato's ghost lurks everywhere in the verses of the Romantic poet. Instead of writing about love for his actual wife Mary Shelley, Percy Bysshe Shelley has chosen to write about an Ideal source of Beauty found in a woman with whom he will never come into sexual relation. The poem's romance is all imaginary. The poet's relationship with Emilia is celibate.

But Shelley's passionate climax does not erupt before he anticipates the Modern Era in poetry. Before the poem's conclusion, Shelley finds that the mysteries of love he has tried to put into print defy language:

> . . . Woe is me!
> The winged words on which my soul would pierce
> Into the height of Love's rare Universe,
> Are chains of lead around its flight of fire. . . .[419]

In these penultimate words, Shelley anticipates the Modern Era of T. S. Eliot. Eliot will claim that language has lost its power to express meaning because culture has become too fragmented to provide a context for it. And in Eliot, impotence and the death of God are predominant metaphors. Already, in Shelley, Platonic reasoning and actual Romance have given way to poetic imagination and celibate, self-enclosed fantasy. The Ideal world is becoming located within the human mind. It takes only a little more cultural fragmentation to result in self-enclosed subjective minds alienated from each other. Shelley's long, complex reverie on love and Idealism paves the way to existential isolation.

---

419. *Ibid.*, ll. 587-590.

CHAPTER X. THE DEATH OF GOD, THE END OF LOVE: T. S. ELIOT'S *THE WASTE LAND*

"April is the cruellest month." So T. S. Eliot begins his epic poem *The Waste Land*.[420] And with that opening line, Eliot sets himself against millennia of love traditions, from Plato and Longus up through the Romantic era in the nineteenth century. April represents springtime for Eliot; and the blossoming of flowers and the warming air awakens the hearts of lovers. Eliot continues, "breeding/Lilacs out of the dead land, mixing/Memory and desire, stirring/Dull roots with spring rain."[421] One wants to ask, "What's wrong with that?" Shouldn't one be happy with the new life that springtime generates in nature, and calls forth from the human heart?

But T. S. Eliot is a counter-Romantic. His claim is that the modern era can no longer sustain those dear encounters that lovers treasure. He prefers the metaphor of winter: "Winter kept us warm, covering/Earth in forgetful snow."[422] The religious and cultural traditions that grounded our feelings of love have become fragmented. The new findings of science, the doctrine of evolution, Modern Biblical criticism, the destruction of the old world order with World War One, the destruction of the tradition of noble birth, the rise of the United States of America into a world power and with it the elevation of the common man over nobility, and the lack of shared cultural values make the modern era one in which love has no tradition in which to ground raw biological passion.

---

420. T. S. Eliot, *The Waste Land and Other Poems* (New York: Harcourt Brace & Company, 1962).
421. Eliot, *The Waste Land*, ll. 1-4.
422. *Ibid.*, ll. 5-6.

Eliot illustrates the Modern fragmentation of tradition and the death of spirituality by referring to the Biblical prophet Ezekiel. In the middle of the desert, God appeared to Ezekiel and gave him his Word to say to the children of Israel:

> He said to me, "Son of man, stand up on your feet and I will speak to you." As he spoke, the Spirit came into me and raised me to my feet, and I heard him speaking to me.
> He said, "Son of man, I am sending you to the Israelites, . . . Say to them, 'This is what the Sovereign LORD says.'"[423]

T. S. Eliot emphasizes the word "say" from the Ezekiel passage. Ezekiel is commanded to say to the children of Israel the very words he hears from God — a huge statement about the power of language. Language, Ezekiel's words, will connect the people of Israel with God. But in Eliot's Waste Land, there is only desert without God. And instead of God's Word, the "Son of Man" can say nothing, for he knows only "A heap of broken images." Culture's fragmentation leaves the Modern "Son of Man" unable to comprehend divinity or speak the Word of God:

> What are the roots that clutch, what branches grow
> Out of this stony rubbish? Son of Man,
> You cannot say, or guess, for you know only
> A heap of broken images, where the sun beats,
> And the dead tree gives no shelter, the cricket no relief
> And the dry stone no sound of water.[424]

Eliot concludes his masterpiece with another comment on the demise of Western culture and the fragmentation of society: "London Bridge is falling down falling down/ . . . These fragments I have shored against my ruins."[425]

The structure of Eliot's *Waste Land* merits consideration. From the point of view of style, Eliot is an "imagist." That is, the meaning in his poem is built upon pictorial images and disconnected phrases. These images and phrases all pile up to create an overall tone. Many of these pictures and phrases are disembodied quotes; Eliot had two purposes for citing so profusely from the history of

---

423. Ezekiel 2:1-3, 4. New International Version (Grand Rapids, Michigan: Zondervan Bible Publishers, 1979).
424. Eliot, *The Waste Land*, ll. 19-24.
425. *Ibid.*, ll. 427, 431.

Western literature. One reason was to illustrate the fragmentation we now experience in Modern culture. Hence his poem presents these phrases disembodied from the works and culture that generated them. Another reason is more complicated; Eliot wanted the citations he selects to carry resonances with them from the literary context in which they initially appeared. If he quotes from an Elizabethan play about love, Eliot wants the context of love to be imported into his poem. Some of the finest parts of The Waste Land are constructed by juxtaposing sharply contrasting contexts brought into the poem by phrases from larger works. These juxtapositions often generate a profound feeling of spiritual debasement. Of course, if one doesn't know where the quotes came from, one won't understand the contexts they represent; so, in an afterthought, Eliot included footnotes at the end of his poem.

Some critics claim that the need to supply footnotes indicates that the poem is flawed. But I think that the unique structure of The Waste Land itself only shows the radically subjective nature of our fragmented culture. Eliot chose quotes that were meaningful to him, and we are unable to make a bridge from our mind to Eliot's. The very structure of the poem, then, shows how separated each modern mind is from another. We all make meaning in our lives from broken traditions and are unable to share with each other our unique attempt to piece together culture's fragments. Accordingly, as Eliot's poem is isolated from its readers without notes, so each modern individual is separated from others by a lack of shared values. The structure of Eliot's poem is its very meaning:

> I have heard the key
> Turn in the door once and turn once only
> We think of the key, each in his prison
> Thinking of the key, each confirms a prison. . . .[426]

But the cultural forces that alienate individual from individual do something more dangerous. Breaking up long held traditions also breaks up traditions about God. An underlying theme to the whole poem is the idea that God is dead. Eliot accepts the doctrine from Plato and Longus both that love is divine. Plato considers his Ideal Form of the Good divine. And for Longus, Daphnis and Chloe's love is inspired by the Greek god of love, "Eros." But with the death of God, love dies as well.

---

426. Eliot, The Waste Land, ll. 412-415.

The whole visible landscape of the Waste Land is constructed around an ancient myth about God. Eliot based the structure of *The Waste Land* around the anthropology of Sir James Frazer. Frazer's Golden Bough[427] is a vast study of primitive myths and rituals. The first myth in his work concerns the dying and resurrected God. Is it a coincidence that for Christians Jesus was resurrected in Easter, in the springtime? The rebirth of nature in the spring was thought in ancient times to be caused by a resurrection of God. Frazer refers to many traditions to expound this myth. He refers to the Egyptian myth of Osiris and Isis, and the Greek myths of Adonis, Dionysus, and Demeter and Persephone. In each of these myths, the God was taken to the underworld, or in the case of Osiris, actually killed. Then, in springtime, the God returned to the world and was reborn. All of nature flourished with the return of the God.

This myth of the dying and resurrected God was applied to kingship in ancient times. The strength and virility of the king was thought to resonate with nature. According to Frazer, in many cultures, such as Mesopotamia, an annual ritual-drama took place in which the king was ceremonially killed and reborn. This ritual-drama ensured the land's fertility.

This same myth can be found in the Chivalric Romance about the Holy Grail; there, the king's testicles have been wounded by a poisoned spear. With the wounding of the king's virility, the land has become barren. Another anthropologist, Jessie Weston, wrote a book entitled *From Ritual to Romance*[428] employing Frazer's ideas. Eliot drew on Weston as well as Frazer in creating *The Waste Land*.

As the title makes clear, throughout Eliot's poem the land is waste and barren. God has died and the king's lands are barren. There is no springtime fertility of the resurrected God in Eliot's Waste Land:

> Here is no water but only rock
> Rock and no water and the sandy road
> The road winding among the mountains
> Which are mountains of rock without water
> If there were water we should stop and drink
> Amongst the rock one cannot stop or think
> Sweat is dry and feet are in the sand
> If there were only water amongst the rock. . . .[429]

---

427. Sir James Frazer, *The New Golden Bough* (New York: New American Library, 1959).
428. Jessie Weston, *From Ritual to Romance* (Princeton, New Jersey: UP of Princeton, 1993).
429. Eliot, *The Waste Land*, ll. 331-338.

This image of desert waste land carries through the whole poem, and is an image of Modern culture.

If Eliot's use of Frazer and Weston did not suffice to image the death of God, the poet also supplies an image from Christianity. He describes a vacant Church, which is not God's home — it is home only for the wind. And within the context of this empty Church, Eliot again refers to Ezekiel's dry bones:

> In this decayed hole among the mountains
> In the faint moonlight, the grass is singing
> Over the tumbled graves, about the chapel
> There is the empty chapel, only the wind's home.
> It has no windows, and the door swings,
> Dry bones can harm no one.[430]

In another passage, a Modern voice mocks the myth of the dying and resurrected God. The voice alludes to springtime and Christ's nails in a profane jibe about Frazer's ancient springtime myth. Rather than God's resurrection in the spring, the speaker fears that a dog will dig up a dead body:

> "That corpse you planted last year in your garden,
> "Has it begun to sprout? Will it bloom this year?
> "Or has the sudden frost disturbed its bed?
> "O keep the Dog far hence, that's friend to men,
> "Or with his nails he'll dig it up again!"[431]

Another way that Eliot shows the spiritual void of Modern society is by illustrating how social amusements can distract people from spiritual depth. His characters are so absorbed in social rituals that they put off deep existential questions. Eliot opens such a section by cheapening Shakespeare into a ragtime passtime:

> OOOO that Shakespeherian Rag —
> It's so elegant
> So intelligent

---

430. *Ibid.*, ll. 386-391.
431. *Ibid.*, ll. 71-76.

After the speaker has been titillated for a while by the Shakespearean rag, he or she wonders what to do when the music ends — "What shall I do now? What shall I do?" Finally, a despairing existential crisis erupts out of the silence, "What shall we ever do?" The answer is escapism through social ritual, "The hot water at ten./And if it rains, a closed car at four."[432]

These social rituals constitute a waste land of social diversion and illustrate the death of God as much as does the desert landscape of *The Waste Land*. Much of *The Waste Land* is set in an urban locale — London, to be specific. London was thought by Eliot to represent the center of world power and culture, as the British Empire had been the world power before World War One. Eliot uses imagery from London to illustrate wasted nature through urbanization. Recall from Chapter 1 how much nature provided the setting in which the love between Daphnis and Chloe flourished. At the end of Longus' story, the couple had the option of moving to the city and inheriting wealth. They chose to stay in the pastoral lands with the nature gods, the nymphs, and Pan. Eliot debases the nature gods by turning nymphs into summer residents of London. Rather than presiding over the river as river-gods, the Modern nymphs pollute the Thames River with empty bottles, sandwich wrappers, cigarette butts and other trash:

> ... The nymphs are departed.
> Sweet Thames, run softly, till I end my song.
> The river bears no empty bottles, sandwich papers,
> Silk handkerchiefs, cardboard boxes, cigarette ends
> Or other testimony of summer nights. The nymphs are departed.[433]

Urban elements crop up again in another extremely compact section that juxtaposes several citations from Western literature. Here, the characters in the poem avoid considering the eventuality of eternity by machines. An encounter with a goddess becomes a banal tryst. Although the issues raised are monumental, the section in Eliot's poem is short:

> But at my back from time to time I hear
> The sound of horns and motors, which shall bring
> Sweeny to Mrs. Porter in the spring.
> O the moon shone bright on Mrs. Porter
> And on her daughter

432. *Ibid.*, ll. 128-131, 134-135.
433. *Ibid.*, ll. 174-179.

They wash their feet in soda water. . . .[434]

This section contains references to Andrew Marvell's "To His Coy Mistress" and to John Day's play, *The Parliament of Bees*. In Marvell's seventeenth-century poem, the speaker complains to his mistress that she is too coy, putting off a consummation of their love too long. Marvell fears that death will come before they celebrate their love. With one line borrowed from Marvell, Eliot recreates Marvell's context, the realization of eternity. Marvell writes: "But at my back I always hear/Time's winged chariot hurrying near:/And yonder all before us lie/Deserts of vast eternity."[435] But in Eliot's *Waste Land*, social distraction takes the mind off eternity. Instead of "Time's winged chariot" beckoning at the poet's back, Eliot's chariot is an automobile, and the tryst contemplated is debased. Eliot's allusion to Marvell is followed by a reference to an Elizabethan play, *The Parliament of Bees*, by John Day. The character in Day's play is already profane, before Eliot demotes him to banality. Day's "Vainglorious" character has made plans to build a mechanical panorama on the ceiling of his palace displaying one of Ovid's myths. (Already, a Latin myth has become a machine.) In Ovid's myth, the mortal named Actaeon witnesses the virgin goddess Diana bathing. The embarrassed and incensed goddess transforms Actaeon into a deer that his own hounds devour; but the blasphemy of seeing a goddess naked is transformed by Day's character into a subject of scandalous titillation. Vainglorious Bee will create a mechanical panorama that will make a perpetual display of the naked goddess. Vainglorious Bee will create,

A noise of horns and Hunting, which shall bring
Actaeon to Diana in the spring,
Where all shall see her naked skin . . .
All this I'll do that men with praise may crown
My fame for turning the world upside down.[436]

Day's Vainglorious Bee shows his profanity by his obsession with his own glory. He has inverted godliness literally, by turning it upside down on his ceiling, even as his own self-absorption has inverted piety by making self, not God, the first priority in his life; but Eliot turns the religious connotations of this

434. *Ibid.*, ll. 196-201.
435. Andrew Marvell, "To His Coy Mistress," in John Ciardi and Miller Williams, *How Does a Poem Mean* (Boston: Houghton Mifflin Co., 1975), p. 379.
436. John Day, *The Parliament of Bees* (New York: Garland Publishing, Inc., 1979), III. 27-29, 33-34.

fragment from Day into banality. In Eliot's *Waste Land* the hunting horns that bring the mortal Actaeon into contact with a goddess have become automobile horns that bring Sweeny to a liaison with Mrs. Porter:

> But at my back from time to time I hear
> The sound of horns and motors, which shall bring
> Sweeny to Mrs. Porter in the spring.
> (ll. 196-198)

Marvell's "deserts of vast eternity" and Day's profane mechanical mockery of a divine encounter have become debased into mere social distraction. Religious symbols have become so desiccated that one can't even be blasphemous in *The Waste Land*.

The Waste Land is structured around Frazer's myth of the dying and resurrected God. Instead of celebrating the rebirth of the god in the springtime, Eliot's poem leaves the reader in the desert, without fertility. The death of God is also depicted by several references to city life debasing nature's beauty. Social ritual has replaced spiritual fulfillment in a desperate attempt to "distract from distraction by distraction."

Eros In The Waste Land

The Waste Land makes three specific allusions to sexuality: impotence, abortion, and loveless sex. The emptiness of spirituality discussed above causes love to lose its potency. If love is a divine gift to humanity, where there is no God, there is no love.

The first reference to love in *The Waste Land* is impotence — both spiritual and sexual. In a powerful short section, Eliot brings in allusions to the Tristan story, the Holy Grail section of Malory's *Morte D'Artur*, and the Biblical Wisdom tradition.

This section from *The Waste Land* begins with a sailor's song from Wagner's opera "Tristan and Isolde":

> Frisch weht der Wind
> Der Heimat zu
> Mein Irisch Kind,
> Wo weilest du?[437]

---

437. Eliot, *The Waste Land*, ll. 31-34.

This song is sung by a sailor who is thinking about his lover, who is on land. Translated, it reads:

> Fresh the wind blows
> To home
> My Irish child,
> Where tarry you?

The section then ends with another selection from Wagner's opera. In the opera, Tristan has been fatally wounded, and he awaits a ship that brings Isolde, the master healer, to cure him. When he asks if her ship can be seen, the response comes, "Vast and waste is the sea" (that is, "*Oed' und leer das mer*"[438]). Eliot selects images of bereft love. The sailor's song is from a man separated from his beloved, and Tristan's question suggests his ultimate death by separation from Isolde. But selecting these passages from "Tristan and Isolde" also sets this selection from *The Waste Land* in a connotation of Romance — "Tristan and Isolde" being a Chivalric Romance tale.

Eliot then begins a section about two lovers who meet in a hyacinth garden. The section is rich with connotations that are drawn from Frazer's *Golden Bough*. The myth of Hyacinth is another one of Frazer's dying and resurrected gods that we have already discussed. The amorous connotations of the passage are thus lifted into spiritual dimensions by the inclusion of the Hyacinth myth. On the mundane level, the section suggests a romantic encounter:

> "You gave me hyacinths first a year ago;
> They called me the hyacinth girl."
> — Yet when we came back late, and your hair wet, I could not
> Speak, and my eyes failed, I was neither
> Living nor dead, and I knew nothing,. . . .[439]

Sexuality is suggested by the meeting in the garden, the wet hair, and flowers of the hyacinth girl. But the lover is impotent to move in the fertile presence of the hyacinth girl. The last line of the hyacinth section suggests a

---

438. *Ibid.*, l. 2.
439. *Ibid.*, ll. 35-40.

deeper spiritual failure by reference to the Wisdom tradition and Malory's Grail Quest:

> . . . I could not
> Speak, and my eyes failed, I was neither
> Living nor dead, and I knew nothing,
> Looking into the heart of light, the silence.[440]

Most commentators on *The Waste Land* recognize "the heart of light" as some kind of spiritual experience — light being so commonly associated with spiritual vision. And this is the very "heart of light" — the source of all illumination. The language and feminine gender of the "heart of light" suggest the Biblical character of Wisdom that we looked at in the preceding chapter. Thus, in this passage of *The Waste Land* the speaker is unable to move sexually in the presence of the Hyacinth girl, and also spiritually in the presence of "the heart of light."

But the language of the speaker's failed response suggests another spiritual context — that of Sir Lancelot in Malory's *Morte D'Artur*. When he views the Holy Grail, Lancelot is unable to move because of his earthly sins. In Malory, the Grail is described as exceedingly bright — seven times brighter than ever daylight shown. The Grail, as the embodiment of God is indeed a "heart of light." As in Eliot's poem, Lancelot is unable to move, and his senses fail:

> Ryght so entird he into the chambir and cam toward the table of silver, and whan he cam nyghe hit he felte a breeth that hym thought hit was entromedled with fyre, which smote hym so sore in the vysayge that hym thought hit brente hys vysayge. And thereewity he felle to the erthe and had no power to aryse, as he that was so araged that had loste the power of hys body and hys hyrynge and syght. . . . and leffte hym there semynge ded to all people.[441]

Thus, within the context of Wagner's opera about the Chivalric Romance "Tristan and Isolde," Eliot narrates a failed sexual encounter between the

---

440. *Ibid.*, ll. 38-41.

441. Sir Thomas Malory, *Works* (Oxford: Oxford UP, 1983), p. 597. Right so he entered into the chamber and came toward the table of silver, and when he came nigh it he felt a breath that he thought was mingled with fire , which struck him so sore in the face that he thought it burnt his face. And therewith he fell to the Earth and had no power to rise, as he that was so frenzied that he had lost the power of his body and his hearing and his sight. . . . and left him there seeming dead to all people.

hyacinth girl and her lover which then suggests spiritual failing through Lancelot's swoon in front of the Holy Grail. We see, then, that the impotence of the speaker in this section of *The Waste Land* is both sexual and religious, and points to a serious degradation spiritual life in the Modern world. The overall meaning that Eliot depicts in this section draws on two fundamental drives — sexual love and mystical transcendence. And both fail. The sexual impotence described in this section is also spiritual emptiness. The failure of sexual love is caused by the wasted spiritual horizon of *The Waste Land*.

The theme of debased sexuality continues as Eliot creates a dramatic dialogue between two women in a bar. One of them, Lil, will soon reunite with her husband, who is being released from the military. Poor Lil is said to look "antique" at the young age of thirty-one. Her appearance is profoundly criticized by her husband — "I swear, I can't bear to look at you." He gave her money with which to buy false teeth — "You have them all out, Lil, and get a nice set." But Lil, already mother of five, has used the money to get an abortion. The pills she took from the black-market chemist to induce the abortion have left her decrepit:

> You ought to be ashamed, I said, to look so antique.
> (And her only thirty-one.)
> I can't help it, she said, pulling a long face,
> It's them pills I took, to bring it off, she said.
> (She's had five already, and nearly died of young George.)
> The chemist said it would be all right, but I've never been the same.
> You are a proper fool, I said.
> Well, if Albert won't leave you alone, there it is, I said,
> What you get married for if you don't want children?[442]

Lil's worn appearance may cause the end of her marriage:

> He's been in the army four years, he wants a good time,
> And if you don't give it him, there's others will, I said. . . .
> Others can pick and choose if you can't.
> But if Albert makes off, it won't be for lack of telling.[443]

---

442. Eliot, *The Waste Land*, ll. 156-164.
443. *Ibid.*, ll. 148-149, 154-155.

The marriage institution is not strong enough to keep Albert's desire for sex gratified by Lil, in her wasted condition — brought on by her abortion that was brought on by his desire for sex.

In a third counter-romance, characters are drawn from the lower class of society. A bored typist and a self-absorbed clerk meet for dinner, served in cans, and then engage in lifeless sex. The couple is even compared to machines.

> At the violet hour, when the eyes and back
> Turn upward from the desk, when the human engine waits
> Like a taxi throbbing waiting. . . .[444]

The conceited clerk arrives at the home of the typist. He is, "A small house agent's clerk . . ./One of the low on whom assurance sits/As a silk hat on a Bradford millionaire."[445] The typist has no erotic feelings, but still does not resist. The clerk's conceit takes the typist's "indifference" as a "welcome."

> The meal is ended, she is bored and tired,
> Endeavors to engage her in caresses
> Which still are unreproved, if undesired.
> Flushed and excited, he assaults at once;
> Exploring hands encounter no defense;
> His vanity requires no response,
> And makes a welcome of indifference.[446]

When the encounter is over, no feelings of ecstasy have erupted. Rather, the typist is glad it is over. She moves like a machine, and rather than sing any song from her heart, she plays a record on the record player:

> She turns and looks a moment in the glass,
> Hardly aware of her departed lover;
> Her brain allows one half-formed thought to pass:
> "Well now that's done: and I'm glad it's over."
> When a lovely woman stoops to folly and
> Paces about her room again, alone,
> She smoothes her hair with automatic hand,
> And puts a record on the gramophone.[447]

---

444. *Ibid.,* ll. 215-217.
445. *Ibid.,* ll. 231-233.
446. *Ibid.,* ll. 236-242.
447. *Ibid.,* ll. 249-256.

This passage is made even more sad by a reference Eliot makes to Oliver Goldsmith's *The Vicar of Wakefield*. In Goldsmith's story, the Vicar's daughter Olivia has returned home after being jilted by a false lover. She sings a song, one evening, about false love from which Eliot borrows a line:

> When lovely woman stoops to folly,
> And finds too late that men betray,
> What charm can soothe her melancholy,
> What art can wash her guilt away?
>
> The only art her guilt to cover,
> To hide her shame from every eye,
> To give repentance to her lover,
> And wring his bosom — is to die.[448]

Moved by her own experience, Olivia falters in her singing. The contrast can hardly be more marked. Olivia's shame and sorrow, evidenced in her broken song, is twisted by Eliot into mere relief that the sexual encounter has ended. Olivia has returned home to the community of family, but Eliot's typist paces around her room alone. And rather than showing any emotional response, Eliot's typist "Smoothes her hair with automatic hand." Mechanical connotations are further heightened by the typist putting a disk on the gramophone, contrasting Olivia's tender singing.

The *Waste Land* is a place utterly devoid of spirituality and love. Carnal interactions bring no passion; religious symbolism brings no meaning or refinement of humanity. This utter lack of significance finds expression in a short phrase in the poem. "I can connect/Nothing with nothing. . . . /My humble people who expect/Nothing."[449] Rather than hope for spiritual rewards, absolutely nothing is expected in the *Waste Land*. There is even a question about whether one can be said to live at all.

> "What is that noise?"
> The wind under the door.
> "What is that noise now? What is the wind doing?"
> Nothing again nothing.

---

448. Oliver Goldsmith, *The Vicar of Wakefield* (New York: New American Library, A Signet Classic, 1961), pp. 127-128.
449. Eliot, *The Waste Land*, ll. 301-302, 304-305.

"Do
"You know nothing? Do you see nothing? Do you remember
"Nothing?" . . .
"Are you alive or not? Is there nothing in your head?[450]

No Gods. No love. The absence of spirituality leaves no actual life in the *Waste Land*. Eliot has written a powerful indictment on the Modern world. And the Modern world responded. *The Waste Land* was an instant success. People resonated with its symbolism and content. It shaped Modern literature as much as it reflected the norms of a wasted society.

To a large degree, the world of *The Waste Land* is with us today. Television provides a constant stream of distraction from spiritual depth with its puerile sit-coms that titillate with adolescent sexual snickers. News media bombard us with sensationalism and scandal, attacking our ability to reason with tiny sound-bites of information. Sex is a tool of Madison Avenue to crassly sell anything from alcohol to automobiles. Film has lost the ability to find tragic struggles of past theatrical works such as Shakespeare or of ancient Greece. Instead, numbing violence, car chases and spectacular crashes distract us from considering the meaningful issues of rich spiritual life. Churches are dwindling in population, except for fundamentalist congregations that would ignore the advances of scientific thought and ask their parishioners to live in a Victorian world of the past. Our Post-Modern world is every bit as debased as Eliot's *Waste Land*.

We flounder about in the fragments of former traditions that no longer cohere into a system of meaning:

> I sat upon the shore
> Fishing, with the arid plain behind me
> Shall I at least set my lands in order?
> London Bridge is falling down falling down falling down . . .
> These fragments I have shored against my ruins. . . .[451]

---

450. *Ibid.*, ll. 118-122, 124.
451. *Ibid.*, ll. 424-427, 431.

CHAPTER XI. ANCIENT VOICES ECHO IN MODERN HALLS: THE RECENT EROTIC SPIRITUALITY OF VATICAN II AND DAVID MATZKO MCCARTHY, KARL BARTH, AND EBERHARD JUNGEL

The voices of recent erotic spirituality come mainly from the cloistered tower of the university, or from real cloisters. Hence they have remained largely insulated from the arid currents of the Waste Land. Recent spirituality has been able to preserve some of the dearest articulations of romance from the past, but along with their nostalgic grasp on the best from the past, some of the problematic traditions in the preceding chapters reverberate even in modern theologies. Some preserve Plato's fear of passion; others echo the ancient Biblical tradition of female subservience to men.

Vatican II

Platonism is still preserved in Catholicism, in his tradition of Transcendental Love. For Catholics, the highest form of spiritual discipline is to merge totally in God, renouncing marital love. But if the highest form of spiritual love means to leave behind a dearly loved human, then what does that say about married life?

A massive convocation was held to re-think many Catholic traditions in the mid-1960s. Since it was the second such convocation held in the Vatican, it is commonly referred to as "Vatican II." While many traditions were challenged, the doctrine of priestly celibacy remained unchanged. The beliefs of Augustine,

Jerome, and Chrysostom, which we looked at in Chapter 4, were retained. Vatican II teaches that the highest bond with God is found by renouncing a dearly beloved mortal — even as Plato sought to bond with the Ideal Form of Beauty. Still, priests are given a contradictory teaching regarding celibacy. They are told, on the one hand, to revere the married estate, and on the other hand, to recognize the superiority of virginity:

> Seminarians should be duly aware of the duties and dignity of Christian marriage, which bodies forth the love between Christ and the Church (cf. Ephesians 5:32ff). Let them perceive as well the superiority of virginity consecrated to Christ, so that by a choice which is maturely thought out and magnanimous they may attach themselves to God by a total gift of body and soul.[452]

This document clearly prefers the celibate life over marriage. In celibacy the priest attaches to God body and soul. In celibacy, the priest grows more maturely, masters soul and body better, and comprehends more blessedly the promises of the Gospel:

> Let them be warned of the very severe dangers with which their chastity will be confronted in present-day society. . . . [M]ay they learn so to integrate the renunciation of marriage into their life and activity that these will not suffer detriment from celibacy; rather, that they themselves may achieve a greater mastery of soul and body, and added growth in maturity; and may comprehend more profoundly the blessedness promised by the Gospel.[453]

We looked at the Platonic origins of this doctrine in Chapter 1; and we followed its severe incorporation into Christianity in Chapter 4, where in the most extreme analogy — put forth by Jerome — marriage was compared to hell itself.

Yet Vatican II softens its discussion of marriage. While Thomas Aquinas discussed the love between married persons only briefly, and was primarily worried about sexual passion, Vatican II provides a touching testimonial to married love. It reads as though written by some romancer of the Chivalric

---

452. *The Documents of Vatican II*, Walter M. Abbott, Gen. Ed., "The Deepening of Spiritual Formation," (Chicago: Follett Publishing Co., 1966), p. 447.

453. *Ibid.*

period, instead of a scholarly, celibate theologian. Vatican II is indeed generous in its treatment of married love:

> Such love, merging the human with the divine, leads the spouses to a free and mutual gift of themselves, a gift proving itself by gentle affection and by deed. Such love pervades the whole of their lives. Indeed, by its generous activity it grows better and grows greater. Therefore it far excels mere erotic inclination, which, selfishly pursued, soon enough fades wretchedly away.[454]

But we still see the justification for marriage that Thomas Aquinas wrote about in the Middle Ages, which we looked at in Chapter 6. The purpose, or should we say excuse, for marriage is to beget children — "Marriage and conjugal love are by their nature ordained toward the begetting and educating of children" (253). Vatican II states plainly that anything that interrupts this purpose is contrary to the marriage contract:

> . . . sons of the Church may not undertake methods of regulating procreation which are found blameworthy by the teaching authority of the Church in its unfolding of the divine law.[455]

Does not the voice of Thomas echo here, who could justify sexual passion only by the procreation of human life?

Finally, what can a thinking person do with these modern teachings from Vatican II? Let's recall our philosophical arguments from Chapter 1. If Plato is right, and in order to merge with the Ideal Form of Beauty we must leave behind any attachment to another mortal, then marriage holds us back from spirituality. If, on the other hand, Longus is right, and married love is a gift from the god of love, then denying personal love is a rejection of God. One can't have it both ways. How, then, can an aspiring priest affirm the dignity of marriage while he himself renounces marriage in order to pursue a greater form of spirituality? Isn't a priest, by his very life, casting a shadow on marriage? Does not Jerome echo in Vatican II? In Chapter 4, we saw that Jerome compares celibacy to gold and marriage to silver. While Vatican II has warmed up to the dignity of marriage and uses none of Jerome's harsh language, the Church still considers Transcendental Love superior to marriage.

---

454. *The Documents of Vatican II*, "Conjugal Love," p. 253.
455. *The Documents of Vatican II*, Harmonizing Conjugal Love with Respect for Human Life," p. 256.

David Matzko McCarthy

A complex and fascinating argument has very recently been put forth by the crypto-Platonic David Matzko McCarthy. I call him crypto-Platonic because his Platonism comes mediated through Catholicism, and one cannot even tell that he is Catholic until one peers through his arguments and counts the references to Vatican II and to popes.

McCarthy's *Sex and Love in the Home*[456] contains wonderful ideas and also alarming ones. His arguments about romance are extremely challenging — so challenging that I felt he needed an answer. Throughout my book, I articulate various traditions of romance from Western civilization. Throughout his book, McCarthy appears to attack these traditions in a crypto-Platonic fashion. McCarthy and I even conflict in our methods of argument. Much of McCarthy's argument is based on his own personal experience, while much of my own work is based on deeply entrenched literary traditions. It's hard to argue with someone who says, "This is what I, myself, experience." But can McCarthy claim that others share his personal experience? Furthermore, can one man's personal experience negate the cultural values that call for the continued publication of literary works from past ages? The texts I have drawn on have lasted because they express deeply held convictions of the human spirit. They have assumed mythic status. They are part of the vocabulary of our culture.

As I have said, McCarthy has some wonderful things to say. His treatment of spiritual love is noteworthy. For him, the highest form of spiritual love conjoins people; it doesn't ask the devotee to merge with an abstract God. It wants to form bonds of communion with fellow humans. Love prompts us to give of ourselves to others. But like all lovers — Aristotle's friends, for instance — we hope for reciprocity. We want to be joined with the other in an ongoing community of giving and receiving. "In the working of reciprocity, giving is completed when giver and recipient receive each other, so that the gift opens the way for common life."[457] The community this form of mutual giving generates is theological — it is the way God's love operates. "[A]t best, love forms a circle of mutual giving and receiving between God, self, and others."[458] The mutual

---

456. David Matzko McCarthy, *Sex and Love in the Home* (London: SCM Press, 2001).
457. David Matzko McCarthy, *Sex and Love in the Home*, p. 137.
458. *Ibid.*

exchange of good will is erotic in the technical sense of general desire. It desires to have the other join with self. This love makes life flourish for everyone. "[B]eing moved by another, being moved by love and compassion, suggests that we are inclined to draw near to him or her. One self-giving act will probably draw us into more such acts, as we are moved to the love of fellowship and common flourishing."[459]

Too often, theological descriptions of love describe it as "disinterested." In these descriptions, one gives without thought of recompense. It is true that love does not expect payback. But a lover does wish to be loved in return. As Aristotle said,

> But it is admitted that we ought to wish our friend's good for his sake, and not for our own. If we wish people good in this sense, we are called well-wishers, unless our good wishes are returned; such reciprocal well-wishing is called friendship or love. . . .[460]

Mutual well-wishing, or mutual gifts from the heart, forms a community of holy love.

As the above suggests, McCarthy is concerned with love as community. With that understood, he wants to locate husband and wife in a wide community of relations. He argues against the traditions of Daphnis and Chloe and Tristan and Yseut in which the lovers form a private world for just themselves, cut off from the rest of the world. He does not think that husband and wife alone can fulfill each other's needs — far from it:

> In contrast to romantic personalism, it is my view and experience that so-called outside relationships are necessary to the internal health of family. Typical descriptions of marriage are so concerned to defend it that they imagine a husband and wife making each other wonderfully complete (giving to the other "totally" and exhausting the other self). This defense of marriage seems to be a formula for failure.[461]

Rather, McCarthy argues for a wide connection of relations between relatives, friends, neighbors, and co-workers.

---

459. *Ibid.*, p. 137.
460. Aristotle, *The Nichomachean Ethics* (Buffalo, New York: Prometheus Books, 1987), pp. 257, 258.
461. David Matzko McCarthy, *Sex and Love in the Home*, p. 215.

Surely, neighborhood life, work, food cooperatives, and networks of friends complete the internal operations of family and multiply its possible configurations. Families work well when we do not expect them to give us all we need, and local connections are internal to how the household works.[462]

McCarthy wants marriage to expand into relations extrinsic to the lovers themselves.

"[C]onjugal union flourishes when opened outward to a wider order of love . . ."[463]

Robert Frost provides a metaphor for McCarthy's holy community of relations. The soul is compared to a tent whose central pole points upward to heaven with the guy lines signifying personal attachments surrounding the spiritual center.

The Silken Tent

She is as in a field a silken tent
At midday when a sunny summer breeze
Has dried the dew and all its ropes relent,
So that in guys it gently sways at ease,
And its supporting central pole,
That is its pinnacle to heavenward
And signifies the sureness of the soul,
Seems to owe naught to any single cord,
But strictly held by none, is loosely bound
By countless silken ties of love and thought
To everything on Earth the compass round,
And only by one's going slightly taut
In the capriciousness of summer air
Is of the slightest bondage made aware.[464]

McCarthy is highly critical of accounts of romance that emphasize only private relations between couples. He calls romantic love between two persons a romantic "dyad." McCarthy defines romantic love as a self-sustaining sphere joining a couple together. "The fundamental aspect of romantic love is not

462. *Ibid.*, pp. 111-112.
463. *Ibid.*, p. 207.
464. Robert Frost, "The Silken Tent," in *The Complete Poems of Robert Frost* (New York: Holt, Rinehart and Winston, 1967), p. 443.

passion itself, but the idea that love is a sphere of its own, that love is a self-sustained connection."[465] When one penetrates McCarthy's difficult prose, one finds that love, as the purpose for uniting a couple, "does not sit well" with McCarthy. His argument becomes complicated by his including of passion in his complaint about love. It is not clear whether passion itself is a problem, or the notion of love as the conjoining drive for marriage.

> Love as passion, in the contemporary sense, is considered a means to cause commitment, unity and mutual responsibility. . . . the goal of love as passion is to sustain its connection through nothing other than the love of connection itself. People are likely to conceive of "relationships" as based, not on a pursuit of common goods, but on the activities of having a relationship as a good in itself. As a sphere of activity and a separate sense of connection, this romantic love does not sit well with us. . . .[466]

McCarthy is clear that he doesn't want lovers to be severed from their outside connections. "Romantic love and 'having a relationship' are oriented as a flight from home, as couples imagine renewing their bond through weekend trips to Bermuda, or dropping the kids off for a weekend at grandmother's."[467] In short, "modern romantic love seeks a liminal place outside the structures of everyday life."[468]

A closer look at McCarthy's complaint against romantic love reveals submerged Platonism. This keen and progressive theologian is yet haunted by Plato's ghost, when examined closely. The traditions we have been looking at are deeply embedded in our culture.

McCarthy is suspicious of passion — which might make us suspicious of McCarthy, after all we have considered so far. In discussing the problem of love as the foundation for uniting with another, which we looked at just above, McCarthy broaches the subject of passion. I repeat that portion.

> Love as passion, in the contemporary sense, is considered a means to cause commitment, unity, and mutual responsibility. . . . As a sphere of activity . . . this romantic love does not sit well with us, and it is certainly inhospitable to home.[469]

---

465. McCarthy, p. 61.
466. *Ibid.*, p. 51.
467. *Ibid.*, p. 154.
468. *Ibid.*, p. 155.
469. *Ibid.*, p. 51.

His attack on passion continues throughout his work. Someone seeking only passion is McCarthy's definition of the lover. "[L]over, if considered a primary description, has no practical context other than the perpetuation of the relationship itself through passion."[470] In another place he disparages desire, adding it to his general complaint against romance. He doesn't think rapture will sustain a personal union.

> The promise of desire is that we will come alive and transcend the ordinary. We will discover a deeper self that is not available in the regular course of life. Illouz points out that this preference for romantic love is incompatible with what constitutes common sense about companionship and mutual happiness.[471]

The rapture of passion is often referred to by McCarthy as a "liminal" experience. The quest for these "liminal" experiences devalues ordinary life, and therefore is problematic. McCarthy looks elsewhere for meaning.

> One striking result of theological romanticism about marriage is that it actually takes the joy out of the regular course of things. We must always be looking beyond for moments of self-discovery, liminal experiences, and total abandon. In order to understand enjoyment and struggles of sex and love in the home, a different approach will have to be taken. We will have to set ourselves to cultivating a social landscape that reproduces love and passion of a different kind.[472]

McCarthy attempts a precise definition of passion but in this he fails. His discussion becomes diffuse. In one place, he defines passion with terms borrowed from capitalist market theory. He claims, and he might be right about this, that our culture teaches us that our desire for desire must stay hungry. With each passionate encounter we find only the desire for more passion.

> Because sexual desire is enlivened by the new and improved, dissatisfaction is key to this grammar of good sex. The need for novel pleasures is accompanied by a need for ceaseless sexual yearning, so that if a person is contented, he or she ought not be.[473]

---

470. *Ibid.*, p. 154.
471. *Ibid.*, p. 53.
472. *Ibid.*, p. 64.
473. *Ibid.*, p. 36.

Using his definition of passion based on market theory, in which novelty is the basis for sexual excitement, McCarthy argues that routine is a threat to passion. But he also includes romantic love in this criticism, mixing it with passion. He complicates his argument further by stating that marriage is a threat both to passion and to romantic love. "From the side of romantic love . . . marriage is a threat to sexual passion insofar as sexual practices become routine and ordinary."[474] He states imperiously that "Love and passion die once partners settle at home."[475] He assumes without question that passion will die in marriage, if we are romantics.

> When romance is the linchpin of a relationship or a marriage, then the couple, after the first wave of passion is gone, will have to work a great deal in order to conjure up passion and spontaneity. The romance is likely to die because one or both partners will become tired of working to restore what is supposed to be spontaneous passion.[476]

We gradually realize that McCarthy is trying to use the term "romance" in a technical sense. A careful reading of his text shows that he means to criticize only a particular form of romance. His complaint is supposed to be with the kind of romance peddled by Wall Street advertisers and the editors of, say, *Cosmopolitan* magazine.

> First, I sustain a critique of market capitalism and the contractual social economy. The market requires that our desires be nomadic, that our long- ing never find a resting place. In the market, our experiences of things and people are considered ideal when they conjure up more desire, and drive us incessantly onward to new things. In order to enliven us, our desires must be continually unsettled. . . .
> Contemporary romanticism is not the selfless love of medieval trouba- dours.[477]

So McCarthy may not be arguing against the medieval tradition of Tristan and Yseut. However, by lumping the romantic "dyad" into his critique of romance, and by his distrust of passion, McCarthy's use of the term "romance" comes to mean more than he wants it to mean. It has been my purpose in the

---

474. *Ibid.*, p. 197.
475. *Ibid.*, p. 64.
476. *Ibid*, p. 163.
477. *Ibid.*, p. 213, 214.

preceding chapters to identify various strains of romantic tradition. The problem with McCarthy is that he blurs the varieties and distinctions that I have been at pains to separate out in my work. We might say that McCarthy is criticizing Ovid's style of romance. If so, we can locate McCarthy in Spenser's "cruel cupid" critique of romance.

If he is suspicious of romantic articulations of love, what, then, is McCarthy after? He clearly says that marriage isn't based on the mutual passion between lovers. Rather, he points our attention to roles, duties, and merely functional relationships we participate in outside the mutuality of romantic love. This comes out in yet another critique of romantic love understood as a passionate emotional bond.

> Romantic love is spontaneous and based in emotion over against utilitarian rationality, cost-benefit analysis and other means of rational control. Through passion, we can find the depth of who we are, apart from roles, duties, and merely functional relationships.[478]

McCarthy would rather see the bond of marriage based on common goals like managing a household, washing dishes, raising children, or coaching soccer teams. "We could say that love is cultivated through activities that are not focused on love, but on common, goal-directed purposes."[479] For him, it is practical matters that bind a couple together. "When a couple has a practical bond, they are free to be less clingy. They will not fear diverting their attention from the romantic gaze."[480] Ultimately, romantic love is optional in McCarthy's account of marriage.

> The irony is that romantic relationships tie passion and spontaneity to strenuous labors in a way that productive and role-oriented marriages do not. When a wife's intimacy with her husband is founded on common practical ends and a shared vocation, she is bound by a different affective regard, and she may be surprised now and then when passion stirs up. Romantic desire may arise, or it may not.[481]

You don't even need to be in love, to be husband and wife.

---

478. *Ibid.*, p. 61.
479. *Ibid.*, p. 157.
480. *Ibid.*, p. 164.
481. *Ibid.*, p. 164.

My wife and I cooperate in home economics, in tasks such as managing finances and taking active roles in our community. She and I might carry on these practical matters quite well without being "lovers."[482]

McCarthy's problem with the "dyadic" couple and his distaste for passion finally are understandable when he accidentally blurts out a blatant Catholicism. "Theologically, the two intrinsic goods of marriage are unity and procreation."[483] This sweeping statement is indeed true for Catholic theology, but not for all theology, as we will see below in Karl Barth and Eberhard Jungel. What McCarthy is referring to are the "marriage goods" of Thomas Aquinas. Is this, then, what it all comes down to? As I said in my introduction, the traditions we have been looking at are deeply entrenched in our culture.

A brief recollection of Thomas's theology will reveal why McCarthy has his antipathy for the "dyadic" couple and his suspicion of passion. For Thomas Aquinas, passion is a problem because it interrupts reason. No wise person would give up something as good as reason unless he derived some other benefit. The excuses for passion are the "marriage goods."

> No wise man should allow himself to lose a thing except for some compensation in the shape of an equal or better good. Wherefore for a thing that has a loss attached to it to be eligible, it needs to have some good connected with it, which by compensating for that loss makes that thing ordinate and right. Now there is a loss of reason incidental to the union of man and woman, both because the reason is carried away entirely on account of the vehemence of the pleasure, so that it is unable to understand anything at the same time, as the Philosopher says (Ethic. Vii. 11); and again because of the tribulation of the flesh which such persons have to suffer from solicitude for temporal things (1 Cor. vii. 28). Consequently the choice of this union cannot be made ordinate except by certain compensations whereby that same union is righted; and *these are the goods* which *excuse* marriage and make it right.[484]

There are three marriage goods: faith, childbirth, and sacrament. Faith means you remain faithful to your spouse, childbirth means that you intend children when you marry and have sex, and sacrament is a divine dispensation

---

482. *Ibid.*, p. 154.

483. *Ibid.*, p. 209.

484. Thomas Aquinas, *Summa Theologica Supplement*, Volume III, *Summa Theologica*, trans. Fathers of the English Dominican Province (New York: Benziger Brothers, Inc., 1948), Question 49, Article 1 (emphasis mine).

("grace") given by the marriage ceremony that allows you to perform the goods of marriage in a holy manner.

For Thomas, sexual pleasure without the intent of procreation is always a sin. "If, however, he seek pleasure within the bounds of marriage, . . . it is a venial sin."[485] We now know why McCarthy sees common functional roles and procreation as the purpose for a couple's uniting. "Up to this point, the current chapter has reversed the typical order of things by locating the unitive end of marriage within the procreative good."[486] This is the case even for couples who haven't yet conceived. "Even for couples who do not have children, openness to procreation signifies a course of life and the character of the home."[487] Thus McCarthy has labored hard to found a theology of sexuality that both undercuts romance and affirms the marriage goods of Thomas Aquinas.

The "dyads" Daphnis and Chloe and Tristan and Yseut, and the romantic ideal they represent, must be problems for McCarthy. They are in love without intending procreation. Their sexual pleasure is a venial sin. Two lovers who find satisfaction in mutual love alone are missing one of the "marriage goods" that excuse sex. Thus all couples who unite through love alone rather than the desire to beget offspring are problems for McCarthy. This is the underlying reason for his critique of romantic love and passion. The chain of influence can clearly be drawn from Father Plato, through Aristotle, his pupil, through Thomas Aquinas (add indirect influence from the Platonist Saint Augustine representing Catholic traditions acting on Thomas), to David Matzko McCarthy.

Karl Barth

Not being bound by Thomas Aquinas' marriage goods, modern Protestant theologians have written more rapturous accounts of sexual love and spirituality. The early Protestant reformers fought to preserve marriage from the contradictions of a system that valorizes celibacy. They demoted marriage from the status of a sacrament and made it a rite. They did this to free marriage from interference of the mediaeval Church which invaded every aspect of life with restrictions and prescriptions; but by devaluing marriage they have taken away some of the sanctifying power with which religion can invest life.

A great modern Protestant theologian named Karl Barth articulated a powerful sexual theology. Being a Swiss, his theology follows a step-by-step logic not unlike the workings of a fine watch.

---

485. *Ibid.*, Question 49, Article 6.
486. McCarthy, p. 209.
487. *Ibid.*, p. 212.

He starts his arguments by asserting that to be a human being is to be in relationship with other humans. We are only humans if we are fellow-humans. "Humanity, the characteristic and essential mode of man's being, is in its root fellow-humanity. Humanity which is not fellow-humanity is inhumanity."[488] And fellow-humanity for Barth is not neuter or sexless. In our essence, we are either male or female. And since we are persons only as fellow-persons, our primary defining relationship is with the other sex. Essential humanity is a relation between man and woman.

> Man never exists as such, but always as the human male or the human female. Hence in humanity, and therefore in fellow humanity, the decisive, fundamental and typical question, normative for all other relationships, is that of the relationship in this [sexual] differentiation. . . . We have to say that man is necessarily and totally man or woman, and that as such and in consequence he is equally necessarily and totally man and woman.[489]

We are who we are, we are defined as people, only as gendered people. And our gender is defined in relationship with the opposite sex. What is male is so only by relationship to what is female, and conversely.

> Nor can he wish to liberate himself from the relationship and be man without woman or woman apart from man; for in all that characterizes him as man he will be thrown back upon woman, or as woman upon man, both man and woman being referred to this encounter and co-existence.[490]

This radical relationship between man and woman exists because of a fundamental duality in God himself. Recall that in Genesis 1, man and woman were created together in the image and likeness of God. The theological implication of this sexual duality is that God himself is a duality reflecting the two sexes. The essential relationship between man and woman reflects an essential relation within God, in whose image man and woman are created. The first relationship humanity is born into is a relationship with God. The second relationship is with fellow humans.

> In God's own being and sphere there is a counterpart: a genuine but harmonious self-encounter and self discovery: a free co-existence and co-

---

488. Karl Barth, *Church Dogmatics*, vol. III.4: *The Doctrine of Creation* (Edinburgh: T. &T. Clark, 1985), 54, p. 117.

489. Karl Barth, *Church Dogmatics*, vol. III.4, 54, pp. 117, 118.

490. *Ibid.*, 54, 118.

operation; an open confrontation and reciprocity. Man is the repetition of this divine form of life; its copy and reflection. He is this first in the fact that he is the counterpart of God, the encounter and discovery in God himself being copied and imitated in God's relation to man. But he is it also in the fact that he is himself the counterpart of his fellows and has in them a counterpart, the coexistence and co-operation in God Himself being repeated in the relation of man to man.[491]

The relationship between man and woman, and God and humans, does not draw humankind away from each other, up into a transcendental immersion in the Absolute. Rather, because God has an interrelationship in his own essence, when humans love God they repeat this divine interrelation by forming relationships with each other. And the fundamental relationship for a human is the relationship between man and woman. So love of God inclines a human toward involvement in the relationship between man and woman.

Barth's insistence on the radical interrelatedness between man and woman leads easily into praise for Romantic Love. Barth speaks passionately about the yearning of the sexes for union. One is not surprised to find Barth drawing on the *Song of Songs* — that most erotic book in the Bible — when he discusses romantic love. Barth speaks of sexual love separately from the social institutions of marriage and family. Sexual love between man and woman has its own life and does not depend on the social demands to continue the clan, family, or the relationship between parent and child. For Barth, the *Song of Songs* is a bold statement of the power of eros between man and woman.

> A comparison of Genesis 2 and the *Song of Songs* does at last reveal that what interested the authors of the creation saga and these love songs was the fact that in the relationship between man and woman — even prior to its character as the basis of the father-mother-child relationship — we have to do primarily with the question of an incomparable covenant, of an irresistibly purposed and effected union. The *Song of Songs* is one long description of the rapture, the unquenchable yearning and the restless willingness and readiness, with which both partners in this covenant hasten towards an encounter.[492]

Barth is decidedly against the Platonic idea that a person could transcend his or her gender and merge with the Absolute by himself. One cannot opt out of

---

491. Karl Barth, *Church Dogmatics*, vol. III.1: *The Doctrine of Creation* (Edinburgh: T. & T. Clark, 1958), 41, p. 185.

492. *Church Dogmatics*, III.1. 41, p. 313.

the fellowship between male and female, and become a sexless, non-gendered or androgynous being. The intention to become a whole being in oneself is a violation of one's sexuality and an attempt to avoid the sexual dualism intended from creation. Barth does not specify the practices he has in mind when he discusses this attempted escape, but he does mention certain schools of mysticism and Gnosticism which are strongly influenced by Plato. No doubt the schools of Transcendental eros we have been examining thus far would fall into this category, and perhaps the psycho-mystical practices deriving from Jung which seek to unite male and female (animus and anima) attributes within the psyche. Such an attempt,

> . . . aspires beyond its own and the opposite sex to a third and suppos-edly higher mode of being, possible to both sexes and indifferent to both. . . . What is sought is a purely human . . . sexless, abstractly human, and to that extent a third and distinctive being as compared with male and female . . . It is no accident that this type of consciousness has been traditionally impregnated with the magic fragrance of so much mysticism, mythology and gnosis. It is a movement in which man and woman aspire to overcome their sexual and separated mode of existence and to transcend it by a humanity which is neither distinctively male nor female but both at once, or neither.[493]

The desire to "embody in myself alone the whole human being" is to desire a neutered sexuality and hence is a flight from "humanity, . . . the fellowship of the sexes."[494] One is even gendered in eternity. "God created man as male and female, . . . an inward, essential and lasting order of being as He and She, valid for all time and also for eternity."[495] Hence the relationship between the sexes takes place on sacred soil — it is not a function strictly of nature or biology.

But for all his romanticism, Barth is yet a man of his time. He reverts to chauvinism when he speaks about the nature of male and female relations. In the interactions between the sexes, it is the will of God that men be the sexual aggressor. "[H]e is a man, . . . and thus precedes and is superior in relation to woman. . . . he is ordered, related and directed to woman in preceding her, taking the lead as the inspirer, leader, and initiator in their common being and action."[496] Barth is working from the old doctrine of Ephesians 5, the passage

---

493. *Church Dogmatics*, III.4. 54, p. 157.
494. *Ibid.*
495. *Ibid.*, III.4. 54, p. 158.
496. *Ibid.*, III.4. 54, p. 170.

that states that the man is the head of the wife as Christ is the head of the Church. These traditions are deeply embedded in our culture. Barth seeks to soften this doctrine by saying that the man is to act in humility and not lord his superiority over the woman:

> Thus the man does not enjoy any privilege or advantage over woman, nor is he entitled to any kind of self-glorification, simply because in respect of order he is man, and therefore A [A precedes B]. . . . This order simply points him to the position which, if he is obedient, he can occupy only in humility, . . . He cannot occupy it, then, for himself, let alone against her, or in self-exultation, let alone in exaltation over her and therefore to her degradation, . . . Only as he accepts her as fellow-man, only together with her, can he be the first in his relationship to her — the first in a sequence which would have no meaning if she did not follow and occupy her place in it.[497]

Barth wants to hold on to his Protestant Biblical tradition that he reads in Paul, but also to soften the impact in order to make his doctrines acceptable to the Modern mind. For all of his progressive thought, Barth is yet a product of cultural forces. The old traditions of chivalry were still operative in society when he was writing; today, we would probably want to reject both Barth and Paul (or, some of us would). Others still value the old dating rituals. We are in the throes of a cultural revolution. Part of the past remains; part of the future emerges. And we flail about in the maelstrom as the past is broken and the future attempts to gain a foothold.

Eberhard Jungel

A rhapsodic theology of love has recently come forth from the halls of the German academy. With the rapture of a poet, Eberhard Jungel keenly observes the dynamics of romance, and includes these dynamics in his theology.

Eberhard Jungel begins with powerful assertions about God, assertions that lead to his conclusions about interpersonal love.

Jungel holds that the fundamental Christian statement is the proclamation that "God is love." In fact this one statement defines all theological discourse. "To think God as love is the task of theology."[498] Jungel's claim is emphatic and sweeping.

---

497. *Ibid.*

498. Eberhard Jungel, *God as the Mystery of the World*, (Grand Rapids, Michigan: William Eerdmans Publishing Company, 1983), p. 315.

To tell about God's being can and may mean nothing else than to tell about God's love. The statement "God is love" must accompany all talk about God . . . if such talk is to correspond to God.[499]

This proclamation has been prominent throughout Christian history. "Christian theology has given many answers to the question of the being of God. But among all those answers, it has always assigned unconditional primacy to this one: God is Love."[500]

Jungel is equally emphatic that the statement "God is love" is inseparable from God's humanity. Through the human Jesus God becomes known to humans. And he is known as love by his self-sacrificing act of surrender to the complete human condition, even to death.

And thus the Crucified One belongs to the concept of God. For the giving up of the eternal Son of God takes place in the temporal existence of one, that is, of this crucified man Jesus. In him, the love of God has appeared (1 John 4:9), because that love has happened in him.[501]

This "once for all" act of incarnation is the event that makes manifest the humanity and the love of God. "The uniqueness, definitiveness, and the 'once for all' nature of the humanity of God are expressed most stringently in the confession 'God is love.'"[502] By the self-sacrificing act of God's incarnation in the human Jesus, the equation between God and love is revealed.

It is then faith in the humanity of God which preserves the identity of God and love. Faith in the humanity of God is the evidence of the identity of God and love.[503]

Thus for Jungel, all thought and word about God must be understood in the light of God as a divine human. "God's humanity belongs to his divinity. This is what theology must finally begin to learn."[504]

Understanding the humanity of God implies possibilities that otherwise might not arise. God's humanity dignifies and sanctifies our human condition. Since God is love and is human, love as humans know it is sanctified. And by

---

499. *Ibid.*, p. 314.
500. *Ibid.*
501. *Ibid.*, p. 372.
502. *Ibid.*, p. 314.
503. *Ibid.*, p. 343.
504. *Ibid.*, p. 37.

sanctifying love as humans know it, God also sanctifies Romantic Love as one particular facet of human love.

In making his claim, Jungel argues against the Transcendental Platonic forms of Christianity that we have looked at earlier. Jungel acknowledges that Platonism has constituted a significant tradition in the history of Christianity; and Plato's Transcendental world located way above the mortal world made God impossible to talk about in earthly language.

> It is the spirit of Plato which is expressed in this fundamental statement, "The Deity, therefore, is ineffable and incomprehensible." Mediated by Neo-Platonism, the basic Platonic decision about the speakability of God made its way into Christianity. It was especially Dionysius the Areopagite (see Acts 17:34) who brought this philosophical decision to its position of influence within Christian theology.[505]

Platonic articulations of God put God far beyond any human conception or any experience that is available to the human condition, into a "transmundane realm" above every earthly reality.

> The Platonic experience of "that which far exceeds the essence" goes beyond the surpassing of being and presents itself as transcendence over everything which exists and every being, into a transmundane realm, "far exceeding everything," so that even the superlative of being has to be surpassed if one wants to arrive at the divine.[506]

Thinking of God as incomprehensible separates God from love and causes love to recede into a "dark background."

> We must bluntly ask whether the logical distinction of subject and predicate in the statement "God is love" is not generally interpreted by theology in the sense of an ontological difference between God and love, so that love certainly "recedes and sinks" into what is truly a "dark background — God."[507]

The God created after Plato's Absolute Good is entirely above all existence also transcends any thought, word, conception or imagining of humankind. Language, then, must resort to only negative words to express God's being, since

---

505. *Ibid.*, p. 233.
506. *Ibid.*, pp. 233-234.
507. *Ibid.*, p. 316.

any word derived from human experience isn't high enough to speak of this transcendent God —

> In that God is the one who is above all thought, he is called incomprehensible. And in that God is that goodness which surpasses all speech, he is called and he is the Ineffable. Because he is a God who can be expressed through no word, whose deity surpasses every word, this Trans-Word is described most adequately as Non-Word, and accordingly, Non-Name and Non-Knowledge (Jungel's paraphrase of Dionysius the Areopagite).[508]

God as described by the Platonic Christians is said to be beyond passion (*apatheia* = apathy) and unchangeable ("immutable"), even as the Neo-Platonic Plotinus described the original One behind all. This is the object of intellectual love with whom the follower of Platonic Christian "Eros" finds himself in relation. As we will see just below, Jungel argues vehemently against Platonic descriptions of God. For him,

> God based on the cross of Jesus has destroyed the axiom of absoluteness, the axiom of apathy, and the axiom of immutability, all of which are unsuitable axioms for the Christian concept of God. . . . the God who is love must be able to suffer and does suffer beyond all limits in the giving up of what is most authentically his for the sake of mortal man. . . .[509]

Platonic descriptions of God are not just cast-off medieval relics. They can be found in the theology of modern theologians such as Karl Rahner. The traditions we have been looking at are deeply entrenched. As with Plato, love of God for Rahner is of an "unconditional and radically unique kind."[510] Love of God for Rahner sounds a good deal like the doctrine Jungel criticized just above, where "love certainly 'recedes and sinks' into what is truly a 'dark background-God'."

> In this love for Jesus . . . what occurs is precisely that unconditional and radical act of human existence, ultimate and unique, in which the human being surrenders to God accepting his eternal brilliance and radically mysterious incomprehensibility. . . . He or she is prepared to commit everything with the dying Lord to the incomprehensibility of God — the whole world and the self — quietly, unconditionally, even if this God seems darker than

---

508. *Ibid.*, p. 234.
509. *Ibid.*, p. 373.
510. Karl Rahner, *The Love of Jesus and the Love of the Neighbor* (New York: State Mutual Book and Periodical Service, 1988), p. 44.

the absurdity upon which the philosophy of a Sartre or a Camus is centered.[511]

One notices familiar terms in Rahner's theology that Jungel has pointed out — "mysterious incomprehensibility," "commit everything — the whole world and the self," "darker than . . . absurdity." And Rahner appears to imply Plato's ladder of love when he remarks that one must commit "unconditionally" to this transcendent God. Doesn't *The Cloud of Unknowing*, which we looked at in Chapter 6, echo in Rahner's words? In *The Cloud of Unknowing*, the devotee is told to give up all human love of created things, all human knowing, and to sink into the dark cloud of God. Rahner's sentence seems to invoke these very teachings,

> Thus the absolute, the utterly unconditional, can only occur, when it occurs in the human being at all, in the surrender of *everything* to the incomprehensibility of God [italics mine].[512]

Jungel's statements about the humanity of God emphatically oppose this kind of theology. God is not, as Rahner has it, incomprehensible. Jungel insists that God is knowable, thinkable, and speakable through his self revelation in the human Jesus.

> The God who has no analogy in all that exists has become accessible to us as God in his Son. He, the Son, is the image of God (II Cor. 4:4), and that means the image of the invisible God (Col. 1:15), the reflection of his glory and the imprint of his being (Heb. 1:3). As such, he is God's self-communication: the Son through whom God has ultimately spoken (Heb. 1:2). In God the Son, God has now expressed himself in such a way that he has become speakable for us. For that reason, he is called, as the eternal Son, also the word of God (John 1:1). In this word God is knowable, speakable, perceivable, as God. For whoever hears the word hears the Father, and whoever sees him who is the eternal word of God sees the Father (see John 14:9; 12:45).[513]

Knowing, thinking, and speaking about God is not exaggerated anthropomorphism. God himself is knowable through his revelation in the human Jesus.

---

511. *Ibid.*, p. 45.
512. Rahner, p. 45.
513. Jungel, *God as the Mystery of the World*, p. 386.

God has shown himself to be human in the execution of his divinity. To think of him as one who speaks, to speak of him as one who speaks, is not a "dogmatic anthropomorphism," . . . but rather the result of that event in which God becomes accessible in language, which the Bible calls revelation. . . . God as the word comes close to man in human words.[514]

These arguments all support Jungel's initial statements about the humanity of God.

[T]he model of human talk to God is based on the certainty of a God who is human in his divinity. God is thinkable as one who speaks because and to the extent that he is human in and of himself.[515]

As we saw just above, for Jungel, God is love. And God as love is seen only in the humanity of God. Jungel waxes exceedingly zealous at the consequences if God and love become detached. Then, a God can be imagined without the predicate of love. When this happens, theology becomes interested in abstract conditions of deity, such as power and hiddenness, which, in turn, allows religious atrocities. Jungel's zeal comes out in a discussion of Ludwig Feuerbach's critique of Christianity.

. . . [D]oes not Feuerbach's caricature hit the mark when it can view the God who is differentiated from love only as a loveless monster? Is not Feuerbach right when he fears that theology is more interested in the "absolute power of God" and in the "hidden God" (*potentia dei absoluta, deus absconditus*) than it is in the truth that God is love? We should not lightly evade this diagnosis of an inappropriate theological distinction between God and love: "So long as love is not exalted into a substance, into an essence, so long there lurks in the background of love a subject who even without love is something by himself, an unloving monster . . . whose personality, separable and actually separated from love, delights in the blood of heretics and unbelievers — the phantom of religious fanaticism!"[516]

We don't know whether Rahner's incomprehensible God delights in the blood of heretics, but we do know that Rahner's God does not think much of Romantic Love. After arguing for absorption into the incomprehensible darkness of God, Rahner "poisons" romantic conceptions of love. He lists a series of

---

514. *Ibid.*, p. 288.
515. *Ibid.*, p. 289.
516. *Ibid.*, p. 316.

neurotic fears that he claims "avowedly or not are tacitly or expressly bound up" in the experience of Romantic Love.

> But let us begin with the fact that human love generally, however unconditional, radical, and definitive it might like to be, is still codetermined in some way by a secret reservation. The lover's fear of "not measuring up" to the beloved, of not doing justice to him or her — or that the beloved could deny the lover requital of love, which the latter requires in order to continue in this love — the terrible fear of loving someone and having it emerge that there is no longer anything about this person to make him or her lovable . . . whether it is not after all really only a transitory infatuation, gradually dying, after all, and killed by time — these and similar reservations or fears, avowedly or not, are tacitly or expressly bound up with one person's human love for another.[517]

Clearly, Rahner is arguing against romance in favor of Platonic Christianity. Rahner brings up these neurotic fears, which he claims are intrinsic to human love, in order to show how much better love for God is. The insecurities in human love are presented to contrast the perfection of total devotion to Jesus. Only devotion to Jesus truly fulfills a human and quenches those objects of necessary doubt in human love. His method of argument, then, is to use the fears which he uncovered in human love to urge the reader's attention away from human relations to a contemplation of perfect, absolute, divine love.

> Our purpose in presenting its fears and difficulties here is to see by contrast what love for Jesus means. . . . The last reservations and insecurities of all human love are transcended in the case of love for Jesus. . . . at bottom this love for Jesus is unconditional and of an inner absoluteness that "fills out," completes, a human being altogether, and truly makes him or her over to Jesus as the uniquely loved human being.[518]

Finally, an indication of Rahner's real position on romantic love can be gleaned by his description of human relations. Rahner dissolves the kind of heartfelt devotion seen in Romantic Love, where lovers express longing only for each other — the feeling that only that one particular other has the special quality that inspires love. This is the love that we saw between Daphnis and Chloe, and between Tristan and Yseut. Yet for Rahner, human relations are

---

517. Rahner, *The Love of Jesus and the Love of the Neighbor*, p. 40.
518. *Ibid.*, p. 41.

arbitrary. One can love, or withhold love indifferently in a community of "replaceable" finite beings. Any one finite being can be replaced by any other.

> For whatever is not identical with God, taken by itself alone, is finite, conditional, and capable of being replaced or expelled by someone else. It can be loved, yes, but it can be denied love, because, precisely, it is finite.[519]

Isn't Rahner's minimizing analysis of romance exactly what Walter Kasper has in mind when he writes, "Sexuality and marriage have frequently been devalued in the history of Christianity"?[520] But history isn't the only source of Christianity's devaluation of sexuality and marriage. Rahner is Modern. Yet he carries on the devaluation of human love that is the mark of Christian Platonism.

The zeal with which we saw Jungel attack Transcendental forms of Christianity is understandable if we recall the conclusion we reached in chapter one. Transcendental eros is utterly opposed to Romantic eros. Both forms of love cannot coexist together. It must be either-or. Since Jungel includes Romantic Love in his theology he must undermine Transcendental love— just as Rahner, who argues for Transcendental love, must undermine Romantic love.

Jungel, then, has established his theology of "God is love," understood exclusively in the humanity of God. He has further contrasted his theology with Platonic articulations of God (which I exemplified by a discussion of Karl Rahner). Jungel then proceeds to a discussion of interpersonal love. He opens his discussion by considering human love in general. His treatment of human love follows from his assumption that God as love is understood only in the humanity of God. Understanding God's humanity dignifies the human condition, bringing humanity close to divinity. "[T]he mystery of the God who identifies with the man Jesus is the increase of similarity and nearness between God and man...."[521] The humanity of God raises human life into God's realm. Spirituality, then, is concerned with the epitome of what can be experienced as good by humans. And the perfect human life is to live in human love, in all its varieties.

Jungel's system, then, emphasizes spiritual love as it is known in human experience.[522] "To think God as love," one must "do justice to the essence of love, which as a predicate of God may not contradict what people experience as

---

519. *Ibid.*, p. 45.

520. Walter Kasper, *Theology of Christian Marriage* (New York: The Crossroads Publishing Company, 1983), p. 7.

521. Jungel, *God as the Mystery of the World*, p. 288.

522. "Earth's the right place for love:/I don't know where it's likely to go better"—Robert Frost

love."[523] There is no need for it to be otherwise. "For, after all, the love which is possible for men is of God" ([1 John 4] v.2).[524] Contrasting the systems of Transcendental eros which have a Universal Good as their object, Jungel's system valorizes the relationship between fellow humans. "Love is an event which does not only occur in relation to God. Love does not only take place between man and God. Love is no less than an interhuman event."[525] Mutual human love is a spiritual experience. Such a statement is true because the believer is then participating in who and what God is. He or she then "belongs" to God. "And thus he can be called on to love. In that he does that, he is of God."[526] A generalized love between all humans includes the specific expression of Romantic Love, and recognizes the spirituality of it as well.

In Jungel, the central place that erotic love holds in general human love is given serious consideration. The intensity of mutual love between a loving I and a beloved Thou is a part of God's love for and with humans. Unlike the shyness with which McCarthy and Rahner approached the romantic aspects of love, Jungel openly includes romantic desire in spiritual love. And he does so by denying "disinterested" forms of love that don't seek reciprocity.

> Before we pursue this further, it must be noted that love is not identical with absolute selflessness. Love is oriented toward a specific Thou. It desires this Thou and not anyone. It looks with pleasure on the beloved Thou and is by no means blind. . . . And the way in which love looks is a very intensive form of the desire to take possession, for which reason that look can be equated with adultery (Matt. 5:28). In short, love includes the desire or lust of love.[527]

In Jungel, genuine love desires to have the beloved, or to belong to the other. Some Christian writers are afraid to talk about mutual belonging between lovers. They want spiritual love to be all-giving. But for lovers, this is not the case. For them, love is directed at one specific beloved, and they want that one and no other.

In deeply interpersonal love, one's sense of self dissolves. One's "self" becomes more and more replaced by an intense valuing of the other. One's desire for self pales before the desire for other, and in a very real way one loses oneself

---

523. Jungel, p. 315.
524. *Ibid.*, p. 326.
525. *Ibid.*, p. 337.
526. *Ibid.*, p. 326.
527. *Ibid.*, p. 318.

through desire for the beloved. Having one's beloved is more valuable than having one's own self. But just as strongly as one wants one's beloved, one wants to be loved in return. We want the other to want us just as much as we want the other.

> In such surrender . . . I do not want to have anything from anyone, not even myself. Rather I want to be had [a rather unfortunate rendering of the original German]. Self-possession, self-having, is replaced by being possessed. But the same is true of the beloved I. . . . For the beloved Thou can "have" the loving I only to the extent that it is had by it as well.[528]

The turning toward the other is thus a turning away from self. In (mere) affection, the I remains with itself, and I suggest that the same is the case in friendship. But in love, the self-turning becomes radical and is properly called "surrender." "For the I who truly loves [turns] . . . to the beloved Thou in such a way that it is turned completely away from itself. The turning away from oneself and the turning to someone else are now radical. We are now speaking of surrender."[529]

In the intense ardor of love, the beloved is considered closer than one is to oneself. "In the event of loving surrender, then, a radical self-distancing takes place in favor of a new nearness to oneself — a nearness, to be sure, in which the beloved Thou is closer to me than I am to myself."[530] But since one cannot love without being loved in return, the other person, who has and who holds one, gives one back to oneself. "But the beloved Thou gives me myself in that it has me, so that I have myself again, but in a completely new way."[531]

This dynamic of surrender to the other, then receiving the self back from the beloved, actually transforms the self. The loving and loved one is not the same self that a single person is, who holds his or her own ego. In the experience of love, one surrenders one's ego to the other. One's very being changes. Being changes from a self-possessed ego to one of possessing and being possessed by the other, as the other becomes more dear to one than the self.

> The Thou to which the loving I surrenders itself promises thus a totally new being. . . . Thus, the statement addressed to God is true of every genu-

---

528. *Ibid.*, p. 321.
529. *Ibid.*
530. *Ibid.*
531. *Ibid.*, p. 322.

ine love relationship: "Whom have I in heaven but thee? And there is noth-ing upon Earth that I desire besides thee" (Ps. 73:25). Heaven and Earth — that would be too little, much too little, in comparison with the beloved Thou. Yes, the beloved Thou is more to the loving I than its own exist-ence.[532]

Thus, one has a sense of self, but only one that is given by the beloved, to whom one completely surrenders. This transformation of being, such that self is mutually yielded to and held in the other, is the very essence of eros.

> [T]he self-loss in the event of love is already surpassed by the new being which the loving I receives from the beloved Thou in the act of surrender. In this . . . exchange of being between the self-surrendering I and the Thou who gives me myself anew consists the true desire or lust of love, which cannot be made to happen.[533]

Jungel's Christian theology echoes an ancient tradition that can be found in Chivalric Romance Literature. The language of Chretien de Troyes, the first Arthurian Romance writer, is almost identical to Jungel's. In Chretien, we read Jungel's description that the lover feels "there is nothing upon Earth I desire besides thee," that the beloved is "more to the loving I than its own existence," and the same intense surrender to the beloved. These impassioned lines are spoken by the knight Yvain to his lady:

> . . . my heart never wanders from you or is to be found elsewhere; so that I can't think of anything else; so that I surrender myself entirely to you; so that I love you more than myself; so that, if it is your pleasure, I wish to live and die wholly for you. [534]

Jungel is thus incorporating traditions of Chivalric Romance into Christian theology. Or, put differently, he is recognizing theological value in romance. As with Daphnis and Chloe, for Jungel, Romantic Love is life in God.

This radical transformation of being through mutual belonging happens only in eros. It cannot occur in the disinterested regard for others described by certain theologians. Nor can it occur in the philosophical friendship of Plato. One can't have one's own self and another, too. The transformation of identity in

---

532. *Ibid.*, p. 321.
533. *Ibid.*, p. 322.
534. Chretien de Troyes, "Yvain," in *Arthurian Romances*, trans. D. D. R. Owens (London: J. M. Dent & Sons, Ltd., 1987), p. 308.

interpersonal love is so radical that Jungel says a "yawning chasm" separates the single person from the lover. It is actually a change into a different kind of being.

> Between love and non-love there is a yawning chasm, in comparison with which the contrast between heaven and Earth threatens to lose its significance. Whoever is not "in love" can share in it only through "transformation into another kind" (*metabasis eis allo genus*).[535]

Jungel's form of love is in the tradition of Romantic Love. Eros, for Jungel, is not a love for the Absolute, or even for the neighbor. Rather, is is a love exclusively for two who mutually love only each other — "it is this person and no other." "We shall orient ourselves to the indisputable insight that love opens the eyes. Not for everything, but for the beloved Thou."[536]

> There are two people who have chosen each other. They turn to each other and thus each one away from him or herself. They surrender to each other and forget themselves. . . . In such selflessness, the lovers receive their selves anew, each from the other and only from that one.[537]

Selflessness and surrender are central to Jungel's discussion of eros. Accordingly, demonic aspects of the desire to possess such as domination, are not possible. As Paul Tillich puts it, "One individual can conquer the entire world of objects, but he cannot conquer another person without destroying him as a person."[538] This means that neurotic possessiveness or the extreme of rape are not consistent with the structure of love.

> What is then of great significance ontologically and theologically is that the fact that the loving I wants to have the beloved Thou and only then wants to have itself transforms the structure of having. For the beloved Thou is desired by the loving I only as one to whom it may surrender itself. Love is mutual surrender, and the desire of love is the most extreme enemy of violent assault.[539]

The element of selfless surrender is often considered to be a form of love called *agape*, or Christian charity. In Jungel, it isn't either-or. While arguing

---

535. Jungel, *God as the Mystery of the World*, p. 326.
536. *Ibid.*, p. 319.
537. *Ibid.*, p. 324.
538. Paul Tillich, *Systematic Theology*, 3 Vols., Vol. I, (Chicago: UP of Chicago, 1951), p. 177.
539. Jungel, p. 319.

against a strictly Platonic conception of eros,[540] Jungel asserts that agape, or Christian charity, can accommodate eros; "agape is a power which integrates eros."[541] To express benevolence and self-surrender is not to exclude eros. Rather, "it must be emphasized that love which is fully understood will not exclude eros from itself."[542] And indeed, the specific I-Thou love of eros does not leave the two lovers enclosed upon themselves. Rather, as in McCarthy, eros but wants to "radiate out into the realm of lovelessness."[543]

> . . . the I-Thou relationship itself leads beyond itself. Love wants to radiate. As love, it presses to move beyond the lovers themselves. For that reason, love does not lead into an idyllic retreat from the world, . . . It wants to radiate out into the realm of lovelessness.[544]

These capacities for love, the agapistic and erotic, are finally part of the divine order. We are capable of such love because God is that love, and has composed the world out of such love. Our loves are a participation in God. "The erotic and caritative activities done by men are, for their part, correspondences of the divine being which is love."[545]

Referring to 1 John 4, Jungel parallels the human lover-beloved relationship to God-human relations. We are God's beloveds. "The people who are regarded as believers are pointedly called 'beloved' here (vv. 1, 7, 11)."[546] We are empowered to love God by first being loved by God, "For the beloved is already participating in love in such a way that he is then able to love. And thus he can be called on to love."[547]

While Jungel may be thick to read through, I think his theology is important because Jungel makes Romantic Love religious. Not since Swedenborg have we seen a theologian who favors romantic love so dearly. Jungel's articulation, while perhaps deep and dense, is enraptured nonetheless.

In Jungel, we see the argument that we looked at in the first chapter of this book. By beginning his theology with the assumption that God is love and that God is human, Jungel is able to argue for the spirituality of human love. And

---

540. *Ibid.*, pp. 337-338.
541. *Ibid.*, p. 338.
542. *Ibid.*, p. 338.
543. *Ibid.*, p. 325.
544. *Ibid.*, p. 325.
545. *Ibid.*, p. 339.
546. *Ibid.*, p. 326.
547. *Ibid.*

Romantic Love is included in human love. As with Daphnis and Chloe, the God of love creates Romantic Love for humans. Romantic Love is participating in God. Jungel is clearly in the category defined by Longus.

The theology of sexuality in Jungel is outright opposed to Rahner's theology of sexuality. Jungel is oriented toward Romance while Rahner is oriented toward Transcendence. And in Rahner, as for Plato, God is considered above all mortal thought. He is incomprehensible. Following this idea of God, Rahner is suspicious of human love and describes a series of neurotic fears all human love is heir to. He calls for a complete and total devotion to God. Rahner is clearly in the category defined by Plato. The argument with which we began this book continues even in the present age in theology.

But things get even worse in the Post-Modern age. It's no longer just Longus versus Plato. All the traditions we have looked at become jumbled into fragments that we must struggle to make cohere. While the theologians mentioned in this chapter are informative and inspiring, they are not being heard by the masses. Their teachings are usually heard only by theology students locked up in the high tower of the university. Some modern mainstream divinity students may indeed mention these theologians in the sermons they preach to their aging and dwindling congregations; but their influence pales compared with the onslaught of media bombardment and the apathy of *The Waste Land*. Most people today are living in *The Waste Land*, not the cloister; so the beautiful words of McCarthy or Jungel are drowned out or sloughed off, or missed entirely.

Another reason why theologians like McCarthy or Jungel have a weak influence on our culture is that society has reacted strongly against some of the traditions that we have inherited from the past, including the Church. We have just seen some brilliant modern ideas tarnished with the discolorations of objectionable ancient traditions. The Church has put forth ideas that many reject today — some, for good reason. Many feel the need to break entirely from organized religion, rather than pursue the laborious process of sifting through Church doctrines to decide which they would keep and which they would discard. And even when people attempt to put together the valuable fragments of our traditions in a unique synthesis, do they find a Church willing to accept their privately-defined religion?

Ultimately, the theologians we have looked at in this chapter have too weak a voice to significantly impact the deep traditions of romance our culture has generated, or to account for the world after *The Waste Land*. It is now time to press on in an analysis of Post-Modern society and the challenges for love and spirituality we face in today's culture.

CHAPTER XII. A HEAP OF BROKEN IMAGES? EROTIC LOVE AND SPIRITUALITY IN THE POST-MODERN AGE

We have come a long way from the innocent love of Daphnis and Chloe, and the severe philosophical devotion of Plato. We have sketched Aristotle's well-defined friendship doctrines. We have snickered with Ovid as he scandalously manipulates amorous affairs. We have studied the Bible with its rich and varied statements about marriage. We have observed the strictures of Christian celibacy in Augustine, Jerome, and Gregory of Nyssa. We have seen stories of deep devotion such as that of Tristan and Yseut. We have followed Thomas Aquinas as he tried to champion marriage within the doctrines of Platonic reason, and witnessed Luther's stormy clash with the Catholic doctrine of celibacy. We have traveled with the Swedish visionary Swedenborg into a heaven peopled with married couples who are joined in spiritual union. We have soared with Shelley in his reverie of amorous Platonic poetry. We have languished in the waste desert of the Modern world, dead of God and love, in the poetry of T.S. Eliot. And we have heard ancient echoes in the interpersonal spirituality of the modern cloister.

We suggested that these powerful traditions now exist only in fragments that don't cohere into a complete system of meaning. As Nathan Scott put it, our society experiences a "broken center." We are dead at the center of our spiritual plane. We now live in a de-mythologized universe. The sky is no longer the abode of the Classical gods, nor even of the Christian heaven. Instead, it is an infinitely vast, vacant space sparsely occupied by dead matter. This disjunction from a mythological universe to a material one has left couples with only each other to turn to for romantic inspiration. They can't turn outward to the greater world around them in order to reinforce their personal feelings. There is no complete system to turn to.

Paul Tillich discusses this "end of culture" in an application of what he calls "culture theology." Our culture is characterized by a void, in all its forms. Our cultural void causes Tillich to despair of linguistic expressions, as Eliot does in *The Waste Land*. "Son of man, you cannot say/for you know only a heap of broken images."

> A present theology of culture is, above all, a theology of the end of cul-
> ture, not in general terms but in a concrete analysis of the inner void of
> most of our cultural expressions. Little is left in our present civilization
> which does not indicate to a sensitive mind the presence of this vacuum . . .
> Who of us has never been shocked by this void when he has used tradi-
> tional or untraditional secular or religious language to make himself under-
> standable and has not succeeded and has made a vow of silence to himself,
> only to break it a few hours later? This is symbolic of our whole civiliza-
> tion.[548]

Tillich's despair over modern linguistic resources echoes Eliot's *Waste Land*. "Son of man,/You cannot say, or guess, for you know only/A heap of broken images. . . . " The emptiness of our cultural resources puts tremendous strain on the relationships, having only the internal support of the couple itself and no cultural, spiritual, or mythic support.

Some of this brokenness may be good. We may be throwing off traditions that were too problematic.

Literature, not religion, has remained love's best champion. Romantic Love has always had a tense relationship with religion. While we all intuitively feel a spiritual power in Romantic Love, usually the Church's theology is devoted to other topics. It is as if Romantic Love isn't a proper theological topic. In Swedenborg, Romantic Love finds its first theological champion; but Swedenborg's influence in the history of religions has been slight. He has, however, had a great influence on writers of fiction, the true home of Romantic Love.

It was in fiction and poetry that love was most deeply championed. Longus gave us our earliest known Romance. In his tale of the gentle pastoral peasants Daphnis and Chloe, Longus taught us that love is God's gift. Ovid made love a

---

548. Paul Tillich, *The Protestant Era* (Chicago: UP of Chicago, 1957), p. 60.

center of his creative powers, despite his scandalous treatment. And later, the writers of Chivalric Romance made love almost a religion unto itself. Let's hear Shelley's praise of chivalry again, because one can't overestimate the power that Chivalric Romance gave to love. Shelley claims that the influence of these wonderful works of literature actually made people better humans:

> Love became a religion, the idols of whose worship were ever present. It was as if the statues of Apollo and the Muses had been endowed with life and motion, and had walked forth among their worshippers; so that Earth became peopled by the inhabitants of a diviner world. . . . it were superfluous to explain how the gentleness and the elevation of mind connected with these sacred emotions can render men more amiable, more generous and wise, and lift them out of the dull vapors of the little world of self.[549]

But now it appears that Romantic Love's champion has abandoned it. Eliot's *The Waste Land* displays a vacuous world devoid of God and of love. Where can present-day lovers turn for edification? Can they find inspiration in the glut of sleazy romance novels spewed out from cheap paperback presses — or even major publishing? Can they find a voice in magazines, with their Ovidian tips for improving sex life, getting a lover, dressing right, and enhancing our beauty? We lack a profound literature that will bespeak the deep spirituality lovers intuitively feel — even if it lies deeply buried under a deluge of media images and a surfeit of superficiality, or lies dormant waiting to be aroused. Meanwhile our souls languish in the vacuity of Post-Modern society.

Can anyone find depth in the self-help psychology books that fill bookstore shelves? It seems that psychology has now appointed itself the source for intimacy that the Church once was. Basing its findings on soft science, psychology attempts to provide the modern world with advice in a form that accords with the new foundations of truth. But one can hardly read these works without feeling Nathan Scott's "broken center." There's something dead at the heart of these self-help tracts. Or rather, we feel that there is something more to love than these works give us.

In Post-Modern life we have attempted to create new traditions of sexuality in the vacuum left us from the past. One notable attempt is the women's movement that reached a crescendo in the 1960s and has continued to affect our lives.

---

549. Percy Bysshe Shelley, "A Defense of Poetry," in *The Selected Poetry and Prose of Shelley*, Harold Bloom, ed. (New York: New American Library, 1978), p. 435.

A pioneering exponent of the women's liberation movement was Betty Friedan. Her massive and compelling *The Feminine Mystique*[550] struck a chord in "housewives of all educational levels."[551] The book, written in 1963, is still in print today; in fact, it is so important that it is still used as a text in university courses. Ponderously researched and clearly reasoned, *The Feminine Mystique* is a convincing work that attacks a long-held tradition about women's role, specifically the notion that women's "role was to seek fulfillment as wives and mothers."[552] When she wrote, in 1963, the predominant "mystique" about women was that their very nature was bound exclusively by the role of wife and mother. Friedan cites profusely from cultural sources that served to promulgate this mystique. According to her research, popular women's magazines, Freudian psychiatry, sociology, educators at universities — including exclusive women's colleges — and advertising all perpetuated the doctrine that a woman should aspire to no other calling than mother and wife. Yet everywhere Friedan turned in her interviews with housewives, she repeatedly found housewives sharing a "feeling of desperation" with their lives.[553] Women restricted to "Occupation: housewife" asked themselves, "Is this all?"[554]

The extent to which society enforced the mystique of "Occupation: housewife" as a final be all and end all for woman was insidious. Women's magazines consciously printed articles only about motherhood and marriage. Male editors truly believed that women couldn't understand anything else. " 'Women can't take an idea, an issue, pure,' men who edited the mass women's magazines agreed. 'It has to be translated in terms they can understand.'"[555] Friedan, herself a writer for women's magazines, was aware of this prejudice:

> By the time I started writing for women's magazines, in the fifties, it was simply taken for granted by editors, and accepted as an immutable fact of life by writers, that women were not interested in politics, life outside the United States, national issues, art, science, ideas, adventure, education, or even their own communities, except where they could be sold through their emotions as wives and mothers.[556]

550. Betty Friedan, *The Feminine Mystique* (New York: W. W. Norton & Company, (1997).
551. *Ibid.*, p. 28.
552. *Ibid.*, p. 15.
553. *Ibid.*, p. 28.
554. *Ibid.*, p. 15.
555. *Ibid.*, p. 51.
556. *Ibid.*, p. 50.

Freudian psychology became an intellectual idol by the mid 1940s and exerted its influence through the 1950s. To Friedan, Freud became more than a scientific method for bettering humanity's psyches. "Freudian psychology became much more than a science of human behavior, a therapy for the suffering. It became an all-embracing American ideology, a new religion."[557] And for Freudian psychology in the 1950s, a woman's desire for something greater than wife and motherhood was seen as pathological. It was a symptom of "penis envy." This term means that if a woman was striving for occupations and roles that men occupied (and men exclusively occupied nearly all the professions and vocations), she was responding neurotically to make up for her lacking the male member by emulating men's behaviors. Freud, himself, clearly states this in a lecture on "The Psychology of Women."

> The desire after all to obtain the penis for which she so much longs may even contribute to the motives that impel a grown-up woman to come to analysis, and what she quite reasonably expects to get from analysis, such as the capacity to pursue an intellectual career, can often be recognized as a sublimated modification of this repressed wish.[558]

Sociologists enlisted in culture's efforts to promulgate the definition of women as "Occupation: housewife." Margaret Mead, a brilliant anthropologist, and a woman, became a rallying point when she reinforced the feminine mystique. In a book entitled *Male and Female*, she describes a functional difference between the sexes and concludes that women should not enter men's roles in society.

> It is of very doubtful value to enlist the gifts of women if bringing women into fields that have been defined as male frightens the men, unsexes the women, muffles and distorts the contribution the women could make, either because their presence excludes men from the occupation or because it changes the quality of the men who enter it. . . . It is folly to ignore the signs which warn us that the present terms in which women are lured by their own curiosities and drives developed under the same educational system as boys . . . are bad for both men and women.[559]

---

557. *Ibid.*, p. 123.
558. In Friedan, p. 115.
559. In Friedan, p. 145.

And the conclusion of Margaret Mead's studies of primitive cultures was that, "having a baby is the pinnacle of human achievement."[560]

Under the influence of the feminine mystique, and with a presumption that women who possessed college educations had difficulty adjusting to the life as a wife and mother, colleges began teaching courses on adjustment to the home and changed their curricula to be more mother-and wife-oriented. A belief began to be shared in higher education that subjects like "physics, advanced algebra, analytic geometry, four years of language" were "unfeminine."[561] A 1,000 page study, *The American College*, concluded that, "The identity issue for a boy is primarily an occupational-vocational question, while self-definition for the girl depends more directly on marriage."[562] While Yale was admitting women, a psychiatric consultant to Yale University cautioned against encouraging women to have professional careers. "To urge upon her conflicting goals, to stress that a career and a profession in the man's world should be the first consideration in planning her life, can adversely affect the full development of her identity."[563]

The many manufacturers of home appliances had a vested interest in creating an image of the contented housewife. In studying countless documents of an advertising consultant, Friedan noted that the consultant had a keen awareness of "the empty, purposeless, uncreative, even sexually joyless lives that most American housewives lead."[564] Various techniques were employed to sell women on the idea that life in the home was fulfilling and "a means of expressing creativity and individuality."[565] Housewifery was compared to men's occupations as a more creative outlet for women than a career would be. The consultant Friedan studied sold the idea that, "We help them rediscover that homemaking is more creative than to compete with men."[566] To make a woman feel secure about the drudgery of home life, advertisers put spin on the role of housewife. "We help her think of the modern home as the artist's studio, the scientist's laboratory."[567] The idea was to harness the boredom and monotony of housework into an insatiable hunger to spend.

---

560. *Ibid.*, p. 141.
561. Friedan, p. 161.
562. In Friedan, p. 164.
563. In Friedan, p. 365.
564. Friedan, p. 208.
565. *Ibid.*, p. 222.
566. *Ibid.*, p. 227.
567. *Ibid.*, p. 226.

But a new stove or a softer toilet paper do not make a woman a better wife or mother, even if she thinks that's what she needs to be. Dying her hair cannot stop time; buying a Plymouth will not give her a new identity; smoking a Marlboro will not get her an invitation to bed, even if that's what she thinks she wants. But those unfulfilled promises can keep her endlessly hungry for things, keep her from knowing what she really needs or wants.[568]

Friedan's study revealed that in the 1950s women began to marry and have children at markedly earlier ages than in previous generations. She concluded that this early retreat into the home stilted women's identities. It didn't allow for a full development of a woman's intellectual and personal aspirations. She cited the famous psychologist Erik Erikson, who identified a developmental stage in early adult males in which the young man must define his identity in relation to his own aspirations and the limits society puts on him. Finding out who he is in relation to his personal gifts and the social options open to him constitutes a crisis the youth must resolve to reach adulthood. But Friedan points out that this developmental stage is not defined for women. "But why have theorists not recognized this same identity crisis in women?"[569] A woman's identity is defined exclusively by her sexuality — to have children and marry. Imposing this role on women forfeits their own search for identity and the full realization of their potentials; "our culture does not permit women to accept or gratify their basic need to grow and fulfill their potentialities as human beings, a need which is not solely defined by their sexual role."[570] A woman's very humanity depends on her facing the same identity crisis males face. "I think women had to suffer this crisis of identity, which began a hundred years ago, and have to suffer today, simply to become fully human."[571]

After revealing the social sources for the feminine mystique that mother and wife exclusively define a woman's identity, Friedan outlines her program for liberating women. "First, she must unequivocally say 'no' to the housewife image."[572] The primary way to say "no" to the housewife image is through work. But no ordinary job will do. The job must involve her individual abilities and be of benefit to society. "If a job is to be the way out of the trap for a woman, it must

---

568. *Ibid.*, p. 229.
569. *Ibid.*, p. 79.
570. *Ibid.*, p. 77.
571. *Ibid.*, p. 79.
572. *Ibid.*, p. 342.

be a job that she can take seriously as part of a life plan, work in which she can grow as part of society."[573] A menial part-time job will only add to a woman's despair and bring her little personal satisfaction. The same is true of volunteer work. America doesn't respect someone who doesn't earn money for what he or she does. To find fulfillment, then, a woman needs work that will pay and in which she will be respected by her peers. "But I have noticed that when women do not take up painting or ceramics seriously enough to become professionals — to be paid for their work, or for teaching it to others, and to be recognized as a peer by other professionals — sooner or later, they cease dabbling."[574]

It is important to note that Friedan does not exclude marriage and family from the new woman's life plan. She recognizes them as important aspects of everyone's life. But they need to be integrated into a vocation that will allow women to grow as persons according to their own abilities.

> She must create out of her own needs and abilities, a new life plan, fitting in the love and children and home that have defined femininity in the past with the work toward a greater purpose that shapes the future.[575]

But the struggle for this new feminine identity is not only a problem for individual women. Friedan challenges society to radical reform that will allow equality for women. "There are implications of the feminine mystique that must be faced on a national scale."[576] Recalling all the sources she so eloquently cited as propagators of the feminine mystique, Friedan calls on them to reform their attitudes and policies that reinforce the definition of women as "Occupation: housewife":

> We need a drastic reshaping of the cultural image of femininity that will permit women to reach maturity, identity, completeness of self, without conflict with sexual fulfillment. A massive attempt must be made by educators and parents — and ministers, magazine editors, manipulators, guidance counselors — to stop the early-marriage movement, stop girls from growing up wanting to be "just a housewife," stop it by insisting, with the same attention from childhood on that parents and educators give to boys, that girls develop the resources of self, goals that will permit them to find their own identity.[577]

---

573. *Ibid.*, p. 345.
574. *Ibid.*, p. 348.
575. *Ibid.*, p. 338.
576. *Ibid.*, p. 364.

Her closing remarks suggest that culture will benefit from the contributions of self-fulfilled women.

> Who knows what women can be when they are finally free to become themselves? Who knows what women's intelligence will contribute when it can be nourished without denying love?[578]

In her passion to liberate women from the exclusive definition of wife and mother, Friedan doesn't wish to ruin relations between the sexes. In addition to her career as a writer, Ms. Friedan is also a mother and wife. Her true sentiments can be seen in her dedication to this compendious argument for liberation: "For all the new women, and the new men."

Much good has come from the forceful efforts to liberate womankind from the strong male dominance inherited from ages past. Today women are no longer looked at as helpless weaklings who need men to provide for them. They look at men eye to eye on level ground. Or, at least, that is the aim of the liberators.

Women are now in the workforce and thus less dependent on men for their life options. And society is benefiting. If one accepts the thesis that the psyche of womankind values different norms than men do, our culture is now experiencing an influx of more feminine values. As more and more women attain positions of power, they bring their special outlook into their areas of influence.

But as with all change, these new efforts have left society in a state of turmoil. One particularly tragic consequence is the fragmentation that the woman's movement has left the institution of chivalry. In the past, men looked at women as honored beings who received gentle overtures of delicate manners. Now, however, a man is unsure of just how to regard womankind. In the past, knights fought with their fellows to establish structures of subordination and power. Knight jousted with knight to determine wealth and position in the royal court. In Modern society, men competed with their fellow men for wealth and position. In the presence of ladies, men laid aside their violent behaviors to lavish soft affections and gentle manners upon the ladies they served.

But now, women compete with men in the market place. Can one fight with ladies in the work world for limited wealth and then change one's attitude in social settings? Can their competitors in the work world also become the

---

577. *Ibid.*
578. *Ibid.*, p. 378

treasured recipients of noblesse in leisure? Is it conceivable to act under a divided consciousness such that one seeks to overcome a woman in the field of economic competition and to serve her ladylike preferences in the field of social interplay?

And further, society has not yet decided how to structure life outside the work world. Although women are now competing with men economically, and often find themselves on their own with children to provide for, in married households the men are still largely held responsible to be the primary economic provider — so that social expectations and pressure are added to the need to earn. Some men today are fulfilling the household responsibilities that women used to fill, instead of going to work; but we somehow feel that these men are slackers. Men have traditionally worked their 40 hour workday and let women run the house. Now, when men don't work, we look down on them. If a man is supposed to be the primary breadwinner for a household, what can he do if he loses a job to a woman? Similarly, complicated dynamics come into play when a woman with a higher paying job enables her husband to pursue a more artistic, more intellectual or otherwise satisfying job — although, when that happens in the reverse, traditionally we find it more "normal."

Chivalry is also undermined by a dramatic shift in cultural manners today. Many women resent being treated like an agent of special honor. They are men's equals and want to be treated as such. One notable index of this change in manners is found on television and the silver screen. In scenes that would have shocked John Wayne and the culture of the 1950s, women are warriors — equal combatants with men. Many martial arts films and even children's animated stories have women as heroes, overcoming men in physical combat, engaging in fistfights with men. The movie *Crouching Tiger, Hidden Dragon*, which achieved great popularity, portrays a woman defeating countless male martial artists in physical combat. In earlier years, males were taught, "Never hit a woman." Now we see men hitting women constantly (in fictional programs, at the least). Women are becoming men's equals in astounding ways. Feminism has tried hard to revise the perception of women as weaker and in need of special courtesy from men. That has left little room for courtesies that are offered not in recognition of need, but as an honor. Men seeking to show respect for a lady by opening a door for her may find the woman snapping, "I can open my own door!" And when it comes time to pay the bill at a restaurant, she may prefer to pay her share rather than feel beholden in any way to a man. In the market economy, she may not be comfortable leaving the restaurant owing the man something.

Now, we don't know what to do on dates. After a meal, if the lady makes no move when the bill arrives, the man pays. Can a woman call a man up for a date? Some do. Some see nothing wrong with it, and some enjoy the feeling of being the aggressor. But some feel that it cheapens their position to be the aggressor. Can a woman ask for sex? Some men would be delighted; others, deeply offended. If a man doesn't stand up when the lady enters the room, is he showing bad manners or a modern sensibility? Even among young punk rockers, tattooed, pierced, and dressed in black leather, I heard a young woman declare to the group, "I want to go out on a real date! I want the guy to come to my house, pick me up, take me out and pay for it, and take me home!" Was that behavior appropriate for the general ethics of their social structure? Was she sabotaging her results by the way she comported herself in her peer group? And where did such a Post-Modern woman get such an archaic idea about dating, I wondered.

One of the big problems of chivalry is that both parties have to follow defined roles in order for it to function properly. The gentleman acts in the dominant role, and the lady in the submissive role. The turn-of-the century author Henry James defines the code of chivalry well by a character he draws from the old, genteel, southern society of Mississippi.

> He admitted their rights; these consisted in a standing claim to the generosity and tenderness of the stronger race. The exercise of such feelings was full of advantage for both sexes, and they flowed most freely, of course, when women were gracious and grateful. . . . [He] thought that their softness and docility were the inspiration, the opportunity (the highest) of man. . . .[579]

I don't know whether my punker girl would be gracious and grateful. I suspect that she was not soft and docile. And the chivalry of Henry James' southern gentleman carried a heavy price. He thought "that women were essentially inferior to men, and infinitely tiresome when they declined to accept the lot which men had made for them."[580] Clearly, the price of assumed inferiority is unacceptable to today's woman. And prejudicial, predetermined roles are major complaints feminists have with chivalry. Could my punker girl flout chivalry by dressing in ripped leather and exhibiting coarse manners, and still expect to be the recipient of chivalry when dating?

---

579. Henry James, *The Bostonians* (New York: Penguin Putnam Books, 1984), p. 202.
580. *Ibid.*, p. 202.

A major cultural change in regard to courting and marriage occurred in the 1960s, during what has been termed the "sexual revolution." Many of society's cherished ideals and roles regarding the relationship of the sexes underwent a major revision. It began with the term "free love." This meant that one could love and engage in sexual relations without commitments like marriage or engagement.

Although this movement became publicized in the 1960s, in fact, the idea of free love has been propagated from time to time, and in America began to gain ground just slightly earlier in the "Beat" generation. In that era the ideal of free love began to evolve, and in that generation we can see the struggle for liberation clearly in tension with traditions of marriage. The struggle to disengage from conventional social forms is portrayed by one of the great exponents of that generation, Jack Kerouac. His book, *On the Road*, proclaims the incipient ideals of free love and later became a "hippie Bible" in the Sixties. In *On the Road*, music and drug use become intertwined in the lifestyle that included free love as in the Sixties. The only significant differences were that the music at the center of the "mad" life of the Beat generation was avantgarde jazz and the most common drug was alcohol, occasionally also marijuana.

Kerouac's primary character exemplifying free love was Dean Moriarty. As in Shelley's description of the Chivalric period sex was a religion for Dean Moriarty. "[T]o him sex was the one and only holy and important thing in life."[581] It was likewise a spiritual experience for Sal Paradise, who narrates the book. In describing a sexual experience he has with a Mexican girl with whom he spends fifteen days, Sal resorts to religious metaphors:

> I made love to her in the sweetness of the weary morning. Then, two tired angels of some kind, hung-up forlornly in an LA shelf, having found the closest and most delicious thing in life together, we fell asleep and slept till late afternoon (p. 85).

Sex was Dean's overriding passion, along with a zest for finding excitement everywhere in life. Dean "just raced in society, eager for bread and love."[582]

But despite Dean's liberal attitude toward sex he was unable completely to free himself from social conventions. As an adult he married the woman he currently loved, although marriage held little meaning to him. When the book's

---

581. Jack Kerouac, *On the Road* (New York: Penguin Books, 1976), p. 2.
582. *Ibid.*, p. 2.

adventures begin in Denver, Colorado, Dean is involved with two women at the same time and married to one of them. "Dean was making love to two girls at the same time, they being Marylou, his first wife, who waited on him in a hotel room, and Camille, a new girl, who waited for him in a hotel room.[583] Between his two lovers Dean met with his friends to experience "the goodness and joy of life."[584] Soon Dean decides that he is in love with Camille and that he will divorce Marylou and marry Camille. He apparently has Marylou's love and her blessing on the divorce at the same time. Not too much later in the narrative Dean gets back together with Marylou while he is still married to Camille, "He ran and found Marylou in a hotel. . . . Everything was decided again: they were going to stick. Marylou was the only girl Dean ever really loved. . . . he pleaded and begged at her knees for the joy of her being."[585] This love affair was free and unencumbered by marriage, but it didn't last. In New York, Dean meets a woman named Inez with whom he falls in love. Over the phone he arranges a divorce from Camille so he and Inez can marry.[586] The divorce finally happens in Mexico, where the gang was now traveling, and when he returns to New York, Dean and Inez marry. No sooner does this happen, but Dean jumps on a bus to San Francisco to return to Camille. Kerouac sums up Dean Moriarty's affairs succinctly. "So now he was three times married, twice divorced, and living with his second wife."[587]

Throughout Dean's various sexual escapades language of love is interspersed — albeit sometimes in an abstract beat way. At one point when he is with Marylou he says,

> Darling, you know and I know that everything is straight between us at last beyond the furthest abstract definition in metaphysical terms or any terms you want to specify or sweetly impose or harken back . . . ."[588]

At another point, when Dean and Marylou are separated, Kerouac testifies to their enduring love. "He loved her, he sweated over her" (p. 184). Dean himself comes to that realization under the influence of bad marijuana, "I knew I loved Marylou" (p. 184). Similar language is used on Camille. "Are we straight in the

---

583. *Ibid.*, p. 41.
584. *Ibid.*, p. 134.
585. *Ibid.*, pp. 111-112.
586. *Ibid.*, p. 248.
587. *Ibid.*, p. 303.
588. *Ibid.*, p. 155.

deepest and most wonderful depths of our souls, dear darling?" (p. 43). But as his history demonstrates, Dean loves all women and refuses to stay long with one. One may well question whether the term "love" is appropriate for Dean Moriarty's approach to sexuality. Torn between the marriage traditions he inherited from his society and his drive to liberate himself from permanent commitments, one wonders if he isn't seeking mere sexual gratification, in the long run.

Dean's relationships are important because Kerouac makes him the epitome of what a "beat" life should be. The accolades Kerouac lavishes on Dean Moriarty are superlative. Dean is at once "an Angel" (p. 263), "He was BEAT — the root, the soul of Beatific" (p. 195), "a bastard . . . Dean will leave you out in the cold any time it's in his interest" (p. 170), "mad with a completely physical realization of the origins of life-bliss" (p. 132), "a mystic" (p. 121), "a rat" (p. 302) "because of his enormous series of sins, was becoming the Idiot, the Imbecile, the Saint of the lot" (p. 194), "In myriad pricklings of heavenly radiation I had to struggle to see Dean's figure, and he looked like God" (p. 284), and above all Dean will "cut along and make it your own way" (p. 251).

Dean was unable to completely liberate himself from the traditional institution of marriage, though he clearly operated like a "free love" hippie. Neither was the author completely able to free himself from the tradition of marriage. Sal Paradise, the author's alter-ego, displays a similar attempt to wrestle free from marriage traditions while still holding on to them. His case is interesting because in describing his own process he adds valuable philosophical considerations.

In one place his voice is completely conventional:

> In New York I had been attending school and romancing around with a girl called Lucille, a beautiful honey-haired darling that I actually wanted to marry. All these years I was looking for the woman I wanted to marry. I couldn't meet a girl without saying to myself, What kind of wife would she make? . . . "I want to marry a girl," I told them, "so I can rest my soul with her till we both get old. This can't go on all the time —all this franticness and jumping around" (pp. 116-117).

He never does end up marrying Lucille. In another place, his tone is more liberated from convention. It is a highly significant editorial passage that needs careful consideration:

> Boys and girls in America have such a sad time together; sophistication demands that they submit to sex immediately without preliminary talk. Not courting talk — real straight talk about souls, for life is holy and every moment is precious (p. 58).

This passage brings up several critical ideas: sex, courting, and the soul. In the beat generation sex was as freely indulged in as in the Sixties, according to Kerouac — "they submit to sex immediately." For Sal Paradise, this cheapens sexuality. He wants to capture the sense that "life is holy." He believes that significant preliminary talk can instill a sense of the holy into sexuality. Rebelling against tradition, he does not want "courting talk." He wants to break with the social rituals of courting, in which roles and behavior are defined by culture. He wants "real straight talk about souls."

This latter point raises the most important aspect of sexual love in the beat generation. What is the soul that the author wants so desperately to talk about? And will such talk matter? Sal had such talk with a Mexican girl who lasted fifteen days. "[M]ost of the time we were alone and mixing up our souls ever more and ever more till it would be terribly hard to say good-by" (p. 91). But despite "mixing up" their souls, after fifteen days Sal does say goodbye. All that "mixing up" of souls was not strong enough to make their love endure. Neither, perhaps, did Sal want a lasting love at that point in his life.

The great problem his generation brings up, which persists today, is the nature of the soul. By separating sexual love from cultural traditions such as "courting talk," marriage, and religion, tremendous strain is put on the relationship itself. Soul alone is the only glue binding the couple. Then, as today, the possibility of two souls sharing similar fragments of past traditions is a dubious prospect at best.

This can be seen in the nature of the soul as Kerouac describes it in *On the Road*. Sal Paradise's soul is complex, as is evident from a moment of ecstasy he narrates. It is a peak experience that is represented as a goal he "always wanted to reach." It is so fragmented and unique one wonders if another person could share in it, or even if the author could reach it again himself:

> And for just a moment I had reached the point of ecstasy that I always wanted to reach, which was a complete step across chronological time into timeless shadows, and wonderment at the bleakness of the mortal realm, and the sensation of death kicking at my heals to move on, with a phantom dogging its own heals, and myself hurrying to a plank where all the angels

dove off and flew into the holy void of uncreated emptiness, the potent and inconceivable radiancies shining in bright Mind Essence, innumerable lotus-lands falling open in the magic mothswarm of heaven. I could hear an indescribable seething roar which wasn't in my ear but everywhere and had nothing to do with sounds. I realized that I had died and been reborn num-berless times but just didn't remember especially because the transitions from life to death and back to life are so ghostly easy, a magical action for naught, like falling asleep and waking up a million times, the utter casual-ness and deep ignorance of it. I realized it was only because of the stability of the intrinsic Mind that these ripples of birth and death took place, like the action of the wind on a sheet of pure, serene, mirror-like water. I felt sweet, swinging bliss, like a big shot of heroin in the mainline vein; like a gulp of wine late in the afternoon and it makes you shudder; my feet tingled (p. 173).

Much of this ecstasy is influenced by Yogacara Mahayana Buddhism. This is evidenced in the "Mind Essence" that remains through the numberless births and rebirths, the phrase "uncreated emptiness," which sounds like the fundamental Buddhist doctrine of *sunyata*, and the images of lotus-lands, which are the pure lands emanating from Bodhisattvas. In another part of the book, Kerouac again makes reference to *sunyata*, "All of it inside endless and beginningless emptiness" (p. 254). When he sees his first Mexican city across the border, he is reminded of the Tibetan political and spiritual capital city, "it looked like Holy Lhasa." He considers "Benares the Capital of the World" (p. 280). His Buddhistic influences are much more clearly demonstrated in another book he wrote borrowing the Buddhistic term for truth in the title, *The Dharma Bums*. But Kerouac's religious influences are not only Buddhistic. One can find many references to Christianity, particularly Catholic Christianity. In his ecstatic moment he adds the Christian term "heaven" to his mix. And when he sees the eyes of Mexican Indians in the mountains he is particularly Catholic, "They were like the eyes of the Virgin Mother when she was a child. We saw in them the tender and forgiving gaze of Jesus" (p. 297). Even Dean Moriarty has a mystical awareness of God's existence, "And not only that but we both understand that I couldn't have time to explain why I know that God exists" (p. 120). Finally, Kerouac makes a simple and comprehensive statement that brings his generation right into that of the Sixties, "Love is all" (p. 146). We can now leave Kerouac and his gang in their "ragged and ecstatic joy of pure being" (p. 195) and reflect on the implications for erotic love that his work raises.

Kerouac's unique mix of religious traditions makes community extremely difficult. During the time of Dante, culture agreed on the basic tenets of religious tradition. But with Kerouac's individualized mixture of religious sources, can he find another soul to share his convictions? This is a particularly compelling question since Kerouac sees the soul as the only binding force in a relationship. His problem is also our problem today. As Eliot's *Waste Land* demonstrates our culture retains only fragments of traditions from the past — "these fragments I have shored against my ruins."

Following hard on the heels of the beat generation, a secular "religion" arose that gave a new form to "Eros" during the powerful decade of the 1960s. In that decade, the ideal of "free love" exploded in American media and music. The break with erotic traditions begun in the Beat generation intensified. Now, marriage was no longer an issue even as the ethic of love became the dominant theme for the decade. Love was to be liberated from the restrictions put on it by the Church, family, and society. People were free to love whomever they wanted, when they wanted, and without the encumbrances of social structures they no longer needed.

It was a decade of love. Everywhere, love was the dominant ethic. It was a time when brother embraced brother, sister, sister, and lovers mutually embraced without bowing to any outside authority. People believed that their movement of love would transform society. "They would just spread out like a wave over the world and end all the bull-shit, drown it in love and awareness, and nothing could stop them."[589] Even the cynical, comedic Hunter S. Thompson pauses in his drug crazed narrative to reflect soberly on the mid-Sixties:

> It seems like a lifetime, or at least a Main Era — the kind of peak that never comes again. San Francisco in the middle Sixties was a very special time and place to be a part of. Maybe it *meant something*. Maybe not, in the long run . . . but no explanation, mix of words or music or memories can touch that sense of knowing that you were there and alive in that corner of time and the world. Whatever it meant . . .
> . . . every now and then the energy of a whole generation comes to a head in a long fine flash, for reasons that nobody really understands at the time — and which never explain, in retrospect, what actually happened.[590]

---

589. Tom Wolfe, *The Electric Kool-Aid Acid Acid Test* (New York: Bantam Books, 1999), p. 377.
590. Hunter S. Thompson, *Fear and Loathing in Las Vegas* (New York: Vintage Books, 1971), Pp. 66-67.

One searches in vain for substantial literature that chronicles this time period — because the free love ethic was a movement from the "counter culture." It was fueled by the increasingly influential media of television, radio and the press. People were connected immediately across the country as never before.

Although literature of the time did not capture this movement, its spirit is found in countless song lyrics. While song lyrics of all generations seem to celebrate romance, in the Sixties, romance was part of a greater movement which called everyone together in the spirit of love. "All you need is love" (The Beatles); "Love can make you happy" (Mercy); "I think it's so groovy now that people are finally getting together" (Friend and Lover); "Come on people now, smile on your brother. Everybody get together, try to love one another right now" (Youngbloods); "Hello, I love you, won't you tell me your name" (The Doors); "If you come to San Francisco, summertime will be a love-in there" (Scott McKenzie); "What the world needs now is love, sweet love" (Jackie DeShannon); "It's the time of the season/When love runs high. . . . It's the time of the season for loving" (The Zombies); "Your love is lifting me higher, higher and higher" (Jackie Wilson).

Music proclaimed a new age for humanity. For Scott McKenzie, it was happening now — "All across the nation . . . There's a whole generation with a new explanation." For Tommy James and the Shondelles, a new day would arrive ("maybe tomorrow"), bringing peace, love and brotherhood:

> A new day is comin' people are changin' . . .
> Love, love is the answer . . .
> Maybe tomorrow when He looks down . . .
> All of his children every nation
> There'll be peace and good brotherhood.

An immensely popular rock opera, *Hair*, proclaimed the new Age of Aquarius:

> This is the dawning of the Age of Aquarius . . .
> Harmony and understanding
> Sympathy and trust abounding
> No more falsehood or derisions
> Golden living dreams of visions
> Mystic crystal revelation
> And the mind's true liberation

Aquarius! Aquarius!

Bob Dylan gave words to this feeling of a new consciousness and age as he and countless other youths rebelled against the traditions of their parents:

> Come mothers and fathers
> Throughout the land
> And don't criticize
> What you can't understand
> Your sons and your daughters
> Are beyond your command
> Your old road is
> Rapidly agin'
> Please get out of the new one
> If you can't lend your hand . . .

The counter-culture felt, in Bob Dylan's immortal words, "the times they are a-changin'."

Sex was liberated from old restrictions and prohibitions. Further statements of sexual liberation occur in the opera *Hair* when the whole cast emerges onstage nude to sing, and when it is questioned why various sexual acts are considered "dirty."

In a tender ballad, the Shirelles describe a night of erotic bliss, but also capture the instability of free love:

> Tonight you're mine completely.
> You give your love so sweetly.
> Tonight the light of love is in your eyes.
> But will you love me tomorrow?[591]

This new free love ethic climaxed in the Woodstock music festival. There, half a million youths met to enjoy the ecstatic spirit of music and love. There was no police force present, yet no violence erupted. Half a million people enjoyed the concert in perfect harmony with one another. This is remarkable to consider, since in most barrooms, a minute fraction of Woodstock's attendance cannot coexist without a bouncer on hand to stave off brawls that are likely to erupt at any moment. Or consider society at large, where we all seem to want a police

---

591. I am indebted to the keen memory of William Day for recalling these classic songs and artists.

force ready to protect us from any number of threats from each other. But at Woodstock, love was in the air, and a peaceable atmosphere enhanced everyone's joy, celebrating camaraderie and mutual respect for each other's freedom to express themselves in their own way.

With the death of Jimi Hendrix, Janis Joplin, and Jim Morrison, the children of the Sixties paused from their mind-expanding trips and Dionysian love-ins to question exactly what had happened in the previous decade. Chroniclers took time to reflect and produced significant works that embodied the spirit of the Sixties.

The times, they had changed. This change is particularly evident in sexual practices which persist today. By the early Seventies, many of the counter-culture ethics emerged into mainstream society. Talk about sex was unleashed from bashful closed doors into public discourse. A testament to the new openness about sex was Alex Comfort's *The Joy of Sex*.[592] Published in 1972, the book on sexual techniques was so successful that a sequel came out one year later, *More Joy of Sex*.[593] Marriage traditions took a heavy hit from the free love of the Sixties and hasn't recovered from it today.

One book that made a big splash and captures the increasingly accepted spirit of free love was Erica Jong's *Fear of Flying*.[594] The novel was published in 1973, but sections of it came out in periodicals during the Sixties — the decade in which much of the story takes place.

The novel narrates Isadora Wing's search for sexual fulfillment. Throughout the story, Isadora is torn in three directions. She wants to be an independent woman writer standing on her own two feet without the need to cling to a man; but due to the feminine mystique which holds sway over her, she feels that a single woman appears as a social pariah. Her other two drives involve men. On the one hand, she wants security and love in marriage, which for her is numbed by years of familiarity. On the other hand, there is a hunger in her gut for excitement and hedonistic indulgence.

The book is written under the influence of Freudian psychology, which permeated the intellectual climate of the Sixties and Seventies, so the book is not only a quest for sexual fulfillment; it is also a quest into the mainsprings of the self. Almost an extended literary psycho-analysis session, the book contains descriptions of childhood and family, introspection, free association, dream

---

592. Alex Comfort, *The Joy of Sex* (New York: Crown Publishing Incorporated, 1972).
593. Idem, *More Joy of Sex* (New York: Crown Publishing Incorporated, 1973).
594. Erica Jong, *Fear of Flying* (New York: Signet, 1995).

sequences, inherited social roles, and an attempt to find the nature of her identity.

One of the roles that Isadora wrestles with is marriage. Like Dean Moriarty, Isadora is unable to free herself from the idea that a woman's role is to be married. This comes out in her debate about whether to leave her husband and take up with a psychologist, Adrian, whom she meets at a convention. Even this attempt of liberation is sicklied over with the pale cast of marriage.

> All my fantasies included marriage. No sooner did I imagine myself running away from one man than I envisioned myself tying up with another. I was like a boat that always had to have a port of call. I simply couldn't imagine myself without a man. Without one, I felt lost as a dog without a master; rootless, faceless, undefined.[595]

Yet she is ambivalent about marriage, too. She finds it a stultifying arrangement and despite her need for marriage also deplores the condition of being married.

> Would most women get married if they knew what it meant? I think of young women following their husbands wherever their husbands follow their jobs. I think of them suddenly finding themselves miles away from friends and family. I think of them living in places where they can't work, where they can't speak the language. I think of them making babies out of their loneliness and boredom and not knowing why. . . . I think of them seeing each other less after marriage than before. . . . I think of them farther apart in the first year of marriage than they ever imagined two people could be when they were courting. And then I think of the fantasies starting. . . . Not: when did it all go wrong? But: when was it ever right?[596]

Yet she claims in principle not to be against marriages.

> I was not against marriage. I believed in it in fact. It was necessary to have one best friend in a hostile world, one person you'd be loyal to no matter what, one person who's always be loyal to you. But what about all those other longings which after a while marriage did nothing much to appease? . . . the yearning for dry champagne and wet kisses, for the smell of peonies in a penthouse on a June night, for the light at the end of the pier in *Gatsby*. . . . Not those *things* really — because you knew that the very rich were duller than you and me — but what those things *evoked*. The sardonic, bittersweet

---

595. *Ibid.*, pp. 79-80.
596. *Ibid.*, p. 80.

vocabulary of Cole Porter love songs, the sad sentimental Rogers and Hart lyrics, all the romantic nonsense you yearned for with half your heart and mocked bitterly with the other half.[597]

In addition to wrestling with her own impulsiveness and the thump-hunger in her gut for exuberance, Isadora also wrestles with her vocation as a writer and a wife. She longs to fulfil both callings, but society will not let her. Her sister urges her to give up writing and have children. "I mean you really ought to stop writing and have a baby. You'll find it *so* much more fulfilling than writing."[598] Adrian, her lover, tells her that she will never be able to do both.

> [N]o man wants to be stuck with a lady writer. They're liabilities. They daydream when they're supposed to be cooking. They worry about books instead of babies. They forget to clean the house.[599]

Isadora feels this tension in her own psyche.

> If you were female and talented, life was a trap no matter which way you turned. Either you drowned in domesticity (and had Walter Mittyish fantasies of escape) or you longed for domesticity in your art. You could never escape your femaleness. You had conflict written in your very blood.[600]

At one point, Isadora yields to culture's domestic definition of womanhood. She desires to be the "good" girl that Betty Friedan's feminine mystique preached.

> I suddenly had a passion to *be* that ordinary girl. To be the good little housewife, that glorified American mother, that mascot from *Mademoiselle*, that matron from *McCall's*, that cutie from *Cosmo*.[601]

But she realizes that she will never be that "good" girl.

> Somewhere deep inside my head (with all those submerged memories of childhood) is some glorious image of the ideal woman, a kind of Jewish Griselda. She is Ruth and Ester and Jesus and Mary rolled into one. She

---

597. *Ibid.*, p. 9.
598. *Ibid.*, p. 44.
599. *Ibid.*, p. 131.
600. *Ibid.*, p. 157.
601. *Ibid.*, p. 253.

always turns the other cheek. She is a vehicle, a vessel, with no needs and desires of her own. When her husband beats her, she understands him. When he is sick, she nurses him. When the children are sick, she nurses them. She cooks, keeps house, runs the store, keeps the books, listens to everyone's problems, visits the cemetery, weeds the graves, plants the garden, scrubs the floors, and sits quietly on the upper balcony of the synagogue while the men recite prayers about the inferiority of women. She is capable of absolutely everything except self-preservation. And secretly, I am always ashamed of myself for not being her. A good woman would have given over her life to the care and feeding of her husband's madness. I was not a good woman. I had too many other things to do.[602]

Yet Isadora is not ready for the solitary life. Or should I say, society will not let her live it.

It is heresy in America to embrace any way of life except as half of a couple. Solitude is un-American. It may be condoned in a man — especially if he is a "glamorous bachelor" who "dates starlets" during a brief interval between marriages. But a woman is always presumed to be alone as a result of abandonment, not choice. And she is treated that way: as a pariah.[603]

Women are presumed always to be waiting for Prince Charming to take them away from "all this." And when Isadora asks, "all what?" her true longing for independence emerges. "All what? The solitude of living inside her own soul? The certainty of being herself instead of half of something else?" (p. 11) Isadora considers herself a "free woman" "(a phrase which means nothing without quotes)." But she found herself incapable of life without a man, which challenged her feelings of freedom. "We had more in our lives than just men; we had our work, travel, friends. Then why did our lives seem to come down to a long succession of sad songs about men? Why did our lives seem to reduce themselves to man-hunts?" (p. 100) She searches in vain for role models of truly free women. "Where were the women who were *really* free, who didn't spend their lives bouncing from man to man, who felt complete with or without a man?" (p. 100). Ultimately, Isadora decides that social forces are too strong for her to remain single and to devote herself to writing.

Being unmarried in a man's world was such a hassle that *anything* had to be better. Marriage was better. But not much. Damned clever, I thought,

---

602. *Ibid.*, p. 210.
603. *Ibid.*, p. 10.

how men had made life so intolerable for single women that most would gladly embrace even bad marriages instead (p. 80).

Isadora's preoccupation with fantasy leads to her general philosophy of sexuality. For her, sex is primarily a mental, not a physical event. She criticizes the sex research of Masters and Johnson, and sex manuals such as *The Joy of Sex* because they deal only with the body's reaction to sexual stimuli. For Isadora the mind is the primary erotic organ:

> Masters and Johnson's charts and numbers and flashing lights and plastic pricks tell us everything about sex and nothing about it. Because sex is all in the head. Pulse rates and secretions have nothing to do with it. That's why the best-selling sex manuals are such gyps (p. 34).

After her failed first marriage, Isadora indulges in a succession of sexual relationships which echo the debased stanzas of Eliot's *Waste Land*. Her ideals of love made her actual experiences disappointing:

> All we wanted were men we could share everything with. Why was that so much to ask? Was it that men and women were basically incompatible? Or just that we hadn't yet found the right ones? (p. 99).

Sex ceased to have meaning. "Progressively the two of us got more and more disillusioned. . . . Our disillusionment was such that we slept with men principally to boast to each other about the number of scalps on our belt. . . . They were mostly joyless" (pp. 99, 100). Later in life, Isadora reflects back on the free sex in which she indulged, and finds it superficial and without the liberation that free love promised:

> I could easily see the sterility of hopping from bed to bed and having shallow affairs with lots of shallow people. I had had the unutterably dismal experience of waking up in bed with a man I couldn't bear to talk to — and that was no liberation either (pp. 73-74).

Isadora displays growth in terms of her identity by the novel's conclusion. After leaving her husband and taking off with a lover on a drunken meander through Europe, Isadora is ultimately abandoned by him. This leaves Isadora completely without a man: utterly alone. At this point she reaches down deep into her psyche and finds liberation. "I was nobody's baby now. Liberated.

Utterly free. It was the most terrifying sensation I'd ever known in my life" (p. 271). She reflects back on her trip with Arian and decides that it was a necessary step in finding her own identity.

> Perhaps my finally running away was not due to malice on my part, nor to any disloyalty I need apologize for. Perhaps it was a kind of loyalty to myself. A drastic but necessary way of changing my life.
>
> You did not have to apologize for wanting to own your own soul. Your soul belonged to you — for better or worse (p. 288).

Isadora questions her former love relationships and finds that she was using love in order to escape her own self.

> I wanted to lose myself in a man, to cease to be me, to be transported to heaven on borrowed wings. Isadora Icarus, I ought to call myself. And the borrowed wings never stayed on when I needed them. Maybe I needed to grow my own (p. 300).

She realizes that another person cannot complete her being. She needs to find her own completion within her own psyche.

> That was what I had originally wanted. A man to complete me. . . . But perhaps that was the most delusional of all delusions. People don't complete us. We complete ourselves. If we haven't the power to complete ourselves, the search for love becomes a search for self-annihilation; and then we try to convince ourselves that self-annihilation is love (pp. 299-300).

She learns finally "that I was determined to take my fate in my own hands" (p. 304).

Unlike Jack Kerouac, Erica Jong has little place in her novel for spirituality. Isadora's primary religion was Freudian psychology — but she distrusted even that. She distrusted all human systems. "I didn't believe in systems. Everything human was imperfect and ultimately absurd" (p. 128). In a remark about one lover's participation in a dance school, Isadora seems to include religion into her distrust for systems, giving it the same status as a dance membership scam. "It wasn't exactly a racket any more than psychoanalysis or religion or encounter groups or Rosicrucianism can be said to be rackets, but, like them, it also promised an end to loneliness, powerlessness, and pain, and of course it disappointed many people" (p. 217). Her parents had a self-generated religion that was materialistic and Hobbesian, in which the struggle for supremacy was the basic human drive:

> . . . a sort of neo-Hobbesianism in which it is proven that life is nasty, mean, brutish, and short; the desire for status and money and power is universal; territoriality is instinctual; and selfishness, therefore, is the cardinal law of life. ("Don't twist what I'm saying, Isadora; even what people call altruism is selfishness by another name.") (p. 151)

The family celebrated Christmas with a tree and Easter with hidden, colored Easter eggs. But these were celebrations of the natural cycle. Christmas was "The Winter Solstice," Easter was "'The Vernal Equinox,' the Rebirth of Life, the Rites of Spring" (p. 54).

Fear of Flying is ultimately based on self-analysis and erotic searching. One might say that eros itself is the only spirituality in the work. This accords with the spirit of the Sixties, when love became a quasi-religion. However, it also reflects well the utterly debased state of Western culture when it comes to spirituality. Eliot's Waste Land is twentieth and twenty-first century America.

Erica Jong represents the early ethic of the "Me" generation. The psychology of the "Me" generation persists today. Self-realization is the dominant ethic. The development and unhampered expression of complete individuality is its goal. This philosophy was taught by the psychological school of the "human potential movement" and was quickly adopted by the counter culture movement of the Sixties. Anti-conformity was a leading doctrine along with total self-expression. "Do your own thing" was the pop phrase heard everywhere in the counter culture. This lifestyle is exemplified in the communal troupe of "heads" who followed Ken Kesey and called themselves "Pranksters." As they are about to embark on a psychedelic tour of America in a Day-Glo painted school bus, Kesey explains their ground rules:

> "All of us are beginning to do our own thing, and we're going to keep doing it, right out front, and none of us are going to deny what other people are doing."
> "Bullshit," says Jane Burton. . . .
> "That's Jane," he says. "And she's doing her thing. Bullshit. That's her thing and she's doing it."
> "None of us are going to deny what other people are doing. If saying bullshit is somebody's thing, then he says bullshit. If somebody is an ass-kicker, then that's what he's going to do on this trip, kick asses. . . . Every-

body is going to be what they are, and whatever they are, there's not going to be anything to apologize about. What we are, we're going to wail with on this whole trip."[604]

Along with this strong ethic of ego formation and the quest for a totally individual identity comes a doctrine that we are not to try to please others at the expense of pleasing ourselves. The teaching goes that one is unable to please others until one has found one's own individual definition of happiness.

This philosophy causes problems for interpersonal love. If one spends one's efforts discovering oneself and making oneself happy, how does one fit another person into this individual quest? Kesey's commune suffers from this dynamic when it comes to mutual sharing. Pancho, one of Kesey's Pranksters, found a book about oriental rugs that blew his mind. He had the natural response of wanting to share his discovery with the others. "Come on, man! I mean, like, I gotta *share* this thing. I gotta *make* you see it, I can't keep this whole thing to myself!"[605] One might expect that the commune would be interested in psychedelic rugs from the East, as their whole commune is psychedelically decorated and Kesey himself wore a jacket with a yin-yang on its back. But when Pancho shows Kesey the book, the cold response is, "Why should I take your bad trip?" The rejected Pancho is hurt and throws his book of oriental rugs on the floor. The rugs weren't Kesey's "thing," so he saw no reason to try to appreciate another's joy. Radical individuality can become an obstacle to the very bonds of community that the troupe of Pranksters sought to foster.

The erosion of deep traditions of love we have been discussing thus far is noted by Allan Bloom. He identifies democratic social patterns, scientific ideology, diffused "disenchantment" and ultimately the "death of God" *zeitgeist* of our society as causes,

> The de-eroticization of the world, a companion of its disenchantment, is a complex phenomenon. It seems to result from a combination of causes — our democratic regime and its tendencies toward leveling and self-protection, reductionist-materialist science that inevitably interprets eros as sex, and the atmosphere generated by "the death of God" and of the subordinate god, Eros.[606]

---

604. Tom Wolfe, *The Electric Kool-Aid Acid Test*, p. 73.
605. *Ibid.*, pp. 160, 161.

For Bloom, these forces have led to a "disastrous decline in the rhetoric of love."[607]

The results of the revolution against tradition and outside authority remain from the Sixties. Sex, love, and commitment now hold tenuous bonds. The deep and enduring romantic traditions that we saw in the tales of Daphnis and Chloe and Tristan and Yseut have faded, leaving only arbitrary connections between the sexes. In some ways, the revolution against tradition of the Sixties may have left a positive legacy. As we have seen in previous parts of this book, many of the doctrines from philosophy and religion have proved too limiting for the Post-Modern mind. But at the same time, by divorcing sexuality from its deeper foundations, couples form increasingly insecure bonds.

A word we hear repeatedly to define the bonds between couples today is the term "relationship." People now have "relationships." Not too long ago, people were husband and wife. Now we are "in" a "relationship" or we are "between" relationships, or just single. A relationship has no defining characteristics to it. No estimated time length. No defined quality of commitment. No sanctioning institution such as Church or court. It's all gray. We must continually prove ourselves in a relationship. We must always test the waters. Always wonder. The bonds of commitment are tenuous; we are free, but freedom is a double-edged sword. We are not bound by a vow or law, we can stay or leave at will — but so can our partner. The Allman Brothers' "Ramblin' Man," a rock song now held to be "classic," seems to capture exactly the spirit of today's relationships. The singer outright tells his beloved that their love is impermanent. "When it's time for leavin', I hope you'll understand that I was born a ramblin' man." Lynard Skynard, in an immensely popular "classic" song, asks his lover, "If I leave tomorrow, will you still remember me?" His champion is "as free as a bird/ And this bird you'll never change." But Skynard gives out a mixed message. If his free bird is leaving, why would he care if his partner still remembers him? Perhaps he seeks more attachment from his partner than he, himself, is willing to give her.

With traditions from the past so fractured, we wonder what can hold couples together. The great Catholic theologian Walter Kasper says,

---

606. Allan Bloom, *Love and Friendship* (New York: Simon and Schuster, 1993), p. 15.
607. *Ibid.*, p. 25.

[T]he radical changes that have taken place in recent years in man's understanding of himself and of the society he lives in and in the relation-ship between the sexes have had such a profound effect [that they] have led to a grave crisis.[608]

In the past, society had boundaries in force. Men were providers, women householders. If the man had steady work, the couple expected to marry, have children, and raise a family. Today, though, the question arises, "What do we value in another?" When coupling begins, we desperately search for common ground. The universe opens up and we are lucky not to experience vertigo. What are your expectations of our "relationship?" Will we move in together, or keep separate residences? How do you feel about spirituality? Past lives? Eastern thought? You're Lutheran? In this day and age? Are you a smoker? Are you into health and fitness? What health club do you belong to? You don't? I see. Am I paying the bill or will you contribute? Do you want to make a lot of money? What about fashion? Do you wear clothes that have someone's name on them? Jeans and a t-shirt? We simply don't know anymore what matters.

The preponderance of our present cultural expressions such as music, film, television, magazines, and literature surrounds us with examples of irresponsible, debased sexual life. It is against this tide that a modern seeker after love and spirituality must strive in order to capture the sense of awe, reverence, or love itself that we saw in earlier traditions in this book.

As we saw in Eliot's poem, sex can degenerate into nothing more than a baseless ritual to be endured without rapture. As Isadora puts it, "our disillusionment was such that we slept with men principally to boast to each other about the number of scalps on our belt. . . . they were mostly joyless."

Consider music. Another "classic" rock song illustrates the point. Bob Seager celebrates adolescent sexual exploration in "Night Moves." Recalling his own youthful introduction to the mysteries of sex, Seager explicitly denies that love played a part in his sexual pleasure — "We weren't in love — oh, no, far from it." It was merely empty sexual gratification — "I used her and she used me and neither one cared/We were gettin' our share." Sheryl Crow, a more contemporary songwriter, echoes the sentiment of Seager's adolescent pleasure. "All I want to do is have some fun/I won't tell you you're the only one." In another song she laments, "What it means to give your life to just one man," and muses,

---

608. Walter Kasper, *Theology of Christian Marriage* (New York: The Crossroads Publishing Company, 1983), p. 2.

"I'd like to watch the sun come up in a stranger's arms." The popular alternative band Tonic epitomizes Bloom's "disastrous decline in the rhetoric of love" with their lyric, "I don't know when I got bitter, but love is surely better when it's gone."

In other areas of our culture we are flooded with sexual imagery to the point of surfeit. Wall Street advertisers parade sex before the public in order to sell the most un-sexual commodities. In television sit-coms, and in film, we see couples sleeping with each other with as little concern for meaning as they would show in selecting a frozen dinner for the evening. Rock music videos display sex in vivid gyrations and revealing clothing song after song. What effect can this flood of sexual imagery have but to cheapen the experience of sex? In the wake of the 1960s free love revolution, sex itself has lost significance.

And that is where we are today. Our journey in these pages is at its conclusion. We have sketched strong crosscurrents that have contributed to our present society. We have delved deep into the origins of sexuality and spirituality in the West. We now have a better understanding of how and why our society looks as it does today.

In our Post-Modern age, we can create meaning for ourselves. That is both our blessing and our curse. We have the freedom to define sexuality in our own fashion and to find the higher power of our own understanding. That is the blessing. The curse, though, is how to find another human that can accord with our unique creations. How can we blend our souls today into a deep union that honors our mutual individuality? With what higher power will we find a connection that can accommodate the society we live in?

These questions, perhaps, help to define the chaos we experience every day. We are on the verge of spiritual anarchy. Perhaps this is why fundamentalist religions are experiencing the astonishing growth we see across cultures and around the world. People struggle to find a foothold in the unsteady ground of Post-Modern society. A secure foundation in a traditional structure can look safe in the face of the abyss that yawns before the individual.

This book has explored options for Post-Modern seekers after love and spirituality. As with so much of our present society, we can pick and choose what ideas make sense to us. By asking the important questions about love and spirituality in their lives, readers can define their personal choices with clarity and precision. Socrates, the subject of our very first chapter, said that "the unexamined life is not worth living." Now, we have little choice but to examine our lives. Society at every turn forces us to choose and define our options. It is my profound hope that this literary offering will help readers to become more self-aware citizens of the Post-Modern Age.

BIBLIOGRAPHY

Abbott, Walter M., General Editor. *The Documents of Vatican II*. Chicago: Follett Publishing Co., 1966.

Ames, William. *Conscience with the Power and Cases Thereof*. London: Printed by E. G., 1643.

Aquinas, Thomas. *Summa Theologica Supplement*. Volume III. *Summa Theologica*. Translated by the Fathers of the English Dominican Province. New York: Benziger Brothers, Inc., 1948.

_____. *Summa Theologica*. Quoted in *Basic Writings of St. Thomas Aquinas*, edited by Anton C. Pegis, vol. I. New York: Random House, 1945.

Aristotle. *The Nicomachean Ethics*. Buffalo, New York: Prometheus Books, 1987.

Saint Augustine. *Concerning the City of God against the Pagans*. New York: Penguin Books, 1981.

_____. *The Confessions of Saint Augustine*. New York: Mentor Books, The New American Library, 1963.

Barth, Karl. *Church Dogmatics*. Vol. III.1: *The Doctrine of Creation*. Edinburgh: T. & T. Clark, 1958.

_____. *Church Dogmatics*. Vol. III.4: *The Doctrine of Creation*. Edinburgh: T. & T. Clark, 1985.

Bernard of Clairvaux. *The Works of Bernard of Clairvaux*. Treatises III. *In Praise of the New Knighthood*. Kalamazoo: Cistercian Publications, Inc., 1977.

_____. *The Works of Bernard of Clairvaux*, Treatises II. *On Loving God*. Kalamazoo: Cistercian Publications, Inc., 1974.

Beroul. *The Romance of Tristan*. New York: Penguin Books, 1970.

Bloom, Allan. *Love and Friendship*. New York: Simon and Schuster, 1993.

Boethius. *The Consolation of Philosophy*. New York: Penguin Books, 1978.

The Book of Common Prayer. New York: Henry Holt and Company, 1992.

Chretien de Troyes. *Arthurian Romances*. Translated by D. D. R. Owens. London: J. M. Dent & Sons, Ltd., 1987.

Cicero. "De Amicitia" in *Loeb Classical Library*. Cambridge: Harvard UP, 1953.

Cleaver, Robert. *A Godlie Forme of Householde Government*. 1603. *The Cloud of Unknowing*. Garden City, New York: Image Books, 1973.

Coleridge, Samuel Taylor. *The Notebooks of Samuel Taylor Coleridge*. Edited by Kathleen Coburn. 3 Vols. New York: Pantheon Books, 1957.

Comfort, Alex. *The Joy of Sex*. New York: Crown Publishing Incorporated, 1972.

_____. *More Joy of Sex*. New York: Crown Publishing Incorporated, 1973.

Day, John. *The Parliament of Bees*. New York: Garland Publishing, Inc., 1979.

De Rougemont, Denis. *Love in the Western World*. New York: Harper and Row, 1974.

Eliot, T. S. *The Waste Land and Other Poems*. New York: Harcourt Brace & Company, 1962.

Emerson, Ralph Waldo. "The American Scholar," Quoted in *Five Essays on Man and Nature*. Edited by Robert E. Spiller. Crofts Classics. Arlington Heights, Illinois: AHM Publishing Corporation, 1954.

Frazer, Sir James. *The New Golden Bough*. New York: New American Library, 1959.

Friedan, Betty. *The Feminine Mystique*. New York: W. W. Norton & Company, 1997.

Frost, Robert. *The Complete Poems of Robert Frost*. New York: Holt, Rinehart and Winston, 1967.

Goldsmith, Oliver. *The Vicar of Wakefield*. New York: New American Library. A Signet Classic, 1961.

Gottfried von Strassburg. *Tristan*. New York: Penguin Books, 1982.

Gouge, William. *Domesticall Duties*. London: John Haviland for William Blader, 1622.

Gregory the Great. "Saint Benedict." Quoted in *The Dialogues of Gregory the Great*. Book II. Indianapolis: Bobbs-Merrill Educational Publishing, 1967.

Gregory of Nyssa. *Commentary on the Song of Songs*. Brookline, MA:Hellenic College Press, 1987.

The Holy Bible containing the Old and New Testaments with the *Apocryphal/ Deuterocanonical Books*. New Revised Standard Version. Oxford: Oxford UP, 1977.

James, Henry. *The Bostonians*. New York: Penguin Putnam Books, 1984.

Saint Jerome. "Letter XLVIII to Pammachius." *http://ccel.org/ccel/schaff/npnf206.v.XLVIII.html*. 9/5/2003.

Saint John Chrysostom. "Homily XIX on 1 Corinthians 7:1,2." *http://ccel.org/fathers/NPNF1-12/Chrysostom/Homilies1/t20.htm*. 2/17/2000.

_____. "Homily XXXVII on 1 Corinthians 14:34." *http://ccel.org/fathers/NPNF1-12/Chrysostom/Homilies1/t38.htm*. 2/17/2000.

Jong, Erica. *Fear of Flying*. New York: Signet, 1995.

Jungel, Eberhard. *God as the Mystery of the World*. Grand Rapids, Michigan: William Eerdmans Publishing Company, 1983.

Kasper, Walter. *Theology of Christian Marriage*. New York: The Crossroads Publishing Company, 1983.

Keen, Maurice. *Chivalry*. New Haven: Yale UP, 1984.

Kerouac, Jack. *On the Road*. New York: Penguin Books, 1976.

Lawrence, C. H. *Medieval Monasticism*. New York: Longman, 1984.

Locke, John. *An Essay Concerning Human Understanding*. Oxford: Oxford UP, 1975.

Longus. *Daphnis and Chloe*. New York: Penguin Books, 1989.

Luther, Martin. "Commentary on 1 Corinthians 7." Quoted in *Luther's Works*. vol. I. Hilton C. Oswald, ed. Saint Louis: Concordia Publishing House, 1973.

_____. *What Luther Says*. Compiled by Ewald M. Plass. Vol. II. Saint Louis: Concordia Publishing House.

Malory, Sir Thomas. *Works*. Edited by Eugene Vinaver. Oxford: Oxford UP, 1983.

Marvell, Andrew. "To His Coy Mistress." Quoted in John Ciardi and Miller Williams, *How Does a Poem Mean?* Boston: Houghton Mifflin Co., 1975.

McCarthy, David Matzko. *Sex and Love in the Home*. London: SCM Press, 2001.

Milton, John. *Paradise Lost*. Norwalk, Connecticut: The Easton Press, 1976.

Michel de Montaigne. *The Complete Essays of Montaigne*. Translated by Donald M. Frame. Stanford, California: Stanford UP, 1965.

The NIV Pictorial Bible. Grand Rapids, Michigan: Zondervan Bible Publishers, 1979.

Nussbaum, Martha *The Fragility of Goodness*. Cambridge: UP of Cambridge, 1987.

Ovid. *The Art of Love*. Translated by Rolfe Humphries. Bloomington, Indiana: Indiana UP, 1957.

Ozment, Steven. *The Age of Reform, 1250-1550*. New Haven: Yale UP, 1980.

Plato. *Phaedo*. Indianapolis: Bobbs-Merrill Educational Publishing, 1978.

_____. *Phaedrus and the Seventh and Eighth Letters*. New York: Penguin Books, 1973.

_____. Plato. *Symposium*. Translated by Alexander Nehamas and Paul Woodruff. Indianapolis and Cambridge: Hackett Publishing Co., 1989.

_____. *Timaeus and Critias*. New York and London: Penguin Books, 1977. "Predator Priests." *Boston Globe Online* 9 May, 2003. *http://www.boston.com/globe/spotlight/abuse/predators*.

The Quest of the Holy Grail. trans. P. M. Matarasso. New York: Penguin Books, 1986.

Rahner, Karl. *The Love of Jesus and the Love of the Neighbor*. New York: State Mutual Book and Periodical Service, 1988.

"Records on 10 clergy released." *Boston Globe Online* 9 May, 2003. *http://www.boston.com/globe/spotlight/abuse/stories4/013103records.htm.*

Rezendes, Michael and Matt Carroll, "More abuse records released." *Boston Globe Online* 11 February, 2003. 9 May, 2003. *http://www.boston.com/globe/spotlight/abuse/stories4/021103records.htm.*

Shelley, Percy Bysshe. *The Selected Poetry and Prose of Shelley*. Edited by Harold Bloom. New York: New American Library, 1978.

Spenser, Sir Edmund. *Poetical Works*. Oxford: Oxford UP, 1983.

Stafford, Margaret. "Priests struggle with fallout from sex abuse crisis." *Naples Daily News* 10 May, 2003, 11A.

Stevens, Wallace. *The Palm at the End of the Mind*. New York: Vintage Books, 1972.

Swedenborg, Emanuel. *Divine Love and Wisdom*. Standard Edition. New York: Swedenborg Foundation, 1928.

_____. *Marital Love*. Translated by William Frederic Wunsch. New York: Swedenborg Publishing Association, 1938.

Thompson, Hunter S. *Fear and Loathing in Las Vegas*. New York: Vintage Books, 1971.

Tillich, Paul. *The Protestant Era*. Chicago: UP of Chicago, 1957.

_____. *Systematic Theology*. Vol. I. Chicago: Chicago UP, 1951.

Weston, Jessie. *From Ritual to Romance*. Princeton, New Jersey: UP of Princeton, 1993.

Wolfe, Tom. *The Electric Kool-Aid Acid Test*. New York: Bantam Books, 1999.

INDEX